Excellence in Communicating
Organizational Strategy

Excellence in Communicating Organizational Strategy

Edited by

Donald P. Cushman

and

Sarah Sanderson King

STATE UNIVERSITY OF NEW YORK PRESS

Published by
State University of New York Press, Albany

For information, address the State University of New York Press,
90 State Street, Suite 700, Albany, NY 12207

Production by Marilyn P. Semerad
Marketing by Anne M. Valentine

Library of Congress Cataloging-in-Publication Data

Excellence in communicating organizational strategy / edited by Donald P.
    Cushman and Sarah Sanderson King.
        p.   cm.
    Includes index.
    ISBN 0-7914-5033-3 (alk. paper) — ISBN 0-7914-5034-1 (pbk. : alk. paper)
    1. Business communication.   2. Industrial management.   I. Cushman,
Donald P.   II. King, Sarah Sanderson, 1932–

HF5718.E96 2001
658.4'5—dc21   00-046419
                                                                            CIP

10 9 8 7 6 5 4 3 2 1

To our brothers, sister, and in-laws:
Albert and Olga Police
Anthony Police
Floyd Police
Sam and Patricia Police
Donna and Gene Hopper,
with whom we have shared many interesting discussions about
achieving excellence.
And to the memory of those who could not be with us today to
argue their points—
Fred, Jimmy, Frank, John, Rosella, Kay, Henry Joe, Esther, and June

Contents

1

Excellence in Communicating Organizational Strategy: An Introduction

Donald P. Cushman and Sarah Sanderson King

Organizations have *goals or desired ends* they want to achieve. Similarly, organizations have *strategies or preferred means* for achieving those goals. In addition, organizations utilize *implementing structures or special organizational processes* aimed at guaranteeing that their preferred strategies are in fact undertaken in the appropriate ways in order to achieve their *desired ends.* This book seeks to shed new light on the communication strategies involved in those processes by providing fourteen chapters that examine, analyze, and execute the communication strategies involved in organizational performance.

For example, at the General Electric Corporation, Jack Welch in the mid-1980s, articulated *GE's organizational goals* as (1) to become the most competitive and (2) to become the most highly valued firm in the world. *GE's communication strategies* or preferred means for achieving these goals were (1) to become the most profitable and (2) to become the most valued firm in the world. *GE's implementing structures* for guaranteeing that the preferred communication strategies were in fact undertaken were (1) to hold and invest in only high-growth businesses in which GE could become number 1 or 2 in market shares in the world and (2) to put in place a continuous improvement program called "workout" which could improve GE's performance by reducing costs and increasing margins, quality, and speed to market in order to become the low-cost high-quality provider of products and services for GE's customers (Cushman and King 1997).

Organizations that function in this manner rely heavily on a *strategy of employing effective communication* in order to integrate, coordinate, and control the information flow to all of an organization's stakeholders, employees, suppliers, investors, and customers. For

1

example, in order to guarantee excellence in its communication strategy, GE put in place three new implementing structures. *First,* Welch revamped GE's organizational culture in order to make employees more self-reliant, rapid in response, and change-oriented. *Second,* Welch developed a world-class education and reeducation system headed by GE's management training center at Croutenville, New York. *Third,* he restructured GE's monitoring and reward system to make it more performance, team, and change-oriented (Cushman and King 1997). Excellence in communicating an organization's strategy results, according to Jack Welch, from a persistent effort over time to clearly articulate a firm's goals and strategies and a leader's passion in monitoring and evaluating the effectiveness of a firm's implementing structures (Welch 1992). Between the mid-1980s and 2000, GE's profits rose from 32nd to first in the world at $10.7 billion, and its stockholder value rose from 45th to first in the world at $480 billion *(Palm Beach Post).*

It will be the purpose of this collection of essays to explore in some detail the theoretic, strategic, and practical linkages for creating excellence in communicating a firm's strategy. This chapter provides an overview or road map of the contributions in this volume, their focuses, major claims, and the data supporting those claims.

Chapter 2 in this book contains an award-winning piece entitled "Stimulating and Integrating the Development of Organizational Communication Through High-Speed Management." Its author Donald Cushman attempts to articulate a general theory of communication called *High-Speed Management* which can serve as an organizing principle capable of integrating all communication research. Such an integrative theory, according to Cushman, must meet three specific criteria. *First,* it must have generality, be simple enough to apply to the wide range of organizational communication activities. *Second,* it must have necessity or account for the driving force in these communication activities. *Third,* such a theory must have explicative power, must explain what governs and guides organizational communication processes.

Cushman then attempts to articulate just such a theory, the theory of High-Speed Management. This theory rests on two simple propositions: *First,* reducing the cycle time an organization takes in getting its product and/or services to customers yields significant organizational outcomes. Decreasing organizational cycle time yields increases in productivity, quality, profits, market shares, management and worker commitment, and customer satisfaction with an organization's products and services. *Second,* improving an organization's communication processes is the central ingredient necessary for reducing organizational cycle time. Reducing communication bottlenecks, standardizing information transfer, and appropriate adaptation to and speed of communication response are the central outputs that lead to decreasing an organization's cycle time.

Next Cushman discusses the implementing structures for locating communication problems and then generating solutions to those problems by utilizing (1) environmental scanning, (2) value chain analysis, and (3) continuous improvement. An example of the use of these three tools is providing by analyzing communications within the General Motors Corporation. Next, data is provided on how improved communication effectiveness leads to reduced cycle time and the positive outcomes previously listed.

Finally, a review of the literature on High-Speed Management is summarized to indicate how this theory can and has stimulated and integrated research in organizational communication. In 1998, this essay was selected as a finalist by the Arizona State University in a contest for developing an original communication theory capable of stimulating and integrating organizational communication research.

Chapter 3 of this collection is by Donald P. Cushman and Sarah S. King on "Killer Strategies for Competitiveness: The Case of Microsoft." Here they analyze what many consider to be the most competitive firm in modern times. Cushman and King begin by providing a conceptualization of sustainable competitive advantage rooted in customer demand, a firm's core competencies, and a breakpoint in product development. Next, they report the results of a large study which locates the most successful strategies employed by multinationals who achieve sustainable competitive advantage. These were (1) locating a domestic product niche with limited exports, (2) exporting high-quality politically supported products, (3) exporting high-quality innovative products, and (4) exporting continuously improved business processes.

Attention is then turned to analyzing Microsoft's unique success in the software industry. Bill Gates, Microsoft's CEO, articulated an organizational goal of pioneering and orchestrating the evolution of mass markets within the computer software industry. Next, he put forward five business strategies for achieving those goals. These involved (1) developing new products, (2) continuously improving old products, (3) pushing volume sales, (4) leveraging industrial standards, and (5) integrating and simplifying products. Finally, Gates introduced four killer implementing strategies for employing communication excellence to guarantee the fulfillment of those strategies in a manner which shut out Microsoft's competitors: (1) the use of Microsoft's unique brand of teamwork to insure effective product development and continuous improvement; (2) the setting of industry standards through product development, acquisitions, and alliances; (3) the volume marketing through competitive pricing, exclusive contracting, and software bundling; and (4) the leveraging of standards to limit competitor sales.

Finally, Cushman and King demonstrate how Microsoft employed its goals, strategies, and implementing structures to gain control of the five gateways for gaining access to the Internet. In so doing they observe how Bill Gates was able to respond to an industrial breakpoint, the rise of the Internet, by turning Microsoft's focus on PC software to Internet software in just six months while shutting out his competitors in controlling access to the five Internet gateways. Microsoft's speed, effectiveness, and dominance of this industrial breakpoint relative to its competitors is a theoretic, strategic, and practical move worthy of careful study. The use of goals, strategies, and implementing structures is different from those employed by GE and may in terms of outcomes be more effective. In 1987 Microsoft earned more profits from less sales than any major firm in the world while moving into the top five behind GE in global stockholder value *(Fortune)*.

In chapter 4, Yong-Chan Kim analyzes *High-Speed Management Strategies for Competitiveness: E-land, a Korean Multinational.* Here Kim provides a communication audit which reveals how a well-developed corporate culture can link communication to organizational outcomes in a powerful and productive manner. The E-land Corporation, a Korean-based multinational conglomerate in clothing and construction, developed a unique corporate culture based on (1) Christian principles, (2) a youth movement, (3) male and female management equality, and (4) a learning organization which provided E-land with a sustainable competitive advantage. The focus on Christian principles avoided the pitfalls or corruption which now plagues most Korean firms. Hiring competent male and female college graduates allowed E-land to strengthen its management team in an area where competition for male graduates created a competitive shortage. Emphasizing a youth movement in which progress from line to top management took half the time of most Korean firms made the organization attractive to competent young graduates, while creating a learning environment which, in turn, created a collegiate spirit in the firm. The implementing structures for linking communication to these values are traditional, but the outcomes, unique. The growth and performance of E-land speaks for itself: sales rose from $500,000 to $1.5 million in just three years. In addition E-land has become one of the most preferred firms for work by new college graduates in Korea. E-land's goals, strategies, and implementing structures may become the model for leading Korean and Asian firms out of their current economic crises rooted in organizational and governmental corruption while energizing Asian youth.

Thomas Florence and Branislav Kovačić in chapter 5 address the issues involved in the "Intersections Between Crises and Management." The authors begin by constructing a crisis management model based upon Lester Thurow's (1996) metaphor involving (1) plate tectonics and (2) punctuated equilibrium as central concepts in understanding chaotic activity. Organizational crises, like earthquakes, cannot be understood in terms of their visible manifestations. Instead, one must look below the surface of the frictions caused by its plate tectonics. In organizational crises a friction develops between (1) organizational ideology, (2) economic stability, (3) cultural business practices, (4) the legal implications of corporate activities, and (5) government intervention. These organizational tectonic plates floating in the molten lava of the mass media rub against each other creating faultlines or public disputes such as (1) labor/management, (2) environmental concerns, (3) competitive alliances, (4) legal issues, (5) income, (6) safety net, and (7) global economic disasters. These disputes surface in and are influenced by the mass media. Such disputes are dynamic and feature a process of punctuated equilibrium which offers openings for the constructive resolution to the conflict. A discussion is then provided of several types of equilibrium and disequilibrium and the types of message strategies appropriate to constructive solutions in each. Issues regarding risk management, public anger, goal management, crisis stages, responses to attacks, and the implementing structures in terms of message design are analyzed.

Chapter 6 by Joseph Pillittere II extends our understanding of excellence in communication strategy during a crisis when he explores "Excellence in Communication During a Crisis: The Case of the Indian Point 3 Nuclear Power Plant." Pillittere argues that action must establish credibility and build trust before, during, and after a crisis or perceived crisis. This is best accomplished by (1) having a crisis management plan in place and practicing it, (2) responding quickly to all inquiries, (3) being truthful, (4) listening carefully with an open mind to a firm's stakeholders, (5) employing simple language with visuals and with prepared messages where possible, (6) if you don't know the answer, saying so, and then finding out and responding, and (7) when possible, distributing in printed form news releases to all stakeholders.

Next Pillittere provides a case study of the effective use of these principles in a perceived crisis by segments of the press in regard to a repair being made at the Indian Point 3 Nuclear Reactor in upstate New York. In the case study a potential crisis with the press was prevented by establishing credibility and trust with local officials, the press, and community leaders. While maintenance was being performed on a reactor, an accident occurred which had no harmful effects. By treating the accident as a potential crisis and keeping its stakeholders clear on what was going on, the nuclear plant prevented a perceived crisis when one newspaper provided misinformation on the problem. When other journalist sources spoke with the government, community leaders, other journalists, and the public, the convergence of these sources provided collaboration for the noncrisis event.

Chapter 7 by Yanan Ju addresses "R&D and Marketing Strategy for Cross-Cultural Cooperation: A Cross-Pacific Study between China and the U.S." Ju begins by asserting that in today's global economy with fax machines, telephones, and E-mail, the U.S. and China are seconds apart in electronic communication. However, they are hours, days, and months apart in understanding the content of communication due to massive cultural differences. To support his claim he examines communication between two firms—Company A (a U.S. firm) and Company B (a Chinese firm) who formed a joint venture to produce electric motor bikes. He explores the differences in terms of tasks, ways of working, and means of communication coordination aimed at developing a value-added relationship between firms. *At the task level,* Company A handled the R&D while Company B handled manufacturing and marketing. The U.S. firm designed a 50cc small bike for sale in China. However, the cost of nickel-metal-hydride batteries was such that the Chinese firm wanted a 125cc bike which could carry passengers. Company A, not understanding Chinese culture, believed it had designed a low-cost bike by U.S. standards. Company B found the basic costs in developing a 50cc and 125cc bike about the same with the Chinese market viewing the costs as high. So unless the bike could be used to carry people or haul heavy loads, it would not sell.

At the work level of coordination even more problems developed. In the U.S. we have a capitalist economy and great respect for the law. In China they have a socialist economy governed by *quanxi*, the giving of financial rewards for favors. In a socialist economy, the communist party is like a mother-in-law. Without the mother-in-law's endorsement, nothing happens, and when it does happen, it follows the preference of the mother-in-law involved. *Quanxi* is a web of blood and social relationships that only works to support 'buddies" who reciprocate favors. In China when people first meet they are strangers; when they meet again, they are acquaintances; by the third meeting they have the potential to become buddies when they reciprocate support. U.S. firms have difficulty understanding this system. They rely on profits and legal contracts. These are not considered important in China. Profits are necessary but only if distributed appropriately among an established network of buddies who reciprocate rewards. In addition, in China oral commitments among buddies are much more important than mere legal documents. In China, the law is easy to change; buddies are not.

At a communication level, understanding is rooted in nonverbal face-to-face communicating among buddies over a meal. In the U.S. it is rooted in verbal agreements among firms that are put in writing. Ju argues that time and trial and error are substantially slowing joint ventures between the U.S. and China. He argues for a more careful study of cultural differences to speed up the understanding process and any increase in the value-added coordination to generate profits and mutual respect.

Chapter 8 by Robyn Johnston explores "Strategies for Survival in the Global Marketplace: A Study of the Australian Pharmaceutical Industry." Johnston explores three national strategies employed in Australia to raise a nation's competitive edge in the global economy. *First,* between 1986 and 1996, the Australian government entered into negotiation with the Australian Council of Trade Unions to liberalize union agreements. These liberalizations included that a portion of wages was to be determined by local performance and awarded at the enterprise level. Work rules were also localized. These included flexible work hours, shift loads, paid holidays, annual leave, and the potential for work on any day of the week. In addition, rigid job specifications were eliminated and work teams allowed. *Second,* the role of manager changed in this same time from monitoring and control to coaching and facilitating organizational improvement. Skills in communication and motivation were increasingly considered central factors in upward mobility. Skills development for managers became necessary for advancement, particularly skills in visioning, strategizing, continuous improvement, and entrepreneurship. *Third,* the nation's educational systems and firm's training system were focused on developing learning organizations. The nation's vocational education and compulsory postsecondary school educational systems became more skills-oriented. Unions began to require firms to train and retrain workers as part of the contract. Nation-wide standards were established for certification of successful skills training. Training agendas were established in labor contracts, and increases in pay were tied to increased skills attainment. Finally, the author traces out how these strategies helped the firms in the pharmaceutical market industry expand Australia's global performances in this industry.

Chapter 9 by Rod Miller entitled "Beyond Benchmarking for Institutional Achievement: Jump-Start to Fund-Raising Excellence" explores the strategies employed to unite a board of directors, the CEO, and a professional development staff of a major Australian university in setting targets, developing fund-raising strategies, and putting in place implementing structures following a benchmarking study of the most successful universities in the world of fund-raising. Strategic targets were set; partnerships were formed with 200 leading organizations in the community, and 500 prominent individuals were selected as prospects for contributions. The activities of the board members and staff in mounting a significant fund-raising effort are then detailed and preliminary results given.

Ernest Martin in chapter 10 addresses the issues involved in "Intuition and Metacommunication Strategies in Times of Change." The author argues that in times of rapid change successful managers develop highly profitable hunches or intuitions which account for their firm's success. Martin then explores how and why productive intuitions are separated from human folly through positive and negative feedback, self-realization, and ethics. Integrity, courage, and ethics are then explored as the personal characteristics behind a firm's vision, values, and action. Next, he expands our conception of effective communication by demonstrating how intuition provides the basis for metacommunication effectiveness. Metacommunication involves energy, a variety of frequency domains, and a multidimensional holographic model of nonverbal communication interpretations. Awareness of these intuitional bases of metacommunication is a refinable skill, a skill which can be developed through training and which provides the energy, motivation, and interpretative processes that underpin an organization's vision, values, and actions.

Chapter 11 by John Penhallurick explores "The Strategic Impact of Affect on Decision-Making." Here the author reviews the literature on emotion and its effect on organizational decision-making processes. Emotion is viewed as a type of intelligence when appraised and expressed properly under controlled perimeters which focus on flexible planning, creative thinking, motivation, and redirecting attention to key problem areas. The often overlooked constructive case for the use of emotion to enhance organizational performance is then put forward.

Susanne and Robert Morris in chapter 12 explore "Training Strategies for Excellence: Selecting the Appropriate Models for the Specific Task." Two critical variables are analyzed, namely, a firm's needs and the time the firm has to learn and implement the training to support those needs. A firm's needs are divided into two levels—known and unknown needs. Time is divided into two levels—unconstrained and constrained. Four models for training are then explored to meet a firm's specific needs and time frame: (1) a general competency model is developed for firms with unknown needs and an unconstrained time frame; (2) a packaged/handbook strategy is developed for firms with unknown needs and a constrained time frame; (3) a professional/specialist model, for known needs and constrained time frame; and finally, (4) a just-in-time model, for known needs and a constrained time frame. Characteristics and examples are then put forward to illustrate the use of each training strategy and the implementing structures involved in each model.

Chapter 13 by Richard Dieker, "Strategies of Leadership Excellence for Corporate Survival," explores the need for a transformation from current need deficiency leadership strategies, which are not working, to transcendental leadership strategies. Harmful effects of deficiency need leadership include aggressive, fearful, or defensive behavior; lack of foresight or vision; an inability to delegate; an inability to take unpopular actions when needed; and damaging motivation by taking personal recognition for others' accomplishments. Transcendental leadership focuses on the development of vision in four major areas: the organization and its mission; the realization of greatness in the members of the organization; continuous monitoring and development of the self as a leader; and finally, the ability to translate this vision into appropriate leadership behavior. Dieker then discusses developing the skills necessary for transcendental leadership by indicating the appropriate implementing strategies leaders must employ to become such a leader. A checklist inventory for measuring progress in developing these skills is provided.

Chapter 14 by Cushman and King provides a conclusion to this collection by abstracting from each of the chapters the central lesson and implications for achieving "Excellence in Communicating Organizational Strategy."

We hope this brief map for exploring the rich and insightful chapters in this book will whet the reader's appetite for what can only be described as the gourmet main course you will find as you read on.

References

Cushman, D. and King. S. S. (1997). *Continuously Improving an Organization's Performance*. Albany: SUNY Press, 42–43.

Fortune (April 28, 1988). The Fortune 500, F7.

Palm Beach Post (January 20, 2000). Jack Welch, Leader of the Century, D1.

Thurow, Lester C. (1996). *The Future of Capitalism: How Today's Economic Forces Shape Tomorrow's World*. New York: William Morrow.

Welch, J. (March 15, 1992). Statement in the Award Report. Quoted in "A Balance Between Values and Numbers," *New York Times*, D1.

2

Stimulating and Integrating the Development of Organizational Communication through High-Speed Management

Donald P. Cushman

What idea or theory has the greatest potential to stimulate and integrate the development of organizational communication? This chapter seeks to answer this question by dividing the issues into three parts: *First,* we shall explore the criteria and operations by which one can judge an idea or theory's potential to stimulate and integrate the development of organizational communication. *Second,* we present one such theory for consideration, the High-Speed Management theory of organizational communication. *Third,* we shall investigate the evidence available that this theory has the potential to stimulate and integrate organizational communication.

Criteria and Operations for Judging an Idea or Theory's Potential to Stimulate and Integrate Organizational Communication

At least three criteria appear in evaluating such proposed ideas and/or theories. *First,* and idea or theory *must have generality.* It must be simple enough to apply to a wide range of organizational communication activities in the private, public, and not-for-profit sectors of organizational communication behaviors. *Second,* an idea or theory *must have necessity.* It must utilize a normative system or belief which can govern and guide the communication activities of all organizational stakeholders, be they investors, voters, contributors, leaders, managers, workers, suppliers, customers, or clients. *Third,* an idea or theory *must have power.* It must govern and guide

(Arizona State Award Winning Essay)

the central communication activities of organizations, namely, their (a) organizational integration processes, or the communication activities involved in leadership, establishing a positive corporate climate, and utilizing effective teamwork; (b) organizational coordination processes or the communication involved within and between organizational units as well as the interactions between stakeholders; and (c) organizational control processes or the monitoring, evaluation, and adjustment to organizational performance.

At least three operationalizations are necessary for employing the above criteria. *First,* we must examine the assumptions that underlie the idea or theory to make sure they are active in organizational stakeholders' thinking and behaviors. *Second,* we must examine the central constructs and relationships between the constructs to make sure they are conceptually and operationally distinct and yield clear and strong observable outcomes. *Third,* we must examine the implementing structures such ideas or theories suggest to be sure they generate the desired communication and limit undesirable outcomes.

High-Speed Management Theory of Organizational Communication

The time it takes to perform an organizational activity, function, or process has become an important measure of that organization's effectiveness. In private-sector organizations, a firm's speed in getting a product or service to market is the chief determinant of organizational success (Fraker, 1984; Stalk, 1988). In the public sector, the time it takes candidates to develop an agenda or image, the time it takes to pass legislation, and the time it takes to deliver a public service to a client have become the chief determinants of a candidate's, legislature's, or agency's effectiveness (Cullin and Cushman, 2000). In the not-for-profit sector the time it takes to raise funds and the time it takes to deliver services have become the chief measure of organizational effectiveness (Miller, 2000). Time has become an important measure of an organization's effectiveness because of its ease of use, its relative lack of bias, and its predictability of other desirable organizational outcomes (Fraker, 1984).

Over the past several years, Drs. Donald P. Cushman and Sarah S. King and associates have developed the theory of High-Speed Management in Organizational Communication as one means for stimulating and integrating all the available theory and research on organizational communication. This effort has been summarized in over thirteen authored and edited books and in over fifty journal articles or chapters in books (see the later section, "An Investigation of the Evidence Available that High-Speed Management Theory Has the Potential to Simulate and Integrate Organizational Management," and the bibliography for documentation). This theory is grounded in two apparently well-supported propositions.

First, reducing the cycle time an organization takes for getting its products and/or services to customers, clients, voters, and aid recipients yields significant organizational outcomes. Decreasing organizational cycle time yields increases in productivity, quality, profits, market shares, and management and worker commitment and customer, client, voter, and aid recipient satisfaction with that organization (Dumaine, 1984; Ruffin, 1992; Vesey, 1991; Stalk, 1988). For example GE reduced the time it took to deliver a washer or dryer to market from three weeks to three days saving millions of dollars in costs and increasing productivity, quality, and customer satisfaction (Ruffin, 1992). Recent surveys conducted by Kaiser and Associates and McKinsey and Company of 50 and 150 multinational corporations located in the U.S., Europe, and Asia found that all listed time-based communication strategies as their top priority for improving organizational performance (Cushman and King, 1994a and 1994b). Why? Because speed of response tends to provide order of magnitude improvement in productivity, quality, and profits and worker, management, and customer satisfaction (Dumaine, 1984; Ruffin, 1992; Vesey, 1991).

Second, improving a firm's organizational communication processes is the central ingredient necessary for reducing organizational cycle time. Removing communication bottlenecks, standardizing information transfer, developing rapid response systems, improving communication quality, and adaptations to customers, clients, voters, contributors, and aid recipients are the central outputs that lead to decreasing organizational cycle time. The research supporting this assumption has been integrated and presented along with actual case studies of private-sector organizations in Cushman and King (1995e). They synthesize the literature on communication and leadership, corporate climate, teamwork, R&D and marketing, manufacturing, Management Information Systems, and MIS interfaces as well as performance monitoring and evaluation. In the public sector Cullin and Cushman (2000) provide an integration of the communication research in this area. They synthesize the communication research across disciplines on agenda setting, image building, campaigns, legislative processes, and the delivery of governmental services to aid recipients by agencies.

For example, Jack Welch, GE's CEO between 1989 and 2001, reengineered all the firm's organizational integration, coordination, and control processes so as to reduce cycle time in delivering product and/or services to market. The first reengineering effort was a quick market intelligence system designed to link customer and competitor intelligence with GE decision makers. Monday through Thursday, issues were generated by GE's sales force regarding customer needs, competitor moves, problems in products and service delivery and quality. On Thursday the manager who had responsibility for each issue made a decision aimed at resolving the issues raised. On Friday, via Internet linkage, the decision maker spoke with the person who raised the issue to see if the solution was satisfactory. If the decision was not satisfactory, the manager adjusted the decision. Similar communication systems were set up to respond to worker problems and suggestions, to manager need for support, and to diffuse successful improvements in communication processes throughout the organization. These new improved communication systems were estimated to have saved GE $500 million a year while improving GE's productivity, quality, and customer, worker, and manager satisfaction with the organization (Donion, 1993:6). Similar results can be found for both large and small organizations in the public, private, and not-for-profit sectors (Cushman and King, 1988a, 1988b; King and Cushman, 1998, 1991, 1994a, 1994b, 1995d, 1997a; Cushman, 2000).

Having explored briefly some of the evidence which underpins High-Speed Management's two basic assumptions, we are now in a position to examine the theory itself.

High-Speed Management Theory

High-Speed Management employs three analytic systems in order to determine what changes must be made in an organization's communication systems, and its integration, coordination, and control processes, in order to reduce that firm's cycle time to the satisfaction of its stakeholders. Let us explore High-Speed Management's three analytic systems: (a) environmental scanning, (b) value chain analysis, and (c) continuous improvement analysis in turn.

Environmental Scanning. Each organization has customers, clients, voter, and/or contributors who must select their products and/or services if that organization is to succeed. Each organization be it private, public, or not-for-profit has competitors or organizations that can provide similar products or services. An audience analysis is required in order to determine the appropriate way of communicating with these customers, clients, voters, and/or contributors effectively. Two concepts are necessary for understanding environmental scanning: competitive dynamics and core competencies.

The competitive dynamics for a product or service are the weighted dimensions along which the customer, client, voter, and contributor chose to exercise their options to act. For example, in 1997, survey and focus group research indicated that in the purchasing of a midsized car, a customer's choice to act was influenced 70% by styling, 20% by brand name, and 10% by quality and performance (compiled from various reports in *Automotive News,* 1997 and 1998). Thus organizations that are to be effective must be prepared to communicate with customers in terms of these choices in an ethical manner (Cushman and King, 1995b; Nicotera and Cushman, 1982).

The core competencies for a product or service consist in the customer, client, voter, and/or contributor perceptions of which organizations can best provide the attributes located in the competitor dynamic. For example, in 1997, the customers who purchased cars thought that Toyota, Honda, and Ford were equally competent in styling: Toyota and Honda were equal in brand name and price; and Toyota was competent in performance. Customers thus turned to these organizations to purchase cars.

In short, an environmental scanning analysis can be provided for customers, clients, voter, and contributors of any organization, be it public, private, and not-for-profit.

Value Chain Analysis. Once an organization has an understanding of its customers, clients, voters, and/or contributors and competitive dynamics and core competencies, it is ready to perform an analysis of its own and its competitors' value chain. Such an analysis allows us to locate where to begin improving an organization's communication processes.

For example, Figure 2.1 and Tables 2.1 and 2.2 contain a value chain analysis of GM and Ford Motors operations in 1997. These data were gathered from financial reports, survey research, and process mapping reports from each firm. Figure 2.1 also contains a chart of GM and Ford's business processes and the cycle time required to complete each process. Note the dramatic time disparity between GM and Ford in product development. This means that Ford can produce two new vehicle models adjusted to customer preferences in the time that GM produces one new model. So attempts to improve GM's performance must begin here. In addition product development is the central process involved in intersecting the key attributes of the customers competitive dynamics.

Figure 2.1
Business Process Level: Time

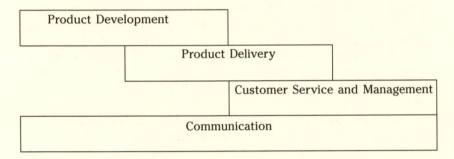

Time for Business Processes
Example: Value Chain to Bring a New Vehicle to Market

Company	Product Development	Product Delivery	Customer Service
GM	3.5 years	9 months	3 months
Ford	1.5 years	4 months	3 months

Table 2.1 contains the central outcomes or performance measures that follow from GM and Ford's cycle time data in regard to productivity, profit, and customer satisfaction. Note GM's shrinking market shares between 1980 and 1998. Each 1% drop in market shares is 100,000 cars in the U.S. market or one factory per year is no longer needed. Also note Ford's superiority in productivity, factory utilization, profits, and labor costs. This suggests the need for a close study of Ford's integration, coordination, and control communication processes involved in the product development process if GM is to halt its declining market shares.

Table 2.1
High Speech Management Outcome Data
for Auto Market 1997

	GM	FORD
% Market Shares 1980 Worldwide	45	20
% Market Shares 1998 Worldwide	31	24
Vehicles Sold Worldwide (millions)	8.7	6.9
Vehicles Sold U.S. (millions)	4.7	3.8
Revenues Worldwide (billions US$)	178	154
Profits Worldwide (billions US$)	6.7	6.9
Factory Utilization (%) Worldwide	60	80
Profits per Car (U.S.) US$	−$105	$1,500
Productivity Unit Output per Worker (U.S.)	27	45
Productivity Increases over 1996 (%) U.S.	4.0	8.2
Labor Cost per Car (US$)	$2,558	$1,500
Administration and Sales Cost as % of Sales	8.2	5.6

Source: Morgan Stanley 1998, Reported in Kerwin, 1998.

Table 2.2 contains a map of the communication strategies employed by GM and Ford in the R&D and marketing coordination process. Note how Ford's integration, coordination, and control process takes less time. This is because the use of product development teams weighted in favor of customers, guaranteeing that the competitive dynamics and core competencies govern the product development process and this creates customer satisfaction.

Table 2.2
Process Mapping of R&D/Marketing
Interface, 1997

TASK	GM	FORD
Strategy	Technology-based	Balanced
R&D Role	Dominant	Balanced
Marketing Role	Limited	Balanced
Customer Role	Limited	Dominant
Form	Division meetings	Production development team
Interactions	Sequential	Coexistence
Topic Focus	Engineering	Customer satisfaction
Timing	6 meetings per year for 3.5 years	Constant interaction 1.5 years

Source: Project Mapping Teams.

Once again a value chain analysis can be performed on any public-sector, private-sector, or not-for-profit organization employing process mapping and communication audits to locate the most appropriate areas for communication improvement. We are now in a position to reengineer the communication process involved in the R&D and marketing interface at GM through continuous improvement.

Continuous Improvement Applications. Improving an organization's basic communication process, the communication involved in organization integration, coordination, and control, normally proceeds in two steps and involves one of several continuous improvement processes.

First, one must locate the data on the best way to restructure the processes involved. Such data can come from three sources: a review of the literature, training by a consultant who has restructured such processes before, or benchmarking an organization that performs this communication process well.

Second, one must design an intervention and implement it through one of two continuous improvement implementing processes—either management-driven contract management or worker-driven self-managed, cross-functional benchmarking or outside linking teamwork.

A review of the communication research on effective R&D and marketing intervention is contained in Table 2.3. A benchmarking of Ford's R&D and marketing interaction processes is contained in Table 2.2. GM has employed the wrong strategy, structure, and topic development to compete effectively with Ford. Note the superiority of a balanced over a technology-driven strategy. Note the advantage of the participation by customers on a product development team. Finally, note the appropriate topics for interaction.

It is clear from this analysis that if GM is to improve its performance relative to Ford it must reengineer its R&D and marketing communication interface. In so doing GM needs to employ a strategy that balances R&D and marketing influences on a product development team where customers hold the balance of power in resolving conflicts. This team needs to employ constant coextensive interaction via computers and to provide the role inputs presented (see Table 2.3). Such a reengineering will reduce substantially the product's development time and improve its focus on the customer's competitive dynamics (perceptions of core competencies and needs), which need to exert a major influence over this communication process if GM is to improve. Such a reengineering should employ both contract management to set cycle time reduction targets for

Table 2.3
Most Effective R&D/Marketing Structures

Strategy	Balanced between R&D and marketing
Form	Team
Interactions	Coextensive
Role of Customer	Dominant
Topic of Dominance	Customer satisfaction

Interaction Topics

Marketing's Role	R&D's Role	Customer's Role
1. Provide customer requirements to R&D	1. Get involved with marketing to develop products according to market needs	1. Provide competitive dynamic
2. Provide customer feedback on product performance	2. Involve marketing in setting new product goals and priorities	2. Provide perceptions of core competencies
3. Provide competitors' strategies to R&D	3. Involve marketing in screening new product ideas	3. Evaluate market segmentation
4. Share test market results with R&D	4. Modify product according to market recommendations	4. Evaluate market strategy
5. Find commercial applications for new product ideas or technologies	5. Involve marketing in generating new product ideas	5. Provide information on customer needs

Sources: Cushman and King (1995a: 16–19) and Gupta, Raj, and Wileman (1985).

improving the product development process and cross-functional and outside linking teams to improve outcomes characteristic through improved communication processes. These changes will significantly improve the integration, coordination, and control communication processes at GM. GM is currently with the assistance of consultants undertaking just such continuous improvement changes.

Continuous improvement applications can be performed on public-sector, private-sector, and not-for-profit organizations aimed at reducing cycle time through improved communication processes.

We are now in a position to evaluate High-Speed Management communication as a powerful tool for stimulating and integrating organizational communication.

An Investigation of the Evidence Available that High-Speed Management Theory Has the Potential to Stimulate and Integrate Organizational Communication

The latter half of the twentieth century has witnessed another revolution in communication. This communication revolution has introduced into the academic arena a marketplace of the practical and technological world with the premise that that which is most valuable is that which can be applied. . . . Knowledge is therefore perceived as the adaptation of theory and research to the arena of practical activities. Truth is that which works in application.

—King (1989:3)

Organizational communication theory and research, like a living organism, always grows and evolves in response to the challenges and opportunities of the times. Thus any attempt to stimulate and integrate organizational communication must foster this growth and evolution by allowing this process to proceed in as open and non-political marketplace as possible. We have argued here that High-Speed Management provides just such a stimulative and integrative device. When time is taken as a measure and studies in cycle time reduction as an outcome variable, just such an open and nonpolitical process for inquiry is created. This process allows for multiple philosophic assumptions, a variety of communication constructs and relationships, and numerous implementing procedures for improving communication outcomes.

Evidence supporting this claim can be drawn from the activities of a small set of academics, managers, and consultants from across disciplines and across cultures. A group of forty researchers from five continents—North America, Europe, Asia, Africa, and Australia—have focused on researching public, private, and not-for-profit organizations. They have over the past six years (a) held conferences and produced publications aimed at stimulating and integrating the organizational communication literature, (b) conducted case studies and benchmarked organizational communication processes of the most successful firms in the world, and (c) undertaken major consultancies aimed at testing High-Speed Management as a communication theory in use. Let us briefly review each of these efforts.

Conferences and Publications

Each year between 1993 and 1998 a conference has been held in different parts of the world which has brought together between thirty and forty participants (not always the same people) aimed at presenting research papers that stimulate and integrate organizational communication theory and research. These conferences have been supported by national governments, private-sector organizations, educational institutions, European business associations, and the U.S. Fulbright Commission. Several books and journal articles have been published which report the most significant research presented at these conferences. Edited books include Kozminski and Cushman (1993) *Organizational Communication and Management: A Global Perspective;* King and Cushman (1994c), *High-Speed Management and Organizational Communication: A Reader;* Cushman and King (1995b), *Communicating Organizational Change: A Management Perspective;* King and Cushman (1997), *Lessons from Recession;* and Cushman and King (2001), *Excellence in Communicating Organizational Strategy.*

In addition to the research published from these conferences, researchers became interested in integrating the communication literature in specific areas of High-Speed Management theory. Cushman and King (1995a) mapped the communication processes involved in the integration, coordination, and control of private-sector organizations. Cullin and Cushman (2000) mapped the communication processes involved in governmental organizations. King and Cushman (1992) mapped the leadership communication processes employed by Socialist nations (Poland, Armenia, Yugoslavia, and China) in moving from a socialist to capitalist economy. Ju and Cushman (1995) mapped effective communication in the teamwork processes. Obloj, Cushman, and Kozminski (1995) mapped the effective communication processes involved in various continuous improvement programs. These publications individually and collectively document a stimulation and integration of organizational communication within a High-Speed Management theoretic perspective.

Case Studies and Benchmarking

Frequently public, private, and not-for-profit organizations discover through rapid adaptations to the issues and competitors facing them more effective communication processes than researchers reveal. It is therefore becomes necessary to develop case studies of outstanding organizations from throughout the globe. Case studies and benchmarking of these firms represent an important contribution to the communication literature on effective communication processes. Cushman and King in a series of journal articles in *International Communication Focus* (1995–1997) and *Focus on Management Change (1995–1998)* have presented case studies of GE, ABB, Microsoft, Toyota, Chrysler, IBM, and Dell. Each of these studies chronicles a high-performance communication integration, coordination, and control system. In addition, Cullin and Cushman (2000) include studies of U.S., British, Singapore, and Australian governmental communication processes. Finally, in a new volume by Cushman and King (in press), case studies of various organizational communication functions (e.g., leadership, teamwork, and marketing) from throughout the global economy are presented. Such case studies attempt to stimulate and integrate organizational communication.

Consulting: Education and Interventions

Over the past several years Cushman, King, and associates have been involved in significant education and intervention projects in the private and public sectors. First, Cushman and King have been invited to present five-day seminars on High-Speed Management in nine ABB international MBA programs and a three-day seminar in Siemens' internal MBA program. In addition, three to five-day High-Speed Management seminars have been presented to public and private-sector organizations in the U.S., Bolivia, Australia, Italy, Germany, Hungary, Poland, Singapore, Indonesia, Japan, Korea, Malaysia, Thailand, and China.

Cushman and King have been involved in several major interventions including a five-year restructuring of the Victoran Public Service in Australia; a five-year benchmarking of the U.S., Singapore, and German education systems for Malaysia followed by a reengineering of the Malaysian National Education system; a one-week reengineering of a multinational corporation's corporate culture in Bolivia; a six-week downsizing of a medical center in the U.S. by $20 million dollars; and a five-year project to privatize governmental agricultural farms in Egypt. This sampling of consulting interventions from Cushman and King is aimed at demonstrating the effective use of High-Speed Management theory applications in the global economy.

High-Speed Management is therefore a stimulating and integrative force in organizational communication. In conclusion, as Cushman and King (1995c:1) wrote

> The purpose of human communication is to share symbolic information, to establish, maintain, and terminate relationships among people and human institutions. Occasionally, very occasionally, a research scholar will pose a question or raise an issue regarding the communication process that when an answer is provided will attract the attention and focus the energy of a group of scholars over a short period of time. . . . Less frequently, but perhaps more significantly, a question is posed, an issue raised, an answer provided by a group of scholars employing diverse methodology that must be considered controlling in its insightfulness and enduring in its suggestiveness and thus foundational to the study of human theory.

References

Automotive News (compiled from various reports, 1997 and 1998).

Cooper, R. (1985). Overall corporate strategies for new product programs, *Industrial Marketing Management, 14,* 179–183.

Cullin, R., and Cushman, D. P. (2000). *Managing Governmental Competitiveness: Speed, Consensus and Performance.* Albany: SUNY Press.

Cushman, D. P., and King, S. S. (1988a). High-technology and the role of communication in High-Speed Management. *Informatologia Yugoslavia,* 20:241–249.

Cushman, D. P., and King, S. S. (1988b). The role of mass media in world community. In *The World Academic Conference of the Seoul Olympiad 88: The World Community in Post-Industrial Society,* Korean Olympic Committees, Seoul Korea, 326–349. Reprinted in *Informatologia Yugoslavia,* 20:131–151.

Cushman, D. P., and King, S. S. (1993). High-Speed Management: A revolution in organizational communication in the 1990s. In S. Deetz (ed.), *Communication Yearbook 16,* 209–237; reprinted in M. Goodman (ed.), *Corporate Communication: Theory and Practice,* SUNY Press, 1994; and reprinted in Y. Ju and D. P. Cushman, *Organizational Teamwork in High-Speed Management,* SUNY Press, 1995, 15–38.

Cushman, D. P., and King, S. S. (1994a). High-Speed Management and high performance organizations. *Management,* November/December: 2–3.

Cushman, D. P., and King, S. S. (1994b). Communication and change. In W. Cummings and M. Cross (eds.), *Proceedings of the Seventh Conference on Corporate Communication.* N.J.: Fairleigh Dickinson, 41–51.

Cushman, D. P. and King, S. S. (1995a). *Communication and High-Speed Management.* Albany: SUNY Press. Reprinted in Malaysian in Malaysia.

Cushman, D. P., and King, S. S. (eds.) (1995b). *Communicating Organizational Change: A Management Perspective.* Albany: SUNY Press.

Cushman, D. P., and King, S. S. (1995c). Organizational ethics. In A. Kent (ed.), *Encyclopedia of Library and Information Science,* vol. 56. New York: Marcel Dekker, 301–317.

Cushman, D. P., and King, S. S. (1995d). High-Speed Management and organizational communication theory. In B. Kovačić and D. P. Cushman (eds.), *Watershed Research Traditions in Human Communication Theory.* Albany: SUNY Press.

Cushman, D. P., and King, S. S. (1995e). High-Speed Management cycle time reduction and high-performance organizations. *Focus on Change Management,* April: 3–6.

Cushman, D. P., and King, S. S. (1995f). Reengineering high-performance organizations. *International Communication Focus—North America,* April: 9–11.

Cushman, D. P., and King, S. S. (1995g). The accidental king of corporate turnaround: Lou Gerstner of IBM. *Focus on Change Management,* October: 17–22.

Cushman, D. P., and King, S. S. (1996a). Toyota: The renaissance of a world leader. *Focus on Change Management,* March: 8–12.

Cushman, D. P., and King, S. S. (1996b, December/1997, January). Excellence in communicating organizational competitiveness: The case of Microsoft. *Focus on Change Management,* 22–25.

Cushman, D. P., and King, S. S. (1997d, December/1998, January). Creating implementing structures that generate winning performance. *Focus on Change Management,* 3–9.

Cushman, D. P., and King, S. S. (1997c, December/1998, January). GE: Increasing productivity through effective internal communication. *International Communication Focus,* 8–9.

Cushman, D. P., and King, S. S. (1997b). The Repositioning of Asea Brown and Boveri. *Focus on Change Management,* March: 11–16.

Cushman, D. P., and King, S. S. (1997a). *High-Speed Management: The Role of Communication in Continuously Improving an Organization's Performance.* Albany: SUNY Press.

Cushman, D. P., and King, S. S. (2001). *Excellence in Communicating Organizational Strategy.* Albany: SUNY Press.

Cushman, D. P., and King, S. S. (in press). *Benchmarking Organizational Communication Processes.*

Donion, J. P. (1993). Alfred Sloan, move over. *Chief Executive Magazine,* 1–8.

Dumaine, B. (1984). How managers can succeed through speed. *Fortune,* February 13, 119, 54–59.

Fraker, S. (1984). High-speed management for the high-tech age. *Fortune,* February 13, 119, 34–60.

Gupta, A., Raj, S., and Wileman, D. (1985). R&D and marketing dialogue in high-tech firms. *Industrial Marketing and Management* 14, 289–300.

Ju, Y., and Cushman, D. P. (1995). *Organizational Teamwork in High-Speed Management.* Albany: SUNY Press.

Kerwin, K. (1998). GM: It's time to face the future. *Business Week,* July 27, 26–28.

King, S. S. (1989). Communication: Roots, visions, and prospects. In S. S. King (ed.), *Human Communications as a Field of Study.* Albany: SUNY Press, 1–12.

King, S. S., and Cushman, D. P. (eds.). (1992). *Political Communication: Engineering Visions of Order in the Socialist World.* Albany: SUNY Press.

King, S. S., and Cushman, D. P. (eds.). (1994). *High-Speed Management and Organizational Communication: A Reader.* Albany: SUNY Press.

King, S. S., and Cushman, D. P. (eds.). (1997). *Lessons from Recession.* Albany: SUNY Press.

Kovačić, B., and Cushman, D. P. (eds.). (1995). *Watershed Research Traditions in Human Communication.* Albany: SUNY Press.

Kozminski, A., and Cushman, D. P. (eds.) (1993). *Organizational Communication and Management: A Global Perspective.* Albany: SUNY Press.

Miller, R. (2001). Beyond benchmarking for institutional advancement, Jump start to fund raising excellence. In D. P. Cushman and S. S. King (eds.), *Excellence in Communicating Organizational Strategy.* Albany: SUNY Press.

Nicotera, A., and Cushman, D. P. (1992). Organizational Ethics: A Within-Organization View. *Journal of Applied Communication Research*, November 10:437–463.

Obloj, K., Cushman, D. P., and Kozminski, A. (1995). *Winning: Continuous Improvement in High Performance Organizations.* Albany: SUNY Press.

Ruffin, W. (1992). Wired for speed. *Business Month*, January, 56–58.

Stalk, G., Jr. (1988). Time—The next source of competitive advantage. *Harvard Business Review*, July/August, 66:41–51.

Vesey, J. (1991). The new competitors: They think in terms of speed-to-market. *Academy of Management Executives* 5, 22–33.

3

Killer Strategies for Competitiveness: The Case at Microsoft

Donald P. Cushman and Sarah Sanderson King

Competition is a lot like cod liver oil. First it makes you sick. Then it makes you better.

—American Micro Devices (1996:22)

The emerging global economy has forced a very serious reconsideration of our understanding of the economic basis of sustainable competitive advantage.

First, quick market saturation, unexpected competition, and the rapid succession of technological breakthroughs have each in turn served to create a volatile global economic environment by significantly shortening the time frame within which any one firm can maintain a competitive advantage.

Second, attempts to constrain this global economic volatility have served to further undermine our traditional understandings of product cost, differentiation, and scope as the basis for a sustainable competitive advantage. For example, the development of integrated manufacturing systems which can produce 1 or 100,000 of a product at the same cost has undermined our traditional notion that high volume leads to a sustainable competitive advantage based on low cost. Similarly, reverse engineering and a dramatic reduction in the cycle time it takes to develop a new product and get it to market has seriously called into question the ability of product differentiation to serve as a basis for sustainable competitive advantage.

Third, technological breakthroughs and the effective computerization of many organization tasks have led to transformational

27

changes in the types of organizational skill required to compete effectively. This in turn has led to both continual and rapid shifts in the core competencies a firm must develop either internally or by external alliances, rendering problematic stable core competencies as a basis for sustainable competitive advantage.

Finally, all of these trends taken collectively have led some thoughtful observers or organizational competitiveness to proclaim the death of sustainable competitive advantage. For example, James F. Moore (1996) in his provocative book, *The Death of Competition: Leadership Strategy in the Age of Business Ecosystems,* argues that former bitter rivals must now learn how to collaborate or they will not survive given the structural economic forces at work in the emerging global economy. He then cites Microsoft Corporation, AT&T, Hewlett Packard, and Netscape Communication Corporation as support for his claim.

It will be the purpose of this chapter to (1) develop a conceptual and empirical basis for understanding sustainable competitive advantage in the global marketplace, (2) apply that conceptual and empirical analysis to Microsoft Corporation's dominance of the PC software industry, and (3) draw some conclusions regarding the significance of this conceptual and empirical framework for establishing a firm's excellence in communicating organizational competitiveness.

Developing a Conceptual and Empirical Basis for Understanding Sustainable Competitive Advantage

Sustainable competitive advantage can be a considerable asset if it truly confers a lasting benefit and helps toward achieving the objectives set by a company's business strategy.

—Coyne (1996:1)

Business strategies are created in order to determine the way in which organizations can move from their current position to a new and stronger position vis-à-vis their customers and competitors. This is what is meant by improving a firm's competitiveness. A universal conception of competitiveness does not exist. Some view competitiveness as a communication process, the ability to persuade customers to choose their offerings over some other alternatives. Others view competitiveness as the ability to continuously improve a firm's value chain responsiveness to environmental change and competitors' activities. Still others believe a firm must develop certain core competencies relative to other firms in the same industry and market (Feurer and Chaharbagh, 1994:49). Our attempt to resolve these issue will proceed in two stages: (1) providing a conceptual framework for understanding what a sustainable competitive advantage is and (2) providing an empirical operationalization of the organizational strategies capable of yielding such an advantage.

Conceptualizing Sustainable Competitive Advantage

Central to an understanding of sustainable competitive advantage are the concepts of (a) competitive dynamic, (b) core competency, and (c) industrial breakpoints. *Competitive dynamic* refers to the weighted dimensions along which customers evaluate a product or service when making a purchase. For example, in the U.S. auto market in 1995, the competitive dynamic for purchasing a car included the automobile's style (40 percent), a car's price (30 percent), brand loyalty (20 percent), and vehicle quality (10 percent) (*Automotive News*, 1996:21). Collectively, these dimensions determine customer purchasing patterns.

Core competencies are the skills a firm has which customers are persuaded best provide the above desirable dimensions in a product. Note that core competencies include two separate elements: (1) a communicated expectation that a given firm can deliver on the appropriate dimensions and (2) the reality of the firm's ability to meet these expectations in the required area. If customers' expectations are not met, the core competencies of the firms are adjusted appropriately in the next customer evaluation. The composite of each firm's customer evaluation along with all the competitive dynamic dimensions yields the industry's core competency leaders in market shares. For example, in 1995, U.S. customers of medium-sized cars (e.g. Lumina, Camry, Taurus, Accord, and Intrepid) associated auto style (40 percent) with (1) Honda, (2) Ford, and (3) Chrysler; price (30 percent with (1) Chrysler, (2) Honda, and (3) Ford; and auto quality (10 percent) with (1) Toyota, (2) Honda, and (3) GM. Overall, Honda edged out Ford in the customers' perception of core competencies and in sales, followed by Chrysler, Toyota, and General Motors (*USA Today*, 1996:B1).

An *industrial breakpoint*, according to Stroebel (1995:11–12),

> is characterized by a new offering in the market that is so much superior in terms of the value perceived by the customer and the delivered cost of the offering that it changes the rules of the competitive game. A breakpoint is typically accompanied by a sharp shift in the industry's growth rate and a dramatic realignment of market shares.

Industrial breakpoints appear to be divided into two main types, divergent and convergent. *Divergent breakpoints*, according to Stroebel (1995:12),

> usher in an increasing variety of competitive product offerings. They occur, initially, at a discontinuous juncture in an industry, when the direct innovation of entrepreneurs and others results in divergent experiments, with competitors racing to develop the new products and or services which will redefine the industry standards.

For example, Chrysler's development of the Jeep Cherokee sports vehicle or Toyota's development of the Lexus midprice-range luxury cars represent divergent industrial breakpoints. *Convergent breakpoints* involve a more standardized set of offerings, with competition being focused on improving an organization's business systems in delivering existing products in a more effective manner. For example, Toyota's lean manufacturing with its *Kaisan* and *Kaban* systems and Limited's point of sale inventory system represent continuous industrial breakpoints.

Table 3.1
Types of Industrial Breakpoints

Divergent	*Convergent*
Product centered	Organization process centered
Direct innovation	Process integration
R&D or acquisition created	Continuous improvement created
Stakeholder network	Process reengineering

Taken collectively, the concepts of competitive dynamics, core competencies and industrial breakpoints allow for a very specific operationalization of the basis of a conceptual sustainable competitive advantage. Such a conceptualization has three components:

- *First,* customers must hold a relatively stable view of the dimensions constituting a product or service's competitive dynamics.

- *Second,* customers must perceive a significant difference between competing firms in regard to their core competencies.

- *Third,* the differences the customer perceives in regard to the core competency gap can be expected to endure at least until the next industrial breakpoint. For example, Chrysler's development of the minivan ten years ago has yielded that firm a sustainable competitive advantage which has existed awaiting the next industrial breakpoint.

Having conceptually and operationally defined sustainable competitive advantage, we are now in need of an empirical specification of model strategies capable of yielding and then maintaining a sustainable competitive advantage in the global marketplace.

Empirical Description of Successful Competitive Strategies

Allan Morrison and Kendall Roth (1992) provide just such a specification in their seminal monograph, "A Taxonomy of Business Level Strategies in Global Industries." Two basic questions are addressed in their research: (1) what are the distinct patterns of business level strategic behaviors that differentiate competitors in the global industrial context and (2) do economic performance difference exist among the distinct patterns? They surveyed 144 executives of firms operating in eleven manufacturing and consumer goods industries of the global economy.

Morrison and Roth (1992) employed eighteen measures of strategic positioning, multiple measures of internationalization (i.e., investment, coordination, and political scales), and multiple measures of a firm's economic performance (i.e., return on assets [ROA], return on investment [ROI], and increase in sales). This data was then factor-analyzed yielding four distinct models of successful competitive strategies operating in the global economy. These four models employed strategies which explored (1) a domestic product niche with limited exports, (2) exporting high-quality politically supported offerings, (3) exploring high-quality innovative products, and (4) a continuously improved business process exporting strategy. The models presented in table 3.2 indicate the strategic positioning, internationalization, integration, and economic performance measures which clustered in each model.

Table 3.2
Global Strategies for Achieving Market Shares

Model 1: Domestic: Product Niche with Limited Exports
a. Lowest percent of exports (12%) to total sales normally involving only one other country
b. Lowest international investment, political influence, and integration scores.
c. Narrow product specialization focus
d. Emphasis on manufacturing leadership due to process innovation and efficiency
e. High quality, reasonable cost, mature products
f. Lowest ROA, ROI, and second lowest sales growth

Model 2: Exporting High Quality Politically Supported Offerings
a. Exports 33% of total shares to two other countries
b. Low levels of internationalization of finance and integration
c. High level of political influence to support exports
d. Minimal attention to manufacturing leadership and cost controls
e. Production mainly in home country along with reliable distribution
f. Lowest or next to lowest ROA, ROI, and sales growth

Model 3: Exporting High-Quality Innovative Products
a. Second highest percent of exports (37%) to total sales, going to ten countries
b. High internationalization of finance, political influence, and integration
c. Minimal political influences from home government
d. Emphasis on reputation for quality and marketing
e. Narrow high-priced product specialization
f. R&D focuses on costly bells and whistles which influence marketing more than product technology
g. Highest or next to highest in ROA, ROI, and sales growth

Model 4: Continuously Improved Business Process Exporting Strategy
a. Highest percent exports (59%) total sales going to fourteen countries
b. Highest percent of foreign assets to total assets 24%
c. Highest in international political influence and integration
d. Emphasis on innovations in manufacturing and marketing processes
e. Tight capacity utilization
f. Strong emphasis on skilled sales force
g. Strong emphasis on control of distribution channels
h. Either highest or next to highest in ROA, ROI, and sales growth

These then are the empirically established strategies employed by successful global competitors in eleven industries aimed at establishing a sustainable competitive advantage. The Exporting Innovative Products Strategy (Model 3) and the Continuously Improved Business Process Exporting Strategy (Model 4) appear equally successful from an economic performance perspective and closely parallel our conceptualization of divergent and convergent approaches to capitalizing on industrial breakpoints. However, the empirical models refine our conceptual analysis by pointing out that the *Divergent Product Innovation Model* frequently takes a distinct marketing flavor by focusing on bells and whistles rather than product superiority alone and that the *Convergent Continuous Improvement of Business Processes Model* focuses on advances in manufacturing, distribution, and sales.

We have conceptualized sustainable competitive advantage through the precise definition of (1) competitive dynamics, (b) core competencies, and (c) industrial breakpoints. We have operationalized the empirical strategies employed in the global market to obtain a sustainable competitive advantage as (1) a domestic product niche with limited exports, (2) exporting high-quality politically supported offerings, (3) exporting high-quality innovative products, and (4) a continuously improved business process strategy. We are now in a position to apply our conceptual and empirical analysis of sustainable competitive advantage to the Microsoft Corporation's attempts to dominate the PC software industry.

Analysis of Microsoft's Attempts to Establish a Sustainable Competitive Advantage

I personally believe that Microsoft is the most powerful economic force in the United States in the second half of the 20th century. Some of Microsoft's control over competing, at all levels, is obvious. Much, however, is invisible. Even longtime insiders are just beginning to understand the nature of that power, how Microsoft acquired it, preserves it, and exercises it.

—Schmidt (1996:51)

Microsoft's competitors within the computer industry speak of their will to dominate markets (i.e., seek a sustainable competitive advantage) with concern, fear, and admiration. Michael Kapar, CEO of Lotus

Development Corporation, argues "The question of what to do about Microsoft is going to be a central public policy issue for the next twenty years. Policymakers don't understand the real character of Microsoft yet—the sheer will to power that Microsoft has." (Gleick, 1995:39) Lawrence Ellison, CEO of Oracle, another Microsoft competitor argues that "Bill Gates and Microsoft do not just want to compete in the computer industry. Rather, they seek to dominate every aspect of the market, to eliminate their competition." (Cortese, et al., 1996:86) In 1994, *Fortune* magazine conducted two polls of managers, customers, and stockholders. The *first* found Microsoft *to be the most innovative firm in America*. The *second* found Microsoft *to rank second as the most admired firm in America* (Jacob, 1995:54).

The Microsoft Corporation is considered by most observers to be one of the most competitive firms in the world. In just twenty-one years its CEO, Bill Gates, went from a Harvard dropout to amass a $15 billion fortune and become one of the richest men in the world. The Microsoft Corporation in the same timeframe went from a two-person firm with $16,000 in sales to one of the world's most powerful corporations with 18,000 employees, $5.3 billion in sales, and $1.4 billion in profits. In addition, over 3,000 of its employees are now millionaires based on their stockholder value in Microsoft (Jones, 1995:14–15.

Each day 170 million people use personal computers. Each day 140 million of them begin by entering Microsoft MS DOS operating systems. Seventy million PC users then enter Microsoft Windows operating systems on IBM-compatible, Apple, Macintosh, and Power Mac's PCs. Then, 100 million users select one of Microsoft's many software application packages to begin their work. Microsoft holds an 85% market share in computer operating systems, an 80% share of the office applications market, a 64% of the word processing market, and 80% of the business spreadsheet market (Schlender and Kirkpatrick, 1995:87). In addition, Microsoft's 25% profit margins are significantly higher than most firms in the industry. In order to understand how Microsoft obtained such a sustainable competitive advantage, let us (1) explore the firm's macro competitive strategy, (2) explore the operationalization of that strategy or tactics employed in the marketplace, and (3) trace the firm's competitive positioning at one breakpoint in the computer industry.

Microsoft's Macro Competitive Strategy

Microsoft's products and services are aimed at empowering people and organizations by providing them with an easy way of finding and using information. In order to compete successfully in the software industry, Bill Gates believes that Microsoft must *"pioneer and orchestrate evolving mass markets"* (Cusumano and Selby, 1995:127). This involves pioneering in software applications and operating systems which can dominate their respective markets while forging an industrial consensus among key stakeholders in the global marketplace as to "appropriate standards" needed to regulate the application interface (API). Microsoft employs five strategic principles in guiding their macro competitive strategy.

1. Enter evolving mass markets early or stimulate new markets with good products which can become the industry standard.

2. Incrementally continuously improve products and periodically make old products obsolete.

3. Push volume sales to ensure that products become and remain the industry standard.

4. Leverage the industrial standard to develop new products and market linkages.

5. Integrate, extend and simplify products and services to reach new mass markets. (Cusumano and Selby, 1995:127)

"Microsoft is one of those rare companies where leadership, strategy, people, culture and opportunities come together to create an extraordinary effective organization" (Cusumano and Selby, 1995:400). To see how and why this happens, we need to explore the firm's focus on (1) the benefits of continuous improvement programs and (2) a focus on setting industry standards.

Unique Economics of Information

Benefits of Continuous Improvement. Developing a "good" product in the software industry is a complex activity. It involves working within several rather fixed and important parameters. *First,* there are technological parameters to the hardware, what the basic architecture of the hardware can do. *Second,* there are historical parameters involving past applications, operating systems, and marketing segments which must be preserved in a new program to maintain or expand a mass market. *Third,* there are the emerging areas for new operating systems, applications, and market segments needed to create or maintain a mass market. *Fourth,* there are the strengths and weaknesses of various interface capabilities between these parameters and their users. *Finally,* computer software is a rapidly evolving business where in three years all the products, services, and knowledge we have today may be outdated, thus timing in getting a product to market which fits all these stakeholder needs is a challenge.

In order to successfully navigate all these important parameters plus the normal volatility in the global economy of unexpected competition, quick market saturation, and/or technological breakthroughs, it is necessary to get products out in the market and then use your resources as a large, financially sound, and rapidly responding firm to develop and/or acquire existing and/or new technologies in order to meet your stakeholder needs more effectively than your competitors. That is why most initial Microsoft offerings are not industry leaders but through continuous improvement achieve the status of industrial standards. That happened with Q-DOS and MS-DOS, Windows and Windows 95, Word and Office Systems, and others.

A second ingredient is required in order to create a mass market.

Focus on Setting Industry Standards.   The age of mass production for mass markets could not begin until the world agreed on standards for nuts, bolts, parts, and their interface. Establishing standards acts as a catalyst for economic development. In the past, many of these mass production standards were set by governments, international organizations, or industry consortia, but seldom by a single firm. The more complex the products, the more precise the standards must be, and computer software is a very complex product. In understanding the two-decade history of Microsoft's increasing control over the computer industry, nothing matters more than its strategic management of the creation, marketing, and manipulation of standards.

It works like this. In order to successfully work within all the parameters for creating software listed above, all the key players in an area of the industry must meet and negotiate a common standard which includes the integration of their past, current, and future products and technologies. Let us say you are an expert in a small firm in voice recognition and turning that recognition into a printed text. One day you get an invitation from Microsoft to come to a set of meetings on standards. You cannot not go or your products and interests could be excluded. Then under Microsoft's guidance, you and several other firms negotiate the rules governing the applications program interface (API). Not many large firms have the power to call such a set of meetings, but Microsoft does.

The result, according to Gleick (1995), is that Microsoft in co-operation with virtually the entire speech software industry, will release next year the Microsoft Speech Software Development Kit containing all the necessary tools to develop applications which meet the standards set.

The problem of setting new standards which will create a mass market is solved. However, in these standards meetings, Microsoft receives and files away an enormous body of intelligence on the speech software industry. It discovers where the competitors have been, where they are going, and how they will get there. It then has the competitive intelligence necessary to develop a balanced software program for meeting the complexities of the parameters in a given area. Microsoft has held such conferences on standards in such areas as E-mail, network integration, and multimedia applications. Microsoft is not the only firm attempting to set standards, but it is one of the largest and most effective at doing so.

Cusumano and Selby (1995:163) in their seminal study of Microsoft's competitive effectiveness summarizes our analysis when they argue:

> Microsoft's goal was emphatically not the maximization of revenue or even market share; it was creating relationships with customers, software developers and microprocessor firms like Intel to give as many reasons as possible to support—strategically, financially, and technically—Microsoft's operating systems. These networks of relationships are what makes a standard something more than a product. The standard is not the product of a company, it's the byproduct of these networks. Managing standards means managing networks.

What happens if you support Microsoft in setting these standards? Many firms prosper. Intel, DEC, Compaq, and others have profited immensely. And what happens if you oppose Microsoft's standards and support a competing standard? Again, some firms have prospered such as Sun, Netscape, and Oracle, by setting internet browser standards. However, other firms have dramatically lost market shares, as in the case of Lotus 1-2-3, Borland International's Paradox, and IBM's OS/2 operating system. Standards confer near monopoly power in most areas of computer software. Recently, several banking and networking firms have asked the U.S. government to examine Microsoft's competitive strategies as a possible violation of the antitrust laws. However, evidence is hard to come by since almost all competing firms in the industry have some type of alliance, joint venture, or licensing agreement with Microsoft and realize that Microsoft is a "good" friend and a "bad" enemy. This has led some observers of the software industry, like Jerry Kaplan a former Lotus executive to argue, "What we need in the business is a witness protection program" (Schlender and Kirkpatrick, 1995:90).

Having explained in some detail Microsoft's macro strategies for developing a sustainable competitive advantage by exploiting (1) the benefits of continuous improvement programs and (2) a focus on setting industrial standards, we are now in a position to explore Microsoft's operationalization of these strategies into tactics in the global marketplace.

Operationalizing the Linkages between Macro and Micro Competitive Strategies

How does Microsoft succeed in dominating the global software industry? *First* and foremost, "Bill Gates may be the shrewdest entrepreneur and the most underrated manager in American industry today," (Cusumano and Selby, 1995:23) *Second,* Microsoft's leadership team like that of GE and Intel is filled with talented, highly motivated, and creative managers who provide the tactical linkages between leadership, corporate strategy, and the workers. *Finally,* all employees of Microsoft understand that although knowledge and technology are important, it is more important how that knowledge and technology can make money. "They are interested in bang for the buck and mass markets, and they believe that delivering value to the customer will make the most money" (Cusumano and Selby, 1995:104). Let us explore four of the linkages developed by Microsoft's management team for operationalizing competitive strategy at the workforce-market interface. In so doing we will observe the creative and efficient manner in which Microsoft develops a sustainable competitive advantage.

Product Development and Continuous Improvement Linkage to Microsoft's Unique Brand of Teamwork.   To manage creative people and technical skills in an efficient manner, to produce new and continuously improved products in a manner that sets the industry standard, Microsoft employs a unique form of teamwork. This form of teamwork established functional specialities within small modular teams with overlapping responsibilities. *Product managers, soft-*

ware developers, and testers are the main functional specialists within a product unit.

> Within the product unit, program managers, developers and test work side by side in small "feature teams" These typically consist of one program manager, three to eight developers, and a parallel features testing band whose members are paired with developers. (Cusumano and Selby, 1995:74)

In addition each product team also contains *product managers,* who are marketing specialists; *customer support engineers,* who provide technical assistance to users and analyze customer feedback; and a *user education staff,* who prepares manuals and helps with documentation. Program managers can lead several features teams, and product managers can lead several program teams. Group and division managers supervise and review all program and product team progress. Bill Gates supervises and reviews all group and division leader efforts. Such parallel and synchronous teams with overlapping functional responsibilities and multiple layers of review have several unique competitive advantages. *First,* they are self-correcting based on overlapping functions, parallel synchronization, customer and stakeholder feedback, and multiple levels of review. *Second,* they can be expanded, contracted, eliminated, and redirected quickly due to their modular structure. *Third,* they are uniquely responsive to the marketplace demands of customers. When parallel programming and testing functions are guided by the competitive intelligence gained from the API interference standards meetings, Microsoft can then take an initial product offering and transform it through upgrade to a market standard which better meets customer and stakeholder parameters than its competitors.

Setting of Industrial Standards Linkage to Microsoft's Unique Acquisitions, Product Development, and Alliance Policies.   Central to setting industrial interface and product standards is state-of-the-art technology and strong partners who will support the standards which Microsoft puts forward. For example, currently, there are five gateways onto the information highway: computer operating systems, digital video disk technology, video games technology, digital music disk technology, and inter/intranet browser/server technology (Taylor, 1996:D6). Microsoft is attempting to obtain the technology and form the alliances necessary to set standards for the applications program interface and develop standard products in each of these gateways. Their strategy is to (1) set the interface standards, (2) develop interface tool kits for application development, and (3) develop dominant products which act as the standard for the interface.

In the *Computer Operating System Gateway*, the competition is between Microsoft's Windows 95 and Apple's Macintosh OS and IBM's OS/2. Apple's Mac OS holds an edge in terms of functionality, but runs only on Apple machines. IBM's OS/2 is technologically more robust, but has a limited range of applications programs. Windows 95 currently holds an 85% market share with Apple's MAC OS and IBM's OS/2, each holding 7% of the market share (Taylor, 1996:D5). Microsoft has set the API standards, developed an applications tool kit, and marketed the dominant product in the gateway Windows 95 and developed an upgrade in Windows NT. In operating systems, Microsoft currently controls the gateway.

In the *Digital Video Disk Gateway*, the competition is between SONY along with Phillips Electronics and the Toshiba Corporation along with Matsushita. In September of 1995 manufacturers agreed on a single format for both high-capacity video disks. Windows 95 and NT contain an API standard for the interface between video disk technology and computers. In November 1992, Microsoft released Video for Windows, a tool kit for playback which could incorporate, edit, and create digital video access across all implementations of Windows. By February 1993, Microsoft announced the release of visual control Pack, an easy-to-use collection of nineteen customer controls for visual basic. This was followed in March 1993 by the release of a multimedia Windows publishing kit. In November 1994, Microsoft formed an alliance with ten partners to develop interactive TV software. These included Hewlett Packard, TCI, Intel, US West, Telstar, Deutsche Telecom, Alcatel Cable, Anderson Consulting, Lockheed, Nippon Telephone and Telegraph, and Olivetti. In June 1994, Microsoft acquired Soft Image, a leading developer of both performance 3-D computer animation and visualization software. In March 1995, Microsoft joined with ABC and Dreamworks to help develop content for video, film, and computer game disks. In March 1995, Microsoft joined with Toshiba and Matsushita to develop an API interface for its video disks. In May, Microsoft formed an alliance with Time Warner, Comcast cable, and French, German, Australia, and Singapore cable to design and API cable interface to use Windows 95 and NT for cable TV. In April 1995, Microsoft joined Sony to develop video on demand for home TV and computer delivery. Microsoft appears to be in a position to exert considerable control over the video disk gateway both in its interface with Windows 95 and NT and in developing the content, form, delivery, and interactive applications for customers.

In the *Video Games Gateway*, the competitors are SONY's Playstation, Sega's Saturn, and Nintendo system. Here again no single firm dominates. In July 1993, Microsoft released Arcada, a replication of five of the most popular arcade games from Atari. In February 1995, Microsoft entered the market with an applications tool kit for developing professionals game applications based on Windows technology. Microsoft has its own computer games unit which has marketed several very popular games including Flight Simulator, Golf, Dinosaurs, and others. Several video games developers and makers of PC equipment for games have joined in an alliance with Microsoft to develop applications and hardware for this market. In February 1993, Microsoft joined with Sega Video Games Corporation to provide operating systems for games. In April 1995, Microsoft released its upgraded operating systems for fast-moving multimedia games. The Video Games Gateway is still involved in heated competition. Microsoft came late to the game but is ready to release its first upgrades of initial products and with Dreamworks and others involved in developing the next generation game content. Its API standards and applications tool kits are putting Windows 95 and NT at the center of the computer games interface and expanding Microsoft's influence in this gateway.

In the *Digital Music Gateway*, SONY and Philips have developed competing technologies with competing formats. This diversity has customers confused. SONY sold 92,000 compressed minidisks last year; Philips, 409 million compact disks. In this area, Microsoft has written API standards for its Windows interface and developed application kits. In October 1992 Microsoft released Musical Instruments, the first multimedia title resulting from a joint venture with Dorling Kindusky of London. In addition, Microsoft in March 1995 joined with Dreamworks to develop music and multimedia content for CD roms, cable, and the internet. Microsoft, again, is well-positioned to influence the interface, content, and delivery systems in this gateway. However, at this point in time, no firm or group of firms control the gateway.

In the *Browser/Server Gateway* to the inter/intranet, Netscape's Navigator controls 85% of the browser market with Microsoft Explorer just entering the market holding a 7% market share. Novell's Netware has 53% of the server market share, with Windows NT holding 9% (Clark, 1995:B8). The browser and server markets are still in their infancy. Firms are still developing the technology and adding features as they begin to understand their potential. The market is expected to triple in size each of the next three years as large corporations spend a projected $54 billion per year on multiuser software (Clark, 1995:B8).

All firms are scrambling to form alliances, make acquisitions, and upgrade products. Microsoft's browsers and servers have just entered the market and will be made part of Windows 95 and NT. In addition, Microsoft has made their browser and server systems available free on the internet. This has put pressure on Netscape and Novell which obtain most of their revenues from their browser and server sales. We will explore the browser/server gateway in detail when we investigate Microsoft's competitive positioning in the computer industry's next breakpoint. Currently, this gateway is involved in heated competition and it will take five years for the market's growth to level off and the technology to mature before a winner will be able to emerge.

For Microsoft, its acquisition, product development, and alliance strategies have allowed the firm to become a dominant player in two of the gateways, operating and video disk systems; to become an expanding and influential player in two of the gateways, computer games and musical disk systems; and to become a new player in one of the gateways, browsers/server systems. However, Microsoft is the *only firm* with a strong presence across all gateways, placing them in a position to achieve an integration of these technologies which would yield a sustainable competitive advantage on the information highway.

Volume Marketing and Distribution Linkage to Competitive Pricing, Exclusive Contracting, and Software Bundling.   Volume sales are critically important to the competitiveness of a software firm. Bill Gates tells why: "It's all about scale economies and market share. When you're shipping a million units of Windows software a month, you can afford to spend $300 million a year improving it and still sell it at a low price." (Cusumano and Selby, 1995:158). Executive Vice President of Microsoft, Steve Ballmer, elaborates: "Software businesses are all fixed cost businesses. And so volume is absolutely everything . . . because you have to amortize that fixed cost very broadly" (Cusumano and Selby, 1995:158). The result is that no PC software firm can match Microsoft's financial resources. The company spent $830 million on R&D in 1995 and has salted away $4 to $5 billion for acquisitions and joint ventures.

Windows and Windows 95 used aggressive pricing, licensing, and contract tactics to obtain volume sales. Windows 95 sold at retail outlets for about $95.00. For high-volume wholesalers, it sold at about $35.00. For hardware makers they could reduce the price to about $30.00, if they agreed to preinstall Windows 95 on 50% or more of their PC shipments and adopt the Windows 95 logo (Cusumano and Selby, 1995:161). Thanks to such preinstallation contracts, Windows 95 was preloaded on 70% of all PCs sold in 1995.

In addition to volume purchase price reductions and preshipment installation contracts, Microsoft developed a competitive strategy called applications bundling. Microsoft Office Suite features an integration of the most commonly used desktop applications word processing (Microsoft Word), business spreadsheets (Microsoft Excel), computer graphics (Microsoft Power Point), database management (Microsoft Access), and electronic mail (Microsoft Mail) into a single package selling for about $250. Retail price for each of the products in Office Suite sold independently was about $300 each. Once again further price reductions were possible with preshipment installation contracts. Many hardware providers signed such contracts. The net effect of such bundling and reshipment contracts is that each of these independent products leads its software category in sales.

The effect on competitors was devastating. Word Perfect, Lotus 1-2-3 and others had led the word processing and spreadsheet market, but Microsoft's Office Suite reduced their market shares to close to nothing, placing the firms in financial jeopardy. Microsoft has employed pricing, preshipment contracts, and bundling in the desktop publishing, multimedia, shop floor automation, and home, banking, and computer games applications markets. Microsoft's use of pricing, preinstallation contracts, and software bundling has served to create mass markets for Microsoft in a manner that limits its competitors, capacity to compete, helping to create a sustainable competitive advantage for Microsoft products.

Leveraging Standards to Limit Competitors' Sales and Link Microsoft Products to New Mass Markets. Three examples will serve to illustrate Microsoft's use of this strategy. Cusumano and Selby (1995:160) wrote:

> Digital Research, CPI M-86 (developed in the early 1980s) might have become the dominant PC operating system; reportedly, it had better memory management features and other advantages over MS-DOS. Microsoft, however, was the leading language producer, and it did not rush to deliver versions of its languages compatible

with CP/M86. When it did ship compatible languages, Microsoft priced them 50 percent over DOS-compatible versions, and they sold in low volumes. Microsoft also sold an inferior version of Basic, stripped of graphics. As a result, applications developers found it difficult to write anything but MS-DOS, and CP/M-86 failed as a competing product.

Windows 95 contains an icon and input capability for accessing Microsoft online, a network feature to the program. When a Window's user employed the icon, they obtained access to both Microsoft online and the Worldwide Web. When a user employed another online service for the linkage to Windows 95, the program disconnected the input system and made it inoperable. Microsoft's competitors who are network providers filed a restraint of trade claim against Microsoft for the Windows 95 disconnect function (Cusumano and Selby, 1995:181).

Finally, when one PC operating system controls 85% of the PC market, most independent firms writing PC applications programs will find it most lucrative to develop their products first for compatibility with that system. Then if time and resources permit, the firms will develop applications for competing systems. Windows 95 is so dominant in the PC market that most software development firms do not write Mac OS and OS/2 applications for their products because the market shares are too small to warrant the effort. Both Apple and IBM have had and continue to have trouble getting independent software firms to write applications for their operating systems. Firms that provide operating systems with a limited number of applications have trouble selling those systems. The result is that Windows 95 comes preinstalled on all Apple and IBM computers along with each firm's own operating system. This prevents Apple and IBM from making a serious attempt to increase its market shares and limits the sale of their own hardware systems. In addition, Microsoft was having trouble getting independent software firms to write application programs for its Windows NT workstations operating systems. It solved the problem by requiring every firm which developed a program for Windows 95 by contract to deliver the same program adapted to the Windows NT architecture. The result, Windows NT has the most extensive applications library of any workstation operating system.

We have reviewed four of Microsoft's linkages between its macro competitive strategy and their tactical operationalization at the worker/market interface: (1) the product development and continuous improvement linkages to teamwork; (2) the setting of industrial standards linkage to acquisitions and alliances; (3) the volume marketing and distribution linkages to pricing, contracting, and software bundling; and (4) leveraging standards to limit competitor sales and link Microsoft products to mass markets. In each area, these strategies are employed to provide Microsoft with a sustainable competitive advantage over other firms. Attention is now directed to surveying Microsoft's use of their macro strategies and operational tactics to position their firm relative to their competitors in the next computer industry breakpoint.

Positioning Microsoft to Influence a Computer Industry Breakpoint

By early 1995, the sensation of the computer industry had become the internet and intranet, a 13-year-old government-designed electronic playground that was emerging as "the de facto medium of the Digital Age" (Schlender, 1995:70). The intranet is a privately owned and secured model of the internet for corporations. With the sudden popularity of both the World Wide Web, the Internet's multimedia Main Street, and the emergence of Fortune 500 firm proprietor intranets, we see a rise in computing on these nets. A transformation has occurred in computing. The inter/intranet, it turns out, is an inexpensive and yet powerful alternative form of communication, and a competitive alternative to conventional computer setups. The rise of the inter/intranet represents a potential paradigm shift in the computer industry, a *divergent industrial breakpoint* marked by a large number of new product offerings so much superior in terms of the value perceived by customers that it changes the rules of the competitive game.

The rise of the internet and intranet has already generated a dramatic realignment of market shares which, according to Bill Gates, "threatens all Microsoft has accomplished." The internet and intranet popularity is forcing traditional computer industry powerhouses like AT&T, Hewlett Packard, IBM, and Microsoft to rethink the basic assumptions of their businesses. Meanwhile firms previously viewed as niche players like Sun Microsystems (workstations), Silicon Graphics (workstation software), Oracle Systems (database software), Netscape (a web browser provider), Sybase (a network software router firm), and Novell (a Web server software provider) have doubled, tripled, and even quadrupled sales and stockholder value over the past two years (Schlender, 1995:120). This has led some CEOs of competing computing firms such as Lou Gerstner of IBM and Bill Gates of Microsoft to refocus their firms entire efforts on the inter/intranet and to make them "network centric" to catch the "tidal wave in the sea of change" in the computer industry. Let us explore this industrial breakpoint in three stages: (1) understand the basis for this industrial breakpoint, (2) explore Microsoft's competitive positioning in an attempt to gain a sustainable competitive advantage in the breakpoint, and (3) explore Microsoft's major competitors positioning in the breakpoint.

Basis of the Inter/Intranet Industrial Breakpoint

Consider this possibility. Suppose you could create a corporate intranet or public worldwide internet information environment with the following characteristics. Information is presented in the same format to all software and hardware, pulling all the computer software and database systems into a single interface that enables access wherever it resides. This would create universal access and universal reach for users (Cortese, 1996:77). Suppose further that these networks had an interactive exchange system for data, TV, movies, telephone calls, music, news, computer games, and collaborative work groups. This would create the potential for universal cooperation and integration of these information services for users (Cortese, 1996:77). Suppose further that these networks could be used for banking, marketing sales, and all other types of commerce creating a global shopping mall for users (Cortese, 1996:78). Finally, suppose the software needed to manipulate print, sound, or visual information could be stored on the net so that the computer system for accessing the net could be lean and simple to operate, minimizing the need for training in its use and costing only $500 to $800 per unit. This would allow universal usage (Cortese, 1996:78). This is the potential of the inter/intranets. The basic building blocks for realizing this potential are: (1) an internet communication protocol (TCP/IP), (2) a hypertext markup language (HTML), (3) a network browser software program (Mosaic), and (4) an object computer language (Java).

Bill Joy, founder of Sun Microsystems, as early as 1982 helped develop a version of the Unix AT&T's power network operating system built to link up with the internet. He incorporated the Unix and Internet Communication protocol (TCP/IP) into the architecture of the computer they designed. This hardware could be used to link parts of the world, a firm, or a team together. Joy distributed the TCP/IP protocol free on the internet.

Tim Berneis-Lee, a researcher at the European Laboratory for Particle Physics in Geneva, developed a new type of graphic onscreen document for the internet. The convention he developed, hypertext markup language (HTML) lets authors easily link words or pictures in one document to other documents, whether in the same computer or elsewhere on the net by a mere click of the mouse. Lee distributed HTML for free on the internet.

Marc Andreessen and his colleagues, formerly at the National Center for Supercomputer Applications at the University of Illinois and now CEO of Netscape, found Web documents proliferating at such a rate that it was hard to track them. In 1993 he and his staff put together a piece of software for Sun Workstations called Mosaic. It became the first web browser. It could track down HTML documents anywhere on the net and easily display them in a connected way. Andreessen recently went on to be the cofounder of Netscape which develops browser and server software for Windows, Apple, and OS/2 operating systems.

"Anybody who has gotten hooked on surfing the web can tell you that you go through three levels of enthusiasm," says Bill Joy.

> First, you can't believe the amazing things you're seeing; that you could be looking at the ridiculous home page of some high school kid in Zimbabwe, or checking the weather in Tokyo. Then you realize how chaotic it is and how easy it is to get lost in it because you get distracted along the way. Finally, you realize how truly bad a lot of websites are and how frustrating and slow it can be. That's when you begin to wish that web pages could actually do something once they show up in your computer besides just sit there. (Schlender, 1995:138–39)

That idea led Joy and his colleagues Gassidy to develop a new software language called Java. Java allows a web page to deliver along with its visual content tiny applications programs called *applets* that, once unloaded, bring the page to life. Applets can manipulate data, sound, and visual images, creating dynamic information in the form of updated sports scores and stock prices as well as animated and moving pictures. Suddenly the internet and intranet are the computer. With software programs and documents stored on the Web, one could surf the net in a stripped down computer for $500 to $800. The documents and application are hardware and software independent. Java was given away on the internet free. Java has caught on with software programmers and you can now download thousands of applications from the internet to play on your PC. Sun has now prepared a version of Java that works on Intel microprocessors without the need for Microsoft DOS or Windows operating systems. In addition, Oracle and Sun are developing for commercial use light computers which are ultra cheap and easy to use since users do not have to learn protocols for running different types of application software and the database access protocols.

By April of 1996, inter/intranet computing had become the most rapidly growing segment of the computer business. Most Fortune 500 companies had developed or intended to develop their own internet sites, with most firms involved in developing company intranets to serve as a competing platform for the firm's far-flung operations. By 1997, the market for intranet servers alone reached $4 billion and will double to $8 billion in 1998 (Cortese, 1996:77). Firms on the cutting edge of inter/intranet like Sun, Oracle, Cistco, and Netscape are experiencing double-digit growth. Sun's profits rose 73% in 1995 as revenue grew more than 20% to $6.1 billion. Sun's stock price tripled since 1995 (Schlender, 1995:D4), and analysts say the best is still ahead. It should be apparent by now that these innovations taken collectively represent a major challenge to traditional computing systems and the firms which make them, in particular Microsoft.

Microsoft's Competitive Positioning for the Inter/Intranet

Bill Gates claims that he first became aware of the inter/intranet's potential in April 1993 at one of his Think Weeks, a biannual retreat conducted by Microsoft to consider new developments in the computer industry. Gates did not surf the Internet until his next Think Week in October. During that six months Gates was more impressed by such conventional online services as Compuserve and America Online. What changed his mind was employing Mosaic in February 1994. By then Microsoft was well on its way to setting up its own online server (MSN). By October 1994, Gates had issued his now famous "Sea of Change Brings Opportunities" memo in which he called upon all his division heads to reorient their efforts by focusing on the internet. Gates goes on to argue, "It takes more than guts to bet on the sea of change when you are the market leader, but it is the only way to position yourself for massive upgrades" (Schlender, 1995:B8). He then set an off-site retreat for managers on the potential of the inter/intranet.

In December 1995, Microsoft announced a comprehensive strategy for making existing products internet savvy, "but also to influence future internet evolution." This strategy was designed to meet the customer demand (the competitive dynamic) for (a) universal access to information, which is (b) inexpensive, (c) easy to use, and (d) integrates print, audio, and visual inputs and at the same time demonstrates Microsoft's core competencies in these areas. The strategy was termed "embrace and extend."

The *embrace* side of the plan involved adaptations of existing products and includes

1. Reorganizing Microsoft's business to place priority on the internet

2. Refocusing and moving Microsoft's network (MSN) to the World Wide Web

3. Agreeing to license Sun's Java software for its browser

4. Agreeing to license Oracle's database software for its browser

5. Adding HTML to Microsoft Word programs

6. Adding HTML to Microsoft Excel program

The *extend* side of the plan involves the attempt to influence standards:

1. Forming a joint venture with NBC to provide free at-home news for the Web

2. Taking a 15% stake in UUNet Technologies which sells dial-up internet access services for business customers

3. Acquiring Vermeer Technologies for making and managing web pages

4. Developing an internet browser (Explorer) and giving it away free on the internet

5. Developing an information server (Gibralter) using Windows NT and giving it away free on the internet

6. Developing security software for the intranet (Catapult)

7. Developing banking and consumer software for the internet (Merchant)

8. Developing new generation HTML language for multimedia content

9. Developing along with Computer Associates a database management system for larger computer systems

10. Developing a distribution and sales system for Microsoft's resalers on the internet

11. Signing up America Online's 6 million customers to use Microsoft's browsers

12. Developing a control system for 3-D graphics and multimedia on the internet

13. Developing a software gateway for Windows 95 and NT which allows all internet applications to be shared by multiple users

14. Joining with Toshiba and Gateway 2000 to develop simple interactive computer systems which can transfer data at speeds as fast as 40 million bits a second for the net

Gates reflects on Microsoft's plight:

> If we lose out on the highway we lose everything. Today Windows is the core of our business and Windows must expand to be the superhighway's platform in order to retain our central position. . . . It's a very scary business. No matter how successful you've been in the past, if you fall behind technically there is no guarantee that you'll continue to do well. We have this fear that motivates us. There's someone out there who is working harder than we are who might have thought of something we have not thought of. (Jones, 1995:15)

Gates then set up a new computer research laboratory to keep Microsoft informed on the viability of new directions and processes emerging in the computer industry in an attempt to prevent what happened with the inter/intranets from surprising Microsoft again (Markoff, 1995:D1).

Microsoft's Competitors' Strategic Positioning for the Inter/Intranet. Imitation is the highest form of flattery. In December 1995, Bill Joy and Sun Microsystems held a press conference to announce a long list of companies which have endorsed Java as an interface standard for the inter/intranet. These included IBM, Apple, DEC, Adobe, Silicon Graphics, Hewlett Packard, Oracle, and Toshiba. Sun is developing along with several other firms inexpensive network computers. Sun also dominates the workstation computer market and has developed a sophisticated server system for creating net sites and for managing interactive intranet systems (Dewett, 1996:59).

Netscape's Andrassen has also learned from Microsoft. He has taken Netscape for network browsers and significantly improved it every three months in an effort to stay ahead of Microsoft. He has also linked its operating systems to several new browser's applications system (i.e., a cheap global telephone system, 3-D graphics, and an updated group workware). Netscape acquired Cellular Software and built an advanced groupware feature into its browser. Then Netscape acquired Paper Software to put 3-D virtual reality into its browser. Netscape released tools for creating server content and is rapidly working on publishing and commercial applications. Netscape has increased market shares from 70% to 85% in the browser market by providing inter/intranet customer service and support for building web sites and setting up intranets. Netscape has also developed a cable box browser for AT&T who will distribute it free. Netscape posted strong earnings for the first quarter 1996. Earnings rose to $4.7 million, revenues went from $5.4 million to $55 million (Hof, 1996:82–83; Kim, 1996:B6). Microsoft holds 7% of the browser market (Levy, 1996:48).

Novella's Netware which holds 52% market share in the server market is also upgrading every three months in hopes of staying ahead of Microsoft which has a 9% market share (Clark, 1995:B89).

IBM is planning to bundle a wide array of software and communications services as a link to the inter/intranets. IBM's Louis Gerstner has called upon IBM to completely reorient its firm to become "network centric." This will be a major transformation for a firm whose sales center on mainframes and whose PC division has dropped out of the top five in market shares for the first time in years. IBM's Lotus division is quietly trying to extend its Notes groupware into a total operating system for its browsers and servers (Davis, 1996:4).

The competitive race is on for control of the browser/server Gateway to the inter/intranet. Microsoft is attempting to meet customer demands for inexpensive, low-cost computing which is easy to use on the inter/intranet with nothing short of a major transformation of Microsoft's structure, practices, and products. In so doing, it seeks to establish a sustainable competitive advantage by extending its Windows 95 and NT operating systems to the internet and challenging the core competencies of Sun in network language, Netscape in browsers, Novell in servers, and IBM's Lotus division in groupware, while establishing itself as a standard, for example, in network software, operating systems, multimedia applications, office applications, shop floor automation, electronic mail, and computer games applications. Microsoft is following its traditional macro competitive strategies and operational tactics while it attempts to upgrade both with network adaptations.

We are now in a position to draw some general conclusions regarding our conceptual and operational model of strategies for gaining a sustainable competitive advantage and their application by Microsoft in attempting to control a new industrial breakpoint in the emergence of the World Wide Web.

Some Conclusions Regarding Our Analysis and Inquiry

Competition is a lot like cod liver oil. First it makes you sick. Then it makes you better.

—*American Micro Devices (1996:22)*

Let us review our inquiry into (1) the conceptual and empirical models of global strategies for developing a sustainable competitive advantage and (2) competitive strategies and tactics employed by Microsoft in confronting an industrial breakpoint.

Conceptual and Empirical Inquiry into the Global Strategies for Developing a Sustainable Competitive Advantage

First, our conceptualization of a sustainable competitive advantage employing an analysis of (1) competitive dynamics, (2) core competencies, and (3) industrial breakpoints appears to be extremely useful. Our analysis of Microsoft suggests at least one refinement of that conceptualization. Sustainability which was defined as a firm's capacity to dominate a market until the emergence of the next breakpoint may need to be redefined to involve dominating a market across two or more breakpoints. This would provide a hard test of sustainability, rather than the previous soft test.

Second, our four empirical models for operationalizing the strategies involved in obtaining a sustainable competitive advantage in the global marketplace requires three modifications. Clearly the first two models, the domestic product niche with limited exports and the exporting of high-quality politically supported offerings, may lead to a sustainable competitive advantage in one, two, or three national markets, but they do not lead to a sustainable competitive advantage in the global marketplace. Rather, only two of the models do that, an exporting high-quality innovative products strategy and a continuous improvement of business processes strategy.

Third, the data collected suggested that excellence in the product innovation strategy requires that a firm pay attention to a product's bells and whistles that attract customer support as well as the product technology itself. In regard to the continuous improvement of business processes strategy, the data suggests a focus on manufacturing, marketing, and distribution processes are as important as management processes.

Fourth, our analysis of Microsoft, much to our surprise, reveals that they rely primarily on a Continuous Improvement of Business Processes exporting strategy. While Microsoft appears to employ an innovative product exporting strategy, this strategy more often than not (Windows 95, Office Suite) involved continuous improvement for seamless integration and upgrading of previously developed products. Thus while the continuous improvement and product innovation strategies can be unique approaches, they can also be integrated to yield a sustainable competitive advantage.

Microsoft's Competitive Strategy and Tactics in Confronting an Industrial Breakpoint

First, our analysis of Microsoft's competitive strategies and operational tactics has yielded a rich analysis of sustainable competitive advantage. Recall Microsoft's macro competitive strategy of (1) entering mass markets early with good products which can set industry standards, (2) to incrementally continuously improve the products and make old products obsolete, (3) to push volume sales so as to become and remain the industry standard, (4) to leverage being the industry standard to develop new product and market linkages, and (5) to extend and simplify products and services to reach new mass markets. Taken collectively, this strategy invokes all the substrategies involved in both the exporting of high-quality innovative products model and the continuously improved business processes exporting model. Taken collectively, this strategy entails the need for Microsoft to establish and maintain a sustainable competitive advantage in order to become the industry product standard. This strategy thus assumes that setting an industry standard at one point in time is critical to doing the same at another point in time. While they may be true in a *convergent* breakpoint, it is clearly not the case with *divergent* breakpoints. It therefore appears to be a strategy limited to convergent domains and not useful in establishing sustainable competitive advantage in a divergent domain. This calls into question the effectiveness of Microsoft's attempt to extend Windows 95 and NT as a standard for the inter/intranet and the use of the above strategy in doing so.

Second, recall Microsoft's tactics for operationalizing strategy at the worker/market interface: (1) product development and continuous improvement linkage to Microsoft's unique brand of teamwork; (2) the setting of industrial standards linkage to Microsoft's unique acquisition, product development, and alliance policies; (3) the volume marketing and distribution linkage to competitive pricing, exclusive contracting, and software bundling; and (4) leveraging standards to limit competitive sales and link Microsoft's products to new mass markets. Each of these tactics involves a key communication linking and operating function which involves a high development of very specific communication skills (i.e., teamwork, negotiation, marketing, and persuasion). If these skills are not present at a very high level, each tactic fails in its linking and operating functions. Each of these tactics links Microsoft's strategy to both the firm and the market in an industry-specific way.

Third, each of these strategies and tactics involve the traditional concepts of competitive advantage based on product pricing, differentiation, and scope as outcomes of the communication linkages between strategy and tactics.

Fourth, dominant firms appear to confront divergent industrial breakpoints by attempting to extend their previously successful competitive strategy into this new domain. GM, IBM, Apple, and others have each in turn demonstrated this does not work. Yet Microsoft has sought a similar solution. It will be interesting to observe if this fails and/or if Microsoft is flexible enough to develop a new, more adaptive response.

On January 19, 1996, the Microsoft Corporation reported that its earnings rose 54% in its second quarter, driven in part by sales of Windows 95. The results exceeded analyst projections. "The surprise was that there was no surprise and perhaps that was what people were looking for after the controversy in the quarter regarding Microsoft's lack of a strategy to take advantage of the growing popularity of the internet and reports that Windows 95 sales were not meeting analysts' projections (Fisher, 1996:D2).

Competition is indeed a lot like cod liver oil. First it makes you sick, then it makes you better. We have provided a conceptual and empirical analysis of how to understand and influence the competitive process in order to obtain a sustainable competitive advantage. We have also observed how one of the world's most competitive firms proceeds in attempting to establish a sustainable competitive advantage. Microsoft is getting better. James Clark, cofounder and chair of Netscape, one of Microsoft's main competitors, concludes: "Microsoft doesn't have to fail in order for us to be successful. I don't have anything against them except they want to kill us." That's why Marc Andreessen, CEO of Netscape, claims: "I am totally paranoid about Microsoft, always have been, always will be" (Hof, 1996:82).

References

American Micro Devices. (1996). American Micro Devices advertisement. *Fortune,* March 6, p. 21.

Aley, J. (1996). The theory that made Microsoft, *Fortune,* April, p. 65–66.

Automotive News (February, 1996).

Clark, D. (1995). Microsoft sticks by its tactics despite uproar. *Wall Street Journal,* May 1, p. B1.

Clark, D. (1995). Microsoft Windows 95 is just a sideshow. *Wall Street Journal,* August 24, p. B8.

Clark, D. (1995). Microsoft says it has 43 new partners lined up for its online. *Wall Street Journal,* May 11, p. B4.

Clark, D. (1996). Microsoft adds 10 partners; Discusses plan for new interactive TV selections. *Wall Street Journal,* November 3, p. B8.

Cortese, A. (1996). Here comes the Intranet. *Business Week,* February 26, pp. 76–84.

Cortese, A., Verity, J., Rebello, K., and Hof, R. (1996). The software revolution. *Business Week,* December 4, pp. 75–90.

Coyne, K. (1996). The anatomy of sustainable competitive advantage. *Business Horizons,* June, pp. 1–20.

Cusumano, M., and Selby, R. (1995). *Microsoft Secrets.* New York: The Free Press.

Davis, J. (1996), Microsoft, Novell play catch up to Lotus on Web. *Inforworld,* January 22, p. 41.

Dewitt, E. (1996). Why Java is hot. *Time,* January 22, pp. 58–59.

Feurer, R., and Chaharbagh, C. (1994). Defining competitiveness: A holistic approach. *Management Decisions* 52:49–58.

Fisher, L. (1996). Higher results are reported by Microsoft. *New York Times,* January 10, p. D2.

Gleick, J. (1995). Making Microsoft. *New York Times Magazine,* November 5, pp. 50–64.

Hof, R. (1996). Browsing for a bruising. *Business Week,* March 11, pp. 82–83.

Jacob, R. (1995). Corporation reputation. *Fortune,* March 6, p. 54.

Jones, C. (1995). The genesis and genius of Golden Gates. *European Magazine,* July 7–13, pp. 13–15.

Kim, J. (1996). Netscape posts strong earnings. *USA Today,* August 24, p. B1.

Kim, J. (1995). Software from space plan to gain new edge. *USA Today,* December 6, pp. B1–2.

Levy, S. (1996). The browser war. *Newsweek,* April 29, p. 50.

Markoff, J. (1995). Microsoft quietly puts together computer research laboratory. *New York Times,* December 11, p. D1.

Moore, J. (1996). *The Death of Competition: Leadership Strategy in the Age of Business Ecosystems.* New York: Harper.

Morrison, A., and Roth, K. (1992). A taxonomy of business-level strategies in global industries. *Strategic Management* 13:399–418.

Schlender, B. (1995). Whose Internet is it, anyway? *Fortune,* December 11, pp. 120–42.

Schlender, B., and Kirkpatrick, D. (1995). The valley vs. Microsoft. *Fortune,* March 20, pp. 84–90.

Schmidt, J. (1996). Microsoft network set to man the web. *USA Today,* April 24, p. B1.

Seannell, E. (1996). IBM to bundle servers, network systems. *Inforworld,* January 22, p. 25.

Stroebel, P. (1995). Creating industry breakpoints is changing the rules of the game. *Long Range Planning* 28:11–20.

Taylor, T. (1996). My way or the highway. *New York Times,* March 18, p. D5.

USA Today (May 6, 1996), Ford Taurus dethroned, p. B1.

4

High-Speed Management Strategies for Competitiveness: The E-land, a Korean Multinational

Yong-Chan Kim

The E-land is one of the largest and fastest-growing business conglomerates in Korea, whose main products involve the apparel industry. When the company was established, it was just a very small independent retail store. Due to exemplary moral and cultural values and daring strategies to search for new markets, the E-land had been appraised as the best of the rapidly growing companies of the Korean corporate world, with sales of 1.5 billion US dollars in 1995. The company is also moving aggressively overseas, expanding into Taiwan, China, and the U.S., and in 1995, into the U.K., buying the British duffel coat manufacturer Gloverall (Eisenstadt, 1995). In addition, the company has tried to extend their operations to such fields as construction, real estate, hotel, distribution business, and telecommunications (*Dong-A Daily Newspaper*, September 24, 1995).

Even though the E-land remained outside the Big Thirty companies in Korea during the 1990s, it has been appraised as one of the most promising companies, particularly by Korean college students. Its unique organizational culture looks attractive to the young generation who are often called *Shin Sae Dae*, or "the new generation" (or the Korean counterpart of generation X in the U.S.). According to several polls of senior college students in Korea, the E-land was ranked as the most promising company (*Dong-A Daily Newspaper*, April 15, 1995). The success of the E-land has also been demonstrated in other survey on "the companies where Korean college students admire to be in after graduation," conducted by several Korean recruiting agencies, such as Recruit, Inc., and Intern, Inc. Between 1992 and 1996, the E-land was ranked as the second or third most admired company, followed even by traditional Korean *chaebol* groups (*Hanguk Daily Newspaper*, 29 November 1995). Chaebol groups are Korean giant conglomerates whose total assets amount to $500 million.

Various factors contributed to the success of the E-land during the 1990s. First of all, its strong culture based on the Christian ethics helped facilitating and maintaining the strong motivation of its employees. The company's unique culture system distinguished itself from other typical Korean companies including chaebol groups, such as Samsung, LG, or Hyundai. Second, the company had strong leadership. Sung-Soo Park, chairman of the company, had a charismatic leadership that is based not just on his position as a chairman but on his knowledge about the clothing industry and his ethical and exemplary lifestyle. The third factor that gave the company a competitive edge was the youthfulness of its employees. Finally, the success of the company was rooted in their unique strategies for sales continually trying to find or create niche markets, which will be explained in detail later in this chapter.

Despite the company's relative advantages already mentioned, the company faced several environmental challenges during the 1990s that forced it to cautiously review its operations and create new organizational structures and activities that could survive the turbulent and volatile future environment. The environmental challenges that faced the E-land during the 1990s included:

1. Breathtaking development of clothing technology
2. High competition in both domestic and foreign markets
3. Ever-changing customer needs
4. Local economic bloc
5. Increased labor costs

Table 4.1
The Companies Korean College Students Want to be in after Graduation

Nov. 94		*Nov. 95*	
Company	Response (%)	Company	Response (%)
1. Samsung	37.3	1. Samsung	18.1
2. Korea Telecom	8.7	2. Hyundai	10.7
3. Hyundai	4.3	3. E-land	7.8
4. E-land	3.8	–	–
Total	(n = 7,800)	Total	(n = 7,800)

The purposes of this chapter will be to (1) scan the environment that the E-land faced and to locate the core capabilities of the E-land and its competitors, (2) map the value chain of the E-land, (3) find out the strengths and weaknesses of the E-land from a High-Speed Management perspective, and (4) present the critical success factors that could be introduced for the E-land to be a domestic and world leader in apparel markets.

Most of the analyses presented in this chapter are based on the results of (1) documents from various sources like journals, company publications, and newspapers; (2) in-depth interviews with sixteen employees of Brentano, one of the main brands of the E-land; and (3) a survey of forty-six employees of the same brand. Both of the in-depth interviews and the survey were conducted in early January 1996.

Environmental Scanning

Hidden Opportunities in the Korean Clothing Industry

There was little competition in the Korean apparel market before the early 1980s. Until then, only two companies produced and sold clothing with their own brand names in Korea. In addition, the markets for cheap products and those for expensive brand-name products were clearly separated, but few companies did their businesses in the clothing market for mid-priced products. It was the E-land that successfully located such a market niche between expensive and cheap clothing and exploited the opportunities.

Environmental factors as well as the company's own efforts made a crucial contribution to the success of the E-land during the 1980s. For example, when the company began their business targeting people between the ages of ten and twenty, Korean middle and high schools started to allow students to wear casual clothes, ending the more than 90-year tradition of wearing uniforms.

Since 1990, however, it seemed to be difficult to even stay in business because of the rising competition in the fast-changing domestic and global apparel markets. It looked tougher for a company to survive the maturity stage and lead the apparel industry. Nevertheless, it was acknowledged that the clothing industry of Korea still had flourishing markets that had room for further improvement. The problem was who would win in such a high-speed environment.

Relative Position of the E-land in the Korean Clothing Industry

According to the in-depth interviews with frontline employees of the E-land and previous research on the competitive structure of the Korean apparel industry, the E-land has been acknowledged as the domestic industry leader, especially in corporate culture and domestic sales. The E-land has followed other companies in the area of consumer satisfaction and foreign sales (table 4.2).

The E-land Is the Leader in Corporate Culture. The E-land established and developed a unique and strong culture, which will be explained in more detail later in this chapter.

The E-land Is a Leader in Sales and Market Share. The E-land's sales increased dramatically during the first half of the 1990s (figure 4.1). In 1992, the sale of the company was about $538 million. This increased to about $700 million in 1993 and to about $1 billion in 1994. The company expected to sell up to $1.7 billion in 1995, about $1.4 billion of which would come from fashion and apparel businesses and $300 million from food, hotel, travel, distribution, and furniture businesses (*Joongang Daily Newspaper*, December 25, 1995; *Chosun Daily Newspaper*, July 25, 1995). These figures indicate that the amount of sales of the E-land increased more than three times in just three years. In addition, the E-land possessed the biggest market share (30%) in the middle and low-priced casual clothing market in Korea during the 1990s (*Chosun Daily Newspaper*, December 12, 1994).

Value Chain of the E-land

The value chain of the E-land can be mapped as in figure 4.2. The most crucial aspect in a firm's value chain is to build value-added

Table 4.2
Core Capabilities of the Leading Apparel Companies in Korea

Company	Core Capability
E-land	Culture
	Domestic sales
Competitor A	Consumer satisfaction
Competitor B	Foreign sales

Figure 4.1
Sales of the E-land from 1992 to 1995 (in thousands)

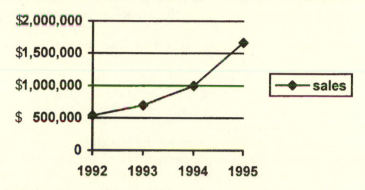

coordination between inside and outside stakeholders. Inside stakeholders of the E-land consist of various functional units such as planning, design, sales and promotions. Outside stakeholders of the company comprise suppliers, manufacturers, merchandisers, and customers. The activities of the E-land to achieve value-added coordination among such stakeholders were a franchising system, globalized sourcing, "little president program" that deals with the relation with stores, and outside linkage strategies such as mergers and acquisitions (M&A).

Figure 4.2
The Value Added Chain of the E-land

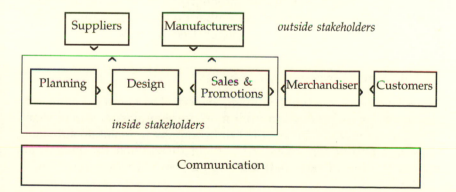

Franchise System

The E-land adopted the franchise system. Without any factory established and fixed capital at hand, the company was able to run a large-scale business. The company did not own any single factory when it initiated its business. This franchise system helped the company to avoid such troubles as labor strikes and high inventory, from which most Korean companies suffered during the late 1980s. In addition, by subcontracting 100% of their supplies, the E-land could reduce their production costs and maintain flexibility within its organizational activities.

What was important in managing the franchising system was to acquire franchisees that could understand the franchiser's strategies and plans and had the capabilities to achieve the goals set by the franchiser. In order to attract the franchisees that were able to give the E-land a greater competitive edge, the company introduced new types of plant evaluation systems (*Joongang Daily Newspaper*, July 10, 1995). With this, the company tried to evaluate its franchised plants by the criteria of management efficiency, quality, and costs.

Global Production System

The company established "the E-land International" as headquarters for global trade, overseas production, and global sourcing. Currently, the E-land International takes charge of production of its thirty fashion brands and produces eleven million pieces (30% of the E-land's total production). In addition, the company has its main factories in China, India, and Sri Lanka. The E-land planned to enlarge the ratio of the manufacture in foreign countries up to 50% of its total production, expecting thereby to cut its production costs by 30%. In 1995, the company had two hundred subcontractors in China and Vietnam and planned to increase its number up to one thousand by the year of 2000 (*Chosun Daily Newspaper*, December 12, 1995).

Global Sourcing System

The E-land has a unique insourcing system. The company acquired resources for its production from more foreign manufacturers than domestic suppliers. This enabled the company to maintain substantially low production costs. The E-land dispatched the industrial experts to China, Pakistan, India, and Italy and others to have them participate actively in global sourcing. By such efforts of global outsourcing, the company expected to multiply, globalize, and specialize the purchasing lines of raw/subsidiary materials (The E-land's brochure, 1995).

Relationship with Stores: "Little President Program"

The E-land introduced a special program called the *sosajang* program, or "little president program," to build more efficient coordination between the company and its franchised independent stores. *Sosajang* were frontline employees who belonged to the sales department and who were supposed to be in charge of two or three neighboring franchised stores. Through establishing and developing "personal" relationships with store owners, the "little presidents" were supposed to gather more accurate information about their assigned stores and find the most appropriate ways to support them. After all, their roles could be defined as helping the company produce and distribute the products which fit each store. That is, this program could lead the company to optimize the production avoiding any overlapping production, reducing unnecessary inventory, and making possible quick responses to the consumer's needs.

Domestic Distribution

In 1994, the E-land opened its first discount outlet, insisting that it would offer customers savings of 50% on clothing and big bargains on household goods. The E-land plans during the next five years to open more than one hundred "next generation department stores" in housing developments that have sprung up around Korea's major cities. With $1 billion in annual sales, the E-land was aiming at a niche between department stores and warehouse stores (Eisenstadt, 1995).

Global Distribution Lines

The E-land established self-sufficient cooperation in Shanghai, China, and has branches in several Chinese cities such as Shanghai, Beijing, and Kwnagju for the purpose of forming a distribution network in that country. In 1996, the company already had distribution networks in Shanghai, Taiwan, New York, and Los Angeles. In addition, the company planned to set up one thousand stores as distribution posts in foreign countries by the year 2000.

Global Linkages

The company had daring plans for globalization. The main strategies of the company to achieve globalization were:

1. Training international agents
2. Global and domestic M&A
3. Pioneering foreign markets
4. Global sourcing
5. Establishing five more outlets (E-land Brochure, 1995)

One of the E-land's main globalization activities was making linkages with foreign companies. In 1995, the E-land took over Gloverall, a U.K. company, which was capitalized at about $2,643,754, and whose sales had been around $6,609,385 per year (*Dong-A Daily Newspaper*, January 16, 1995). The E-land expected that this merger would make it possible for the company to set up, in five years, networks for global sales to both European countries and the U.S. The company also planned to develop the acquired *Gloverall* into one of the Big Three in the U.K. apparel industry. In addition, the E-land was attempting to acquire two or three more U.K. companies in the next three years to use them as posts for approaching the European and U.S. markets. Along with such an acquisitions, the company has tried to build linkages with foreign brands such as Puma (Germany), McGreeger (U.K.), Big John (Japan), and Curezu (French) as a globalization strategy.

Core Capabilities of the E-land: Its Unique and Strong Culture

The core capabilities of the E-land were rooted in its unique and strong corporate culture. The E-land culture was summarized in so-called "the E-land spirit" that was composed of the following eighteen short phrases:

1. Put hard work and sincerity before mere talent
2. Have a willingness to learn
3. Work for pleasure not for money
4. Put humanity before work itself
5. Act God-centered, faith-centered, and Bible-centered
6. Be honest
7. Be faithful

8. Be frugal
9. Take part in teamwork
10. Be thankful
11. Be other-centered
12. Be service-oriented
13. Have a world vision
14. Have a future-oriented mind
15. Have a professional attitude
16. Have a can-do spirit
17. Pursue the best, not just the better
18. Always think in different ways

Characteristic of the E-land Spirit

Company employees sometimes referred to their organizational culture as "three C's," which stands for campus, church, and camp culture. This indicates that the corporate culture of the E-land stressed high motivation, informal relationships, and Christian ethics such as honesty, hard work, and sincerity. The E-land was one of a few Korean companies who allowed (sometimes exhorted) employees to put on casual wear like blue jeans during office hours. Such E-land culture could be summarized as Christian culture, youth culture, feminist culture, and learning culture.

Christian Culture. Around 50% of E-land employees are Christians who have a religious meeting every Monday morning. Most of the employees are expected to spend each morning from 8:30 to 9:00 mediating or praying, regardless of their religion (non-Christian employees often read books suggested by top management during this time). In addition, there were training camps called *soo yang hoe* ("retreat") that are arranged mainly for the Christian employees for four to five days twice in a year. At these camps, the employees are given the opportunities to take a rest and revitalize their working minds. There are various efforts of the company to build harmonious atmosphere among Christians and non-Christians, with such events as song festivals, sports, and parties.

Youth Culture. In 1996, the average age of E-land employees was around thirty-two. Few people are older than forty. Even Sung-Soo Park, chairman of the company is under fifty. Such youthfulness had been the basic source of the unique and strong culture of the company and its innovative strategies.

Feminist Culture.   The E-land is more open to female workers than other Korean firms. Women employees in the E-land amount to 40% of the company. In 1994, the E-land hired a larger percentage (20.3%) of female employees than any other Korean company (table 4.3).

Most of the female employees in the E-land are college graduates and are hired through very tough competitions in which only one out of two hundred is finally employed. After being hired, women workers are supposed to be given equal opportunities of promotion, even after their marriages, which was still unusual in Korean companies.

In addition, the E-land showed the highest ratio of female managers among Korean companies (*Joongang Daily Newspaper,* September 4, 1995). While percentages of female managers higher than the position of *Kwajang* ("Section Chief") in most Korean chaebol groups are around only 1%, over 20% of all managers at the E-land are female (tables 4.4 to 4.6).

Facilitating Willingness to Learn.   One of the major strengths of the E-land culture lies in its continual efforts to build a learning environment. Great amounts of time and money (about $18,750,000 per year) have been invested on educating its employees in management or foreign language skills.

In 1996, the E-land set up a plan to concentrate more on education. According to the plan, the company would (1) assign 600 hours per year to its employees as time for learning, (2) present a list of 300 books and encourage the employees to read them, (3) establish specialized education systems to help employees find and develop their own talents, and (4) recruit 20% more employees than necessary in order to make up for the extra time spent on education (Koh, 1995).

Table 4.3
Percentages of New Women Hires in Korean Companies

Company	% of new female employees (1995)
E-land	20.3%
Samsung	10.0%
Ssangyong	8.0%
Daewoo	6.2%

Source: Chosun Daily Newspaper, August 9, 1995.

Table 4.4
Percentages of Women Taking the Positions Higher than Kwajang ("Section Chief") in Korean Companies

Company	%
The E-land	20.6
Hanjin	5.1
Teapyongyang	3.5
Dongyang	2.1

Table 4.5
Percentage of Women Employees in Each Position in the E-land

	Higher than Kwajang	Kwajang ("Section Chief")	Daeree ("Deputy Section Chief")	Jooyim ("Chief Clerk")	Sawon (Regular Staff)	Total (%)
male	90	85	65	65	50	60
female	10	15	35	35	50	40

Table 4.6
Percentage of Women Employees of the E-land by Department

Sales Departments
male (77%)   female (23%)

Manufacture/Sourcing Departments
male (72%)   female (28%)

Design Departments
male (19%)   female (81%)

Planning departments
male (60%)   female (40%)

The Way to Distribute the Culture Through the Company

The E-land has a unique means to distribute and institutionalize its strong culture. These were well-designed social dramas based on Christian ethics and the unique recruiting and promotion systems of the company.

Social Dramas.   Social dramas (myths and rituals) are organizational mechanisms to make a corporate culture operational. Those mechanisms

demonstrate how the organization's core values are to be linked conceptually to reality (Cushman and King, 1995b: 90–91).

The E-land has several ways to assign social and moral meanings to its employees' efforts. The company interprets its employees' everyday works as fulfilling God's missions or "sacred" services
for the public. In addition, the company defines its efforts to sell
cheaper products as helping the public live "right and frugal" lives
and serving the poor in Korean society.

In line with such efforts to build organizational integration by
providing special meanings to their works, the E-land has tried to
produce value-embedded products. The company insists that it tries
not only to increase sales but also to guide the consumers to the
"right ways of living." The company maintains that it has not produced or sold any products that pampered solely to consumers'
extravagant desires. Instead, the company supplies products such
as leisure, travel, and living materials that were "reasonably cheap
and necessary for living" (*Hanguk Daily Newspaper*, August 18, 1995).

For example, when the E-land entered into the hotel business, it
designed its hotels in a totally different manner from other typical
hotels in Korea. When the company acquired Kensington Hotel located around the Surak Mountain National Park near the Eastern coast
of Korea, they closed down the hotel's night club, even though it
could have been a big money-maker (*Chosun Daily Newspaper*, January 6, 1996). The only reason for shutting down the night club was
that the company thought the club was not consistent with the family
values that the company allegedly tries to keep in their businesses.

Rigid and Unique Recruiting System.   The E-land has a unique recruiting system compared with other Korean companies. Rather than
administering written texts to applicants, which is the traditional
recruiting method, the E-land required applicants to submit very
detailed résumés and personal statements in which they are supposed to clarify their worldviews, long-term and short-term life goals,
personal views on professional life, personalities, and family backgrounds. The interviewers examine personalities and worldviews of
the applicants and try to find out what the candidates think and
need.

Top management believes that a work place should be "a
school" where new social leaders develop and give back to society.
They think that the work place should be a warm and friendly place
where people share responsibilities and workloads. As a way of
implementing this top management philosophy, new employees are

supposed to get special training for three months right after being hired. New employees in these training sessions are advised to find their own answers to such questions as, "Who am I?" "What can I do?" "What are my strong and weak points?" and "What should be my personal lifelong vision?" In addition, the new hires are supposed to take part in various programs that are designed to convert them into "the E-land men and women" (Koh, 1995).

One year after this training program, most employees are supposed to go through another education program in which the E-land spirit is stressed.

Promotion. The E-land provides its employees with various opportunities for promotion (*Chosun Daily Newspaper* December 5, 1995). In 1996, it took about seventeen years for an employee to be promoted to a *bujang* ("department manager") from a *sawon* ("regular staff member") in other typical Korean companies, but it took only eleven to thirteen years for E-land employees to be promoted to the same position.

Although employees are given quick promotion opportunities, and personal preference and aptitude are properly considered and reflected in the job assignment process, they also have to get through a very tough training process. One year or a year and a half after being promoted to *jooyim* ("chief clerk"), employees can get a chance to step up to be a *daeree* ("deputy section chief"). However, they still have to pass through hard training sessions to take the position. For example, they have to pass written and oral tests about several books chosen by the CEOs. In addition, they have to memorize "the E-land Spirits," and submit reports presenting actual cases in which they themselves applied the spirits to real work situations. Even after passing through such an "ordeal," they are supposed to

Table 4.7
Comparison of Average Years Employees Spent Before
Becoming *Bujang* ("Department Manager")
in Korean Companies

Company	Years
Sangyong	18
Samsung	17
E-land	11–13

enter a month-long education program for the position. During the training period, the E-land spirits or values were continuously stressed more than anything.

It is even tougher to be promoted to the position of *kwajang* ("section chief") in the E-land. First of all, if an employee wants to be a section chief, he or she has to be recommended by his or her direct supervisors, who evaluate his or her everyday attitude and character. If recommended by them, the candidate for the position has to pass oral tests usually in front of the Chairman Park. In addition, he or she is supposed to explain clearly a future vision or plans and to present the concrete ways or means to realize them. After being chosen as *kwajang*, he or she is still supposed to go through training programs for the position for one year (Koh, 1995).

What Should Be Improved

Lost Role of Middle Managers as Coordinator

According to the author's in-depth interviews and survey, there is a communication problem between CEOs and the frontline employees in the E-land. In other words, there is a communication stumbling block. The problem seems to result from the company's unclear role for middle managers.

The in-depth interviews reveal that the most important information in the company flows directly from top management to frontline workers. Employees felt that such a type of communication structure should have been changed into a more democratic one. That is, they thought that there should be more chances for frontline workers to input their ideas or suggestions in the process of building core values of the company.

In the survey of forty-six employees in the company, the mean score of responses to the question, "Are you satisfied with communication from top management to employees?" was only 2.767 (5.0 = strongly agree and 1.0 = strongly disagree). In the case of the bottom-up communication, however, the result was more frustrating. The mean score of the responses to the question of "are you satisfied with the communication from the employees to the top management?" was only 1.977 (5.0 = strongly agree and 1.0 = strongly disagree). These scores are much less than the mean scores of companies surveyed by the International Communication Association (ICA). According to the ICA report, the average score of companies in terms of communication between top management and lower levels was around 3.12.

This communication problem seemed to be related with two other problems mentioned by most interviewees. The first one was "too many unnecessary mistakes are made by the employees during their work." Though the employees of the E-land were energetic and young, they lacked working experience. Nevertheless, they had to make lots of decisions and actions based on the flat structure. Without well-planned and organized support from their supervisors or middle management, it seemed that they could not help but make many unnecessary mistakes.

The second problem was a lack of communication across departments. Most of the interviewees mentioned the lack of communication among different departments or brands as one of the main weaknesses of the company. Yim's (1992) research presented similar results in that most employees of the E-land located their most serious problem in the coordination between different company functions.

Lack of Coordination in Planning Manufacturing Marketing Interface

Another weakness the E-land has to overcome in this high-speed management environment is the lack of coordination among planning-manufacturing-marketing functions. As a result of the in-depth interviews and survey, the author found that the company has to improve in the area of design-manufacturing-marketing interface (table 4.8).

Even though the E-land has a strong vision and culture, it is not effectively shared with its customers. According to the survey results, while the scores of "vision sharing with store owners and plants"

Table 4.8
The E-land Workers' Opinions about the
Relation That Should Be Improved

Relation to Be Improved	%
Planning-manufacturing-marketing interface	38.6
Relation with stores	15.9
Relation with plants	4.5
Relation with customers	31.8
Relation with suppliers	4.5

was slightly over the midpoint (3.00), "the vision sharing with customers" was below the midpoint (table 4.9).

In terms of involvement of such stakeholders as customers,
stores, and plants in the process of planning products, all of them
were not fully involved.

Culture and Communication—Lack of Innovative Mind

The third problem of the E-land was located in its culture, which
was often mentioned as a strong point of the company. It should be
admitted that the strong culture of the E-land contributed to the
framebreaking development of the company during the 1990s. However, the E-land has had to continuously reconsider and reconstruct
its culture, especially at the time when the company began to launch
a daring globalization strategy.

The company has stressed the values of change and innovation more than any other value in order to survive and improve in
a high-speed environment. However, change and innovation have
not been stressed enough. Yim's (1992) research showed that the
company stresses mission or good relationships among employees
more than creativity or innovation. While 85.2% of the employees in
the survey for the current study considered missions or responsibilities as the most important in their jobs, creativity or innovation
were mentioned by only 63% of the employees.

Negative symptoms had already appeared in the company's
culture during the 1990s. The most prominent was the potential
strain between Christians and non-Christians. Even if top management kept emphasizing that there was no discrimination because of
their religion and that only the devotion to the E-land spirit matters,
the in-depth interviews showed that non-Christians still felt to be

Table 4.9
Involvement of Stakeholders in the
E-land Culture and Activities

Relation with	Vision-Sharing	Involvement in Planning of Outcomes
Customers	2.814	2.636
Manufacturers	3.659	2.707
store owners	3.091	2.909

(5 = strongly agree, 3 = so-so, 1 = strongly disagree)

treated unequally, especially with promotions to high-level decision-making positions.

Another problem in terms of culture emerged among new employees, who are often called *shin sae dae* "new generation," which is the counterpart of generation X in the U.S. They have different expectations and value systems than the older generation in the company. Such problems with corporate culture extend to customer relations. While the customers always kept changing their values, tastes, and financial status, the E-land spirit seemed to lag behind.

Continuous Improvement Strategies of the E-land

In this chapter, three strategies are recommended for continuous improvement of the E-land. The first one is introducing self-managed teamwork, the second is changing the current leadership style to framebreaking leadership, and the last is benchmarking leading companies for accomplishing consumer-oriented breakthroughs.

Introducing Self-Managed Teamwork

The best way to overcome the problems of the E-land is to build self-managed teamwork. In particular, self-managed teamwork can help the company solve its communication problem between top management and frontline employees and the unclear role-setting of middle management.

I asked forty-six respondents about which teamwork type would be best-suited to their company (self-managed, cross-functional, outside linkage, or benchmarking teamwork). The majority of them (75%) answered that self-managed teams are the best type for solving the problems of their company (table 4.10).

Table 4.10
The E-land's Employees Opinions on the Type of Teamwork Best-Suited to Their Company

Teamwork Type	%
Self-managed teams	75%
Cross-functional team	4.5%
Outside linkage team	4.5%
Benchmarking team	4.5%
Others	4.5%
Total (case)	93 (46)

Self-managed teams are organizational activities to improve the functioning of work units. They are vital as a tool for effective problem mapping. Problem mapping is a team activity oriented toward locating, defining, and solving problems in the workplace. The three most crucial points of the self-managed teams are homogeneity, cross-training, and empowerment (Cushman and King, 1995a, 1995b; Obloj, Cushman, and Kozminski, 1995):

> Homogeneity: Self-managed teams are groups of several participants from the same work units. As a result, self-managed teams are homogenous in terms of work environment and member's tasks.

> Cross-training: Self-managed teams develop their members' knowledge base, experience, and skills through cross-training and common problem solving.

> Empowerment: A necessary condition for self-managed teams is empowerment of the teams. Empowerment should be focused in certain areas, clearly related to problem mapping and problem-solving process.

Framebreaking Leadership

One of the main factors that led the E-land to success is its strong and visionary leadership, especially of Sung-Soo Park, chairman of the company. He has been evaluated as having knowledge-based power. In order for the company to continue to succeed in the global markets, however, the leadership style should change into the framebreaking one that is suited to a high-speed environment.

According to Cushman and King (1995a; 1995b), with the advent of a turbulent global economic environment and the need to deal with discontinuous change, a new high-speed management leader has emerged. They claim that such a high-speed management leader should focus on transformations, network management, and managing organizational discontinuities.

Customer-Oriented, Diffused Breakthroughs

According to Obloj, Cushman, and Kozminski (1995), dramatic and rapid breakthroughs are necessary in the type of turbulent environments that most business organizations face today. A breakthrough means a simultaneous and sharp shift in strategy, power, structure, and controls

(Tushman, Newman, and Romanelli, 1986). The E-land also has to have a capacity to change its strategies, performance, structures, and even cultures for different temporal and spatial situations.

With the already established unique culture, the E-land can introduce consumer-oriented, diffused breakthroughs. The essence of such breakthroughs is "the development of a set of unique, difficult to imitate resources or capabilities spread throughout the organization and reach out into its environment" (Obloj, Cushman, and Kozminski, 1995: 166).

Conclusion

It was the purpose of this chapter to (1) scan the environment that a Korean apparel company faces and locate the core capabilities of the firm and its competitors; (2) map the value chain of the firm, (3) find out the strengths and weaknesses of the firm's communication practices from a High-Speed Management perspective, and (4) present the critical success factors that can be introduced for the firm to be a domestic and world leader in the apparel market.

High-Speed Management (HSM) is a new organizational communication approach that focuses on the issue of value-added interdependence and rapid and accurate coordination within and between organizations. HSM is based on the current trend of global industries toward "interdependence" which could be realized by (1) breathtaking development of communication technology; (2) dramatic increase in word trade; (3) a volatile business climate characterized by rapidly changing technology, quick market saturation, and unexpected competition; and (4) managers' interest in and acceptance of management theories and practices which emphasize innovation, adaptation, flexibility, efficiency, and rapid response (Cushman and King, 1989). Such environmental changes and emergence of HSM have rendered strategies for corporate culture and communication the most important for organizational success, because, in such HSM environments, the competitive edge is not in each task but in the process of coordination among various tasks.

Based on an examination of a Korean apparel firm, the E-land, there were three weaknesses in the coordination of activities. The first was "unclearly defined roles of middle managers." The problem of middle management is closely related with other problems such as lack of communication between the CEO and frontline employees, lack of communication and cooperation across different functions, and inefficiency in storing and distributing knowledge. The second problem concerned the lack of coordination in the planning-marketing-coordination interface. Even though the firm had a strong and unique vision and culture, they were not effectively shared with its customers and franchisees. In addition, the options of the stakeholders such as customers, plants, and store owners were not effectively considered in the process of planning new products. The third problem had to do with its lack of innovative thinking. Even though the strong culture of the firm has contributed to its framebreaking development during the 1990s, the firm has yet to create and institutionalize a new innovative culture that is strategically appropriate for the firm's recently launched daring globalization activities. The new culture should be designed and institutionalized so as to make an efficient integration and coordination among global stakeholders.

In this chapter, three critical success factors as communication strategies to lead the firm to a continuous success in a high-speed management environment have been presented. The first strategy is to form self-managed teams, which have several participants from the same groups, focusing on developing their member's knowledge base, experience, and skills through cross-training, and to empower members involved in problem mapping and the problem-solving process. This self-managed teamwork can help the firm solve the communication problem between top management and frontline employees and the unclear role of middle management. The second communication strategy is to change the current leadership style into the framebreaking ones that are suited to a high-speed environment. The framebreaking leadership should focus on transformation, network management, and managing organizational discontinuities. The third strategy is to introduce consumer-oriented, diffused breakthroughs. The essence of such breakthroughs is the development of a set of unique and difficult-to-imitate resources or capabilities which would be spread throughout the organization and reach out into its environment.

References

Anthony, R. N. (1988). *The Management Control Function*. Boston: The Harvard Business School Press.

Chang, C. S., and Chang, N. J. (1994). *The Korean Management System: Cultural, Political, Economic Foundations*. Westport, CT: Quorum Books.

College women's expectations to be employed (in Korean). (1995). *Chosun Daily Newspaper*, November 11. (Chollian News Database Service).

College women (in Korean). (1995). *Chosun Daily Newspaper*, August 9 (Chollian News Database Service).

Criteria for selecting the company to work for: Welfare or payment (in Korean). (1995). *Dong-A Daily Newspaper*, April 12 (Chollian News Database Service).

Cushman, D. P., and King, S. S. (1995a). *Communicating Organizational Change: A Management Perspective*. Albany: State University of New York Press.

Cushman, D. P., and King, S. S. (1995b). *Communicating and High-Speed Management*. Albany: State University of New York Press.

Cushman, D. P., and King, S. S. (1994a). High-speed management: A revolution in organizational communication in the 1990s. In S. S. King and D. P. Cushman (eds.), *High-Speed Management and Organizational Communication in the 1990s: A Reader*, pp. 5–40. Albany: State University of New York Press.

Cushman, D. P., and King, S. S. (1994b). Communication and management in the global economy. In S. S. King and D. P. Cushman (eds.), *High-Speed Management and Organizational Communication in the 1990s: A Reader*, pp. 291-304. Albany: State University of New York Press.

Cushman, D. P., and King, S. S. (1993). Vision of order: High-speed management in the private sector of the global marketplace. In A. Kozminski and D. P. Cushman (eds.), *Organizational Communication and Management: A Global Perspective*, pp. 69–83. Albany: State University of New York Press.

Cushman, D. P., and King, S. S. (1989). The role of communication in high-technology organizations: The emergence of high-speed management. In S. S. King (ed), *Human Communication as a Field: Selected Contemporary Views*, pp. 151–62. Albany: State University of New York Press.

Cushman, D. P., King, S. S., and Smith, T. (1988). The rules perspective on organizational communication research. In G. M. Goldhaber and G. A. Barnett (eds.), *Handbook of Organizational Communication*, pp. 55–94. Norwood, NJ: Able Publishing Corporation.

Cushman, D. P., and Ju, Y. (1995). *Organizational Teamwork in High-Speed Management*. Albany: State University of New York Press.

Donnellon, A., and Scully, M. (1994). Teams, performance, and rewards: Will the post-bureaucratic organization be a post-meritocratic organization? In C. Hechscher and A. Donnellon (eds.), *The Post Bureaucratic organization: New Perspectives on Organizational Changes*, pp. 63–90. London: Sage Publications.

Eisenstadt, G. (1995). Park Gui-Sook's reading list. *Forbes*, September 11, pp. 72–76.

The E-land. (1995). *The E-land* [Brochure]. Seoul: Author.

The E-land (in Korean). (1995). *Dong-A Daily Newspaper*, September 24 (Chollian News Database Service).

The E-land (in Korean). (1996). *Hanguk Daily Newspaper*, January 19 (Chollian News Database Service).

The E-land (in Korean). (1994). *Chosun Daily Newspaper*, July 25 (Chollian News Database Service).

The E-land adopted sabbatical vacation program (in Korean). (1995). *Chosun Daily Newspaper*, May 23 (Chollian News Database Service).

The E-land established foreign post in UK and China (in Korean). (1995). *Dong-A Daily Newspaper*, January 16 (Chollian News Database Service).

The E-land group set up the brand new personnel program (in Korean). (1995). *Hanguk Daily Newspaper*, June 12 (Chollian News Database Service).

The E-land group: Foster to multiply the activities (in Korean). (1995) *Hanguk Daily Newspaper*, August 18 (Chollian News Database Service).

Etzioni, A. (1964). *Modern Organization*. Englewood Cliffs, NJ: Prentice Hall.

Fahey, L. (1994). Strategic management: The challenge and the opportunity. In E.G. Collins and M.A. Devanna (eds.), *The New Portable MBA*. New York: John Wiley & Sons.

Ketchum, L.D., and Trist, E. (1992). *All Teams Are Not Created Equal: How Employee Empowerment Really Works*. London: Sage Publications.

Kim, K. (1994). Female employees in the E-land (in Korean). *Intern*, April, pp. 177–78.

Female managers in Korean companies (in Korean). (1995). *Joongang Daily Newspaper*, September 4 (Chollian News Database Service).

Focused company, The E-land (in Korean). (1996). *Chosun Daily Newspaper*, January 6 (Chollian News Database Service).

Hoffman K., and Rush, H. (1988). *Micro-Electronics and Clothing: The Impact of Technical Change on a Global Industry*. New York: Praeger.

Huh, E. (1994). A study on the communication process in the clothing manufacture (in Korean). Master's thesis, Ehwa Women's University, Seoul, Korea.

Hwang, S., and Jung, C. (1993). The strategies of the Korean apparel distribution industry to cope with the opening of the domestic market to the foreign companies (in Korean). *Eui Ryu Hak Hoe Ji* 17(2).

Ju, Y. (1994). Organizational teamwork: A high-speed management perspective. In S. S. King and D. P. Cushman (eds.), *High-Speed Management and Organizational Communication in the 1990s: A Reader*, pp. 139–69. Albany: State University of New York Press.

King, S. S. (1994). High-speed management and organizational communication: A road map. In S. S. King and D. P. Cushman (eds.), *High-Speed Management and Organizational Communication in the 1990s: A Reader*, pp. 1–4. Albany: State University of New York Press.

Koh, S. (1995). Education is welfare. *Wol Gan Joongang*, April, pp. 198–209.

Kovačić, B. (1994). High-speed management, environmental spanning, and coalignment of external resources: Strategic alliances. In S. S. King and D. P. Cushman (eds.), *High-Speed Management and Organizational Communication in the 1990s: A Reader*, pp. 69–93. Albany: State University of New York Press.

Kozminski, A. K. (1994). High-speed management and global competition. In S. S. King and D. P. Cushman (eds.), *High-Speed Management and Organizational Communication in the 1990s: A Reader*, pp. 41–67. Albany: State University of New York Press.

Kozminski, A. K. (1993). Global management: A new road to social progress? In A. K. Kozminski and D. P. Cushman (eds.), *Organizational Communication and Management: A Global Perspective*, pp. 185–201. Albany: State University of New York Press.

Mintzberg, H. (1993). *Structure in Fives: Designing Effective Organizations*. Englewood Cliffs, NJ: Prentice Hall.

The most admired company to college seniors (in Korean). (1995). *Hanguk Daily Newspaper*, August 19 (Chollian News Database Service).

New production method—production on orders (in Korean). (1995). *Seoul Economy Daily*, December 1 (Chollian News Database Service).

Nocotera, A. M. (1994). High-speed management and the new corporate culture: IBM and GE: A case study in contrasts. In S. S. King and D. P. Cushman (eds.), *High-Speed Management and Organizational Communication in the 1990s: A Reader*, pp. 113–37. Albany: State University of New York Press.

Nonaka, I., and Takeuchi, H. (1995). *The Knowledge-Creating Company: How Japanese Companies Create the Dynamics of Innovation*. New York: Oxford University Press.

Obloj, K., Cushman, D. P., and Kozminski, A. K. (1995). *Winning: Continuous Improvement Theory in High-Performance Organizations*. Albany: State University of New York Press.

Plant evaluation system in The E-land (in Korean). (1995). *Joongang Daily Newspaper*, July 10 (Chollian News Database Service).

Porter, M. E. (1980). *Competitive Strategy Techniques for Analyzing Industries and Competitors*. New York: Free Press.

Sales (in Korean). (1995). *Joongang Daily Newspaper*, December 25 (Chollian News Database Service).

Samsung is the most preferred company to college seniors (in Korean). (1995). *Joongang Daily Newspaper*, December 7 (Chollian News Database Service).

Seo, J. (1992). Corporate culture and control of labor: A case study of *The E-land*. Master's Thesis, Ehwa Women's University, Seoul, Korea.

Sherriton, J., and Stern, J. L. (1997). *Corporate Culture Team Culture: Removing the Hidden Barrier to Team Success*. New York: American Management Association.

Shin, J. (1995). Strategies for consumer satisfaction: A case study of S apparel company. Master's Thesis, Joongang University, Seoul, Korea.

Tushman, M. L., Newman, W. H., and Romanelli, E. (1986). Convergence and upheaval: Managing the unsteady pace of organizational evolution. *California Management Review* 14(1):29–44.

Companies I want to work for (in Korean). (1994). *Chosun Daily Newspaper*, November 8 (Chollian News Database Service).

Wellins, R., and George, J. (1991). The Key to Self-Directed Teams. *Training and Development Journal* 45(4): 26–31.

Years which are taken to be promoted to the position of senior manager (in Korean). (1995). *Chosun Daily Newspaper*, December 5 (Chollian News Database Service).

Yim, T. (1992). A case study of a middle range priced apparel company. Master's thesis, Hanguk Foreign Language University, Seoul, Korea.

5

Intersections between Crisis and Management: A Case Study

B. Thomas Florence and Branislav Kovačić

The days when corporate public relations worked to keep corporations out of controversy, days of playing it safe, of not offending Democratic or Republican customers, advertisers or associates—those days are done. . . . A major battle will be pitched on quality and prices of consumer goods, targeting particularly on the massive misleading advertising campaigns, the costs of which are passed on to the consumer.

Alinsky (1971: 195)

It is the purpose of this chapter to discuss the issues of (1) organizational crises, (2) organizational communication crisis management, and (3) a possibility to fruitfully theorize about the intersections between organizational crises and their communication management. We will proceed in three steps. First, we will offer a brief conceptualization of organizational crises. Second, we will discuss communication crises management. Finally, we will summarize our argument and offer some conclusions.

Conceptualization of Crises

Our argument in this section will focus on four topics: (1) metaphors and conceptualizations of crises, (2) crisis stages, (3) risk communication management, and (4) the reasons for public anger during crises.

Metaphors and Conceptualizations of Crises

We define organizational crises as events or series of events that violate routine organizational activities, are very often unexpected or unpredictable, and have uncertain consequences that may severely limit organizational options, or even destroy organizations. Outcomes of crises depend on the *turning points* created by the interconnected actions of the major stakeholders. Organizational crises truly become the public concern when defined and influenced by the mass media.

According to Thurow (1996), the conceptual framework of plate tectonics uses the *invisible* movement of the continental plates floating on the earth's molten inner core—the relative movement and jostling of enormous, rigid blocks (plates) comprising the earth's surface—to account for the *visible* present and past *earthquakes* and *volcanism*. Thus, earthquakes and volcanic eruptions may be thought of as the metaphors of organizational crises. The point is that we cannot understand earthquakes and volcanic activities by simply looking at them. We must look below the surface. However, Thurow does not mention a third type of the visible consequence that can be explained by the invisible, relative movement and jostling of plates—mountain-building processes. Such mountain-building processes may constitute a third type of organizational crisis. Nor does Thurow mention that three types of boundaries/margins of the plates help us determine the relative violent nature of the visible crises. First, very narrow boundaries are associated with shallow earthquakes and related volcanic activity. Second, areas where the ridges (narrow elevations) are offset (balanced) are coupled with more violent earthquakes. Finally, diffused boundaries are linked to deep earthquakes. In our case, for example, plates take the form of (1) ideology, (2) economic stability, (3) business practices, (4) legal implications of actions, and (5) government intervention. The molten inner core on which these plates float is made up of the media coverage and the public's response to it. These plates hit each other along such major fault lines as (1) labor-management disputes, (2) environmental disputes, (3) competitive alliances, (4) legal disputes, (5) distribution of income, (6) safety nets, and (7) globalization of the economy. Such clashes disturb a balance between the media coverage and the public's response to it and bring about organizational crises such as (1) downsizing, (2) endangered life, health, and the environment of different stakeholders, (3) mergers/acquisitions/bankruptcies, and (4) large system failures. But let's not forget, crises are media induced, "mediated occurrences."

A second conceptual framework—a punctuated equilibrium—is, according to Thurow (1996) necessary because it depicts organizational crises as rapid developments characterized by flux, disequilibrium, and uncertainty. This is also a time of possible creative solutions to organizational crises. However, Thurow (1996) again glosses over a much debated question of the imperfection of the fossil record. The argument is not about whether gradual or punctuational evolution ever occurs; rather, it is about their relative frequency. This should make us aware of our ignorance of the basic fact—the frequency and distribution of difference types of organizational crises.

Crisis Stages

Although organizational crises have unique dynamics, they all have in common the following four stages: (1) buildup or precrisis period (the symptoms—repeated messages and persistent sets of clues—are detectable), (2) crisis breakout/acute crisis (initial stages), (3) abatement or chronicity of the crisis (charges, countercharges, demonstrations, inquiries, legal actions, and the continuing coverage by the mass media), and (4) termination (back to normal: the crisis is no longer a threat to an organization's operational environment or its constituent publics) (Sturges et al., 1991). From the communication point of view, we conceptualize the crisis life cycle with some help of the media agenda-setting research (Zhu and Blood, 1997). Initially, crises can be described as discrete events. If the crisis continues and acquires momentum and force, links between discrete events are established, a pattern emerges, and events become issues. Finally, the strongest momentum or force is generated when links between issues are generated and issues become agendas. Events would correspond to the build up and outbreak stages of a crisis (Value Jet crash, Intel's Pentium chip, Northeast Utility/nuclear power, and GE's turbines). Issues are analogous to some portion of the chronic stage (FDA's regulation of medical devices such as IUDs, heart valves, pacemakers, and breast implants), and agendas apply to the remaining portions of the chronic stage as well as the crisis termination (Agent Orange, asbestos industry, Dalkon Shield, silicone breast implants, and tobacco industry). At this point we can say that a combination of (1) the stages of crisis, (2) stakeholders' knowledge of the crisis and their specific concerns, and (3) the ways the crisis threatens specific stakeholders shape the range of the most effective message design and implementation strategies. In general, the more the crisis progresses, the less communicative options an organization has.

Risk Communication Management

Related issue concerns involve the (1) risk perception by the lay public, (2) risk assessment by professionals and experts, and (3) risk communication as the link between the two (Susskind and Field, 1996). A fundamental problem is that risk communication management prefers risk assessment to risk perception during the message design and implementation phase.

Reasons for Public Anger

Susskind and Field (1996) discuss six types of anger that are typically displayed in public disputes and crises: (1) when people have been hurt, (2) when people feel threatened by risks not of their own making, (3) when people feel that their fundamental beliefs are being challenged, (4) when people feel weak in the face of more powerful others, (5) when people believe they have been lied to or duped, and (6) when people strategically display anger to manipulate the reactions of others.

Communication Crisis Management

Our argument in this section will focus on three topics: (1) models of communication crisis management, (2) goals of communication crisis management, and (3) message strategies involving message design and implementation.

Models of Communication Crisis Management

There are basically three models of crisis communication management: (1) a marketplace model that argues that crises are caused and solved by economic, political, and legal competition; (2) ideologically based models involving new social movements; and (3) a public participation model based on cooperation among government, private industry, and the public (Gerrard, 1994; see also Susskind and Field, 1996). Our preference is the last model.

Goals of Crisis Communication Management

We outline two main goals of crisis communication management: (1) preventing crises and (2) managing crises. It is our view that crisis communication management should (1) stop the progression of crises from events to issues to agendas or at least shorten the duration of each stage of a crisis and (2) preserve as high a number of effective communication strategic and tactical options as possible. In doing so, we argue that organizations should have two mutually very consistent types of strategies: interpersonal and mass media strategies. The latter should emulate the interpersonal strategies based on honesty and trust and aimed at addressing an organization's stakeholders' specific concerns. In addition, both types of strategies should, if a crisis cannot be averted, help (1) get the necessary attention of the media, (2) define or redefine the perceptual frameworks through which the public sees the crisis, and (3) formulate the frame's cost/benefit tradeoffs as well as its more general consequences.

Message Strategies: Message Design and Implementation

We already stated that a combination of (1) the stages of crises, (2) stakeholders' knowledge of the crisis and their specific concerns, and (3) the ways the crisis threatens specific stakeholders shape the range of the most effective message design and implementation strategies. We also suggested that, in general, the more the crisis progresses, the fewer communicative options an organization has.

We will present our argument in three steps. First, we will hint at how the stages of crises influence the message strategies. Second, we will present one classification of message strategies aimed at responding to attacks on an organization. Finally, we will discuss the role of the mass media formats.

How the Stages of Crises Influence Message Strategies. Cushman and Penhallurick (1983) offer the following important insights: (1) one must understand an audience's processes of selective perception, standard interpretations, filter categories, and information storage and recall; (2) if an audience has little information on a topic, short, well-focused messages may be the most effective (the event stage of a crisis); and (3) if an audience knows a great deal about a topic, long messages which employ a configuration of filter categories similar to and congruent with those of the audience's may be the most effective (the issue stage). However, the agenda stage of a crisis presents a serious difficulty in that all stakeholders most likely have developed extremely negative or positive agendas (filter categories) that are not malleable. This leads us to say that the aim of the effective communication strategy is to locate, seize, and find a way into the specific entry/turning points along the crisis continuum to shape or reverse its direction(s) and outcomes (Crynczyk, MacDougal, and Obloj, 1997).

Message Strategies Aimed at Responding to Attacks.   Attacks on an organization are best formulated in Alinsky's (1971) discussion of rules for rational, that is, calculated, purposeful, and effective, action. His discussion centers on eleven rules pertaining to the ethics of means and ends, five rules on communication, and thirteen rules on tactics.

The eleven rules pertaining to the ethics of means and ends are: (1) one's concern with the ethics of means and ends varies inversely with one's personal interest in the issue; (2) the determination of ethical means is dependent upon the political position of those sitting in judgment; (3) in war, the end [the destruction of enemies] justifies almost any means; (4) judgment must be made in the context of the times in which the action occurred and not from any other chronological vantage point; (5) concern with ethics increases with the number of means available and vice versa; (6) the less important the end to be desired, the more one can afford to engage in ethical evaluations of means; (7) generally, success or failure is a mighty determinant of ethics; (8) the morality of a means depends upon whether the means is being employed at a time of imminent defeat [moral] or imminent victory [immoral]; (9) any effective means is automatically judged by the opposition as being unethical; (10) you do what you can with what you have and clothe your actions with moral garments; and (11) goals must be phrased in general terms (Whitman: "The goal once named cannot be countermandated"). Alinsky (1971) concludes: Means and ends are so qualitatively interrelated that the true question has never been the proverbial [well-known] one, "Does the End justify the Means?" but always has been "Does this *particular* end justify this *particular* means?" (p. 47)

The five rules on communication are: (1) people only understand things in terms of their experience, which means that you must get within their experience; (2) when you go outside anyone's experience not only do you not communicate, you cause confusion;

(3) it is only when the other party is concerned or feels threatened that he will listen—in the arena of action, a threat or crisis becomes almost a precondition to communication; (4) there are sensitive areas that one does not touch until there is a strong personal relationship based on common involvements; and (5) communication occurs concretely, by means of one's specific experience.

The thirteen rules on tactics [doing what you can with what you have] are: (1) power is not only what you have but what the enemy thinks you have; (2) never go outside the experience of your people; (3) whenever possible go outside the experience of the enemy (to cause confusion, fear, and retreat); (4) make the enemy live up to their own book of rules; (5) ridicule is the most potent weapon (it is almost impossible to counterattack ridicule); (6) a good tactic is one that your people enjoy; (7) a tactic that drags on too long becomes a drag; (8) keep the pressure on, with different tactics and actions, and utilize all events of the period for your purpose; (9) the threat is usually more terrifying than the thing itself; (10) develop operations that will maintain a constant pressure upon the opposition (the pressure produces the reaction, and constant pressure sustains action); (11) if you push a negative hard and deep enough it will break through into its counterside; (12) the price of a successful attack is a constructive alternative; and (13) pick the target [single out who is to blame for any particular evil], freeze it [do not let an organization diffuse and distribute responsibility in a number of areas], personalize it [it must be a personification, not something general and abstract], and polarize it [one acts decisively only in the conviction that all the angels are on one side and all the devils on the other]. Alinsky also warns that "[t]iming is to tactics what it is to everything in life—the difference between success and failure" (p. 158).

Benoit (1995) offers six strategies for responding to attacks:

1. *Denial* (the actor did not commit the objectionable act; the actor is not culpable, not deserving of blame) with *simple denial* (the alibi) or *shifting the blame* (victimage: applying guilt to another person; somebody else actually did it; scapegoating)

2. *Avoiding responsibility* (diminish the actor's responsibility for the objectionable act; make excuses) with (a) *provocation* (response to another wrongful act; the actor was justifiably provoked), (b) *defeasibility* (the objectionable act

can be undone or voided because of lack of information about important factors in the situation or control over important factors in the situation), (c) *accidents* (uncontrollable factors that one cannot reasonably be expected to control), and (d) *good intentions* (denial of bad intent)

3. *Reducing the offensiveness of the event* (increase the audience's esteem for the actor or decrease the audience's negative feelings about the act) with (a) *bolstering* (guilt or negative affect/positive attributes of the actor or positive actions in the past), (b) *minimization* (the negative act isn't as bad as it might first appear), (c) *differentiation* (the act is less offensive than similar but less desirable actions), (d) *transcendence* (placing the objectionable act in a different context: justificative strategies of appeal to higher values or loyalties or both), (e) *attack accusers* (the victim deserved what befell him or her), and (f) *compensation* (a gift designed to counterbalance, rather than to correct, the injury; remunerate or bribe the victim)

4. *Corrective action* (addresses the actual source of injury) with an *offer to rectify past damage* or an *offer to prevent recurrence of damage* (one can take corrective action without admitting guilt, e.g., Tylenol)

5. *Mortification* (concessions: admissions of wrong-doing and request for forgiveness; an apparently sincere apology, expression of regret and request for forgiveness; those guilty of wrong-doing probably should accept the responsibility immediately and apologize)

6. *Silence or ignoring accusations* (the hope that if left alone, the image problem may be forgotten; more likely when the actor felt little or no guilt).

Role of Mass Media Formats.   Altheide (1995) discusses the role of communication formats, or the rules for the recognition, organization, and presentation of information and experience. He argues that the mass media formats such as (1) entertainment shows, (2) docudramas, and (3) news reports may be more important than substance because they place events into a format-specific temporal and spatial order.

In such a context, our insistence on the consistency of inter-personal and mass media message strategies has at least two advan-tages: (1) interpersonal communication among organizational stakeholders does rely on multiple communication formats and thus (2) supplies the segments of the public with independent data from outside the media—"extramedia data."

Conclusion

The purpose of this chapter was to discuss the issues of (1) organizational crises, (2) organizational communication crisis man-agement, and (3) a possibility to fruitfully theorize about the inter-sections between organizational crises and their communication management.

First, we offered a brief conceptualization of: (1) metaphors and conceptualizations of crises, (2) crisis stages, (3) risk manage-ment, and (4) the reasons of public anger during crises.

Second, we focused on three topics: (1) models of communica-tion crisis management, (2) goals of communication crisis manage-ment, and (3) message strategies involving message design and implementation.

Finally, what did we learn? We argued implicitly for a particular vision of theory. Let us now make that argument more specific. We may say, as Kovačić and Cushman (1997) do, that theory is a part of a social scientific tradition consisting of (1) philosophical arguments, (2) theoretical arguments (concepts, propositions, and models), (3) empirical arguments, and (4) practical argument (communication skills involving strategies). Our position is, then, that (1) philosophically, crisis communication management is an important type of organiza-tional communication activities, (2) theoretically, we can identify concepts and suggestive models of crisis communication manage-ment, but we cannot specify propositions—a web of relationships between concepts—prior to inquiry, and (3) our main contribution would be an in-depth study of specific message sequences in particu-lar crises with an eye on creating effective crisis communication management.

Let's finish with a statement offered by Alinsky (1971): It can-not "be said that if this is done then that will result. The most we can hope to achieve is an understanding of the probabilities conse-quent to certain actions." (17). To pretend that we can do more at this point would be an unjustified arrogance.

90   B. THOMAS FLORENCE AND BRANISLAV KOVAČIĆ

References

Alinsky, Saul D. (1971). *Rules for Radicals: A Pragmatic Primer for Realistic Radicals.* New York: Vintage.

Altheide, David L. (1995). *An Ecology of Communication: Cultural Formats of Control.* New York: Aldine De Gryter.

Benoit, William L. (1995). *Accounts, Excuses, and Apologies: A Theory of Image Restoration Strategies.* Albany: SUNY Press.

Crynczyk, Arthur, Robert MacDougall, and Krzysztof Obloj. (1997) Lessons in Communicating Change: Some Dilemmas. In S. King and D. P. Cushman (eds.), *Lessons from the Recession: A Management and Communication Perspective.* Albany: SUNY Press.

Cushman, Donald P., and John Penhallurick. (1983). Political Images in the Hawke-Fraser Campaign. In T. Smith, III, G. Graeme, and R. Penman (eds.), *Communication and Government: Issues, Policies and Trends.* Canberra: Conference Proceedings, July.

Gerard, Michael B. (1994). *Whose Backyard, Whose Risk: Fear and Fairness in Toxic and Nuclear Waste Siting.* Cambridge: MIT Press.

Kovačić, Branislav, and Donald P. Cushman. (1997). A Pluralistic View of the Emerging Theories of Human Communication. In B. Kovačić (ed.), *Emerging Theories of Human Communication.* Albany: SUNY Press.

Sturgess, David L., Bob J. Carrel, Douglas A. Newsom, and Marcus Barrera. (1991). Crisis Communication Management: The Public Opinion Node and its Relationship to Environmental Nimbus. *SAM Advanced Management Journal* 56(3):22–27.

Susskind, Lawrence, and Patrick Field. (1996). *Dealing With an Angry Public: The Mutual Gains Approach to Resolving Disputes.* New York: The Free Press.

Thurow, Lester C. (1996). *The Future of Capitalism: How Today's Economic Forces Shape Tomorrow's World.* New York: William Morrow.

Zhu, Jian H., and Deborah Blood. (1997). Media Agenda-Setting: Telling the Public What to Think About. In B. Kovačić (ed.), *Emerging Theories of Human Communication.* Albany: SUNY Press.

6

Excellence in Communication During a Crisis: The Case of Indian Point 3 Nuclear Power Plant

Joseph T. Pillittere II

At the time of this piece, the American people have witnessed several television news reports of three separate mishaps that have killed several hundred people. These incidents would cause that ever-so-popular "fear of flying" to resurface. Gleick (1996) stated that, "every time a commercial airliner meets up with disaster, the flying public is forced to confront dangers it never even knew existed" (p. 40).

Our society is one based on speed. There is a need for people to get where they are going fast and on time. Even the consumer goods one purchases make life faster and simpler. Yet with every advancement there are associated risks. Those risks never seem to bother us until we hear that someone has been injured or killed. There has always been a risk associated with flying—otherwise, people would have been born with wings. Basically, one ignores the associated risks if the perceived benefit is greater. For example, what's interesting—but not surprising—is that AirTran continues to operate. Why is this surprising? In 1996, AirTran's Flight 592 crashed into the Everglades killing 110 people on board. AirTran is the new name for Valujet. When you ask people why they continue to buy tickets, you're told, "It's a great deal!"

Why do people still fly AirTran? First and foremost, the benefit outweighs the risks. Second, the company's communication effort during the crisis has perhaps helped relieve people's fears and concerns, which has given them a renewed sense of trust in the airline industry.

Renewing trust in the airline industry is not an easy task, but excellent communication is part of the solution. Many communication experts know that to be successful, a communication plan is needed. It is this plan that will ensure that all communications will be timely, accurate, and easily understood. Now, let's address crisis communication and how it helped a company maintain its reputation and ease the general public's fear.

Crisis Communication

What is a crisis? According to Bok (1989) "the Greek word *krisis* means "discrimination," "judgment," "decision," "crisis," or "trial." It always involves human perception of an unfolding event . . . but it can also stress the moral element of personal choice which goes along with perception when there is something at stake and opportunity to intervene" (p. 108).

Communication is a major subject of study that continues to fill our bookshelves and advice columns of newspapers. It spawns endless methods, helps to explain and resolve problems, and even assists in educating the public. However, communication is not something you put away until you need it. Gaining the trust and credibility of the general public demands the constant use of communication—good or bad.

Communication in any form in unpredictable. Wurman (1989) states that we are limited by language where words may mean one thing to one person and something quite different to another. Unfortunately, there is neither a definitive way nor an ordained method that will result in the right way to communicate. Gudykunst and Nishida (1986) stated that individuals use direct communication to reduce uncertainty in individualistic cultures.

When companies are faced with a "disaster" how will they deal with the media and the general public? Is the company going to notify the media of its intention to resolve the issue, or will it say nothing and hope no one finds out?

"It takes more than an authoritative presence and a good command of the facts to be an effective spokesperson during a crisis," says Columbia University professor and director of the university's Center for Risk Communications, Vincent T. Covello (USCEA, 1993, p. 2). He continues by stating that, "perception equals reality. It sometimes doesn't matter what the reality is. What does matter is what people perceive the reality to be" (p. 2). People make their judgment of you within the first 30 seconds of an interview. The number one goal is to gain their trust and credibility. The public, according to Covello, "judges trust and credibility based on caring/empathy; competency/expertise; honesty/openness; and dedication/commitment to public health and safety" (p. 3). According to Covello (personal communication, 1993), the public also puts more weight on empathy and caring and only 15 to 20% on the other factors. Whatever one does, telling the truth is better than nothing. According to Dick Winn, a crisis communication consultant, saying something early in a crisis is better than saying nothing, and explaining why you can't talk is better than stonewalling (personal communication, April, 1993).

Nonverbal communication is also important in a crisis communication situation. Covello says it can account for as much as 50 to 75% of the information received by the general public. "People will take a close notice of a spokesperson's nonverbal communication at such a time, and will interpret it negatively" (USCEA, 1993, p. 3). This perception of the spokesperson will eventually move over to the company's reputation. If you doubt bad press can't affect a company's reputation, just look at Exxon. Since the spill that dumped 260,000 barrels of oil into Prince William Sound, the world's third-largest industrial company's reputation is seen as uncaring, incompetent, and a penny-pinching despoiler. Exxon's reputation was based on the perception that television and print reporters portrayed in their stories.

Kant believed that all communications should be based on the truth and that there were no exceptions. As mentioned earlier, many of today's top crisis communication experts believe that truth is not only important, but it is one of the first things one will be judged.

How a company communicates to the general public externally or through the media, will depend largely on the corporate culture the organization has established. As stated by Golden (1968), "On the day that management forgets that an institution cannot continue to exist if the general public feels that it is not useful, or that it is anti-social in the public concept of what is anti-social, the institution will begin to die" (p. 4). Public opinion is extremely subjective with many mood swings. If handled properly, extraordinary events can cause a sudden change from like to hate. Public consent exists because businesses perform in the public's interest, along with an embedded policy of explaining what a business is doing and why. This holds true especially for highly visible corporations. "It takes hard work, harder thinking, an understanding of public moods, and specialists who know something of public attitudes and the many different means of reaching the public" (Golden, 1968, p. 4). This, of course, is not an easy process. It takes commitment and support of upper management to gain the trust of the general public.

Seitel (1994), a senior counselor at Burson-Marstellar, said that public relations has never been more needed, "because the need for positive communications among organizations and their publics in all sectors of society . . . has never been more pronounced" (p. 202).

The general public is smarter and demands more accountability from businesses than ever before. Businesses should be held responsible for their actions and repair the damages they have created. The nuclear accident at Three Mile Island was an unfortunate incident and as Cottrell (1981) states "This playing on public nerves did not start and finish at Harrisburg. It has applied also—and far less justifiably—to all kinds of lesser incidents in nuclear plants, such as small leaks, all the way down to minor occurrences . . . that happen commonly in even the best run of industries" (p. 44). These are usually misrepresented to the general public in the form of dramatic and scary headlines.

A Case Study: Fuel Assembly Incident at Indian Point 3

About Indian Point 3

The Indian Point 3 Nuclear Power Plant is owned and operated by the New York Power Authority. The Power Authority is a nonprofit, quasi-state agency that was created to supply electricity to the State of New York. The plant, a 965,000-kilowatt, pressurized water reactor, is located on the banks of the Hudson River in Buchanan, New York. Besides Indian Point 3, the site is also the home of two other nuclear plants, one of which has been shutdown permanently. The site, known as Indian Point, is approximately 45 miles north of Manhattan, one of the most densely populated areas in the United States. It is for this reason that any incidents, big or small, create media interest instantly.

As stated earlier, Indian Point 3 is a pressurized water reactor. A reactor of this design uses ordinary water for cooling and many tons of uranium to generate large amounts of heat through the splitting of atoms (fission). Water is pressurized in the reactor coolant system to prevent it from boiling. This water is super-heated and then pumped to thousands of tubes contained inside four steam generators. These tubes become hot and transfer their heat energy to a separate supply of water located around them inside the top of the steam generators. This water boils and turns to steam which turns a turbine-generator producing electricity (figure 6.1).

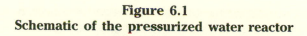

Figure 6.1
Schematic of the pressurized water reactor

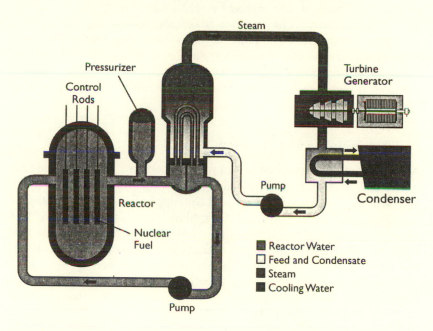

Nuclear power is designed to be safe, if operated in accordance with procedures, regulations, and design basis documents. Indian Point 3, like all nuclear plants, was designed with several multiple barriers and controls to protect the health and safety of the general public and its employees. The uranium fuel, in the form of uranium oxide, is stacked into fuel rods and can withstand high temperatures during plant operations. For example, for a meltdown to occur, temperatures in excess of 5400°F must be reached without cooling. The reactor vessel is eight to ten inches of solid steel, weighs about 433 tons, and is designed to contain the nuclear fuel. The containment dome, which is $3^1/_2$ to $4^1/_2$ feet of steel-reinforced concrete, is designed to prevent the release of radioactivity to the environment in the event of abnormal operating conditions. A steel liner, approximately $3/_4$-inch thick, surrounds the inside of the containment building as a redundant safety measure. There are also several other redundant systems that will help mitigate the likelihood of any significant accident from occurring.

This background information is needed so one can understand that safety measures are part of the plant's design to protect public health and safety in the unlikely event of an accident.

Indian Point 3 was shutdown on September 15, 1990, for its scheduled refueling and maintenance outage. The plant was slated to resume production of electricity on November 19, 1990. During the outage, fifty major modification and 2,000 work items would be completed along with preventive and corrective maintenance of plant systems.

Fuel Assembly Incident At Indian Point 3

After the outage began, work had progressed well and at a moderate pace. The first step in a refueling is to remove the reactor head. Then a large subassembly called the upper internals is removed exposing the top of the fuel assemblies. The assemblies are then removed individually. All refueling operations are conducted under approximately 23 feet of water, which shields workers from intense radiation emitted by the fuel and reactor components.

On Wednesday, October 3, inside the containment building, the reactor head was removed and placed in its normal storage area.

On Thursday, October 4, while lifting the upper internals, two fuel assemblies which should have remained in the core, were inadvertently lifted with the upper internals. The plant staff was aware of the potential for lifting assemblies with the upper internals and was using an underwater camera and visual observation to check. When noticed, the internals had been lifted approximately four feet above the reactor's fuel core and moved five and a half feet horizontally. The two fuel assemblies remained under 22 feet of water in the reactor cavity. All work in the containment building was stopped and workers left as a precaution. Monitoring of air and water samples showed no changes in radiation levels.

The Nuclear Regulatory Commission, the plant's regulator, was notified of the event in accordance with operating procedures.

The event was not classified under the Nuclear Regulatory Commission's four emergency classification levels:

Unusual event: An event(s) are in progress or have occurred which indicate a potential degradation of the level of safety of the plant. No release of radioactive material requiring offsite response or monitoring are expected unless further degradation of safety systems occurs.

Alert: An event(s) are in progress or have occurred which involve actual or potential substantial degradation of the level of safety of the plant. Any releases are expected to be limited to small fractions of the Environmental Protection Agency (EPA) Protective Action Guidelines exposure levels.

Site Area Emergency: An event(s) are in progress or have occurred which involve actual or likely major failures of plant functions needed for protection of the public. Any releases are not expected to result in exposure levels which exceed EPA Guideline exposure levels expect near the site boundary.

General Emergency: An event(s) are in progress or have occurred which involve actual or imminent substantial core degradation or melting with potential for loss of containment integrity. Releases can be reasonably expected to exceed EPA Guideline exposure levels offsite for more than the immediate site area. (NUREG 0654, 1980)

The decision was based on several factors. There was no degradation of plant safety systems, there was no release of radioactivity, and the incident occurred inside the containment building. This building was designed for incidents like this, but on a worst-case scenario.

I had only been with the media relations department for ten months. I was previously at the company's FitzPatrick Nuclear Power Plant in Oswego, New York. The department consisted of the following Public Relations staff: information officer, assistant information officer (myself), information specialist, and a secretary. Periodically, the department would receive support from the media relations staff located in the White Plains and New York City offices.

We were notified of this event immediately by the resident manager in charge of plant operations. I can remember the adrenaline rushing through my body as I was about to be involved in my first "nuclear incident." The first task at hand was to decide what plan of action we were going to take. The information officer called us together to let us know the details of the incident. The first question we had to ask ourselves was, "Since this event did not warrant a classification, did we really need to say anything?"

Before we made a decision we did some quick research. I discovered that similar events had happened at other operating nuclear plants. One incident in particular, had occurred in the United States at a nuclear plant in Connecticut in 1986. Although this incident was not a threat to the general public, it did involve nuclear fuel which could drum up several negative images such as radiation, meltdown, *The China Syndrome* (the movie), Three Mile Island (1979), and Chernobyl (1986). If word of our event was somehow obtained by the news media, the company's reputation and credibility could be damaged.

A decision was made to handle our particular incident like it was a newsworthy event. This decision was based on the company's commitment as a good neighbor that operated the plant with open and honest communications. To withhold information now could only damage our reputation, which could take years to restore.

The staff immediately began to work on developing a news release and talking points. Once this was completed, the staff made internal and external courtesy notifications before distributing the news release. This action on our part, also provided community leaders with timely, accurate, and concise information so they were prepared to answer any potential questions from the news media.

Upon completion of both internal and external notifications, the news release was distributed to our preprogrammed news media list. However, this time we added something to it. Since this particular event involved more technical issues, a picture was created to help demonstrate and clarify what had happened. As the saying goes, "A picture paints a thousand words." This would accompany our first press release (figure 6.2).

The relatively short press release stressed the following points:

- Preparations for refueling were halted until the staff resolved a problem with removal of fuel from the reactor.

- Two fuel assemblies that should have remained in the core were inadvertently lifted with the upper internals.

- The fuel assemblies were suspended from the bottom of the equipment which was still within the water-filled reactor vessel.

- The plant staff was planning to secure and remove the assemblies so that refueling operations could resume.

- The plant has been shutdown for a scheduled refueling outage since September 15.

The calls received from the media that evening were few, and lacked the questioning that we had originally anticipated. The phones

Figure 6.2
Containment Building

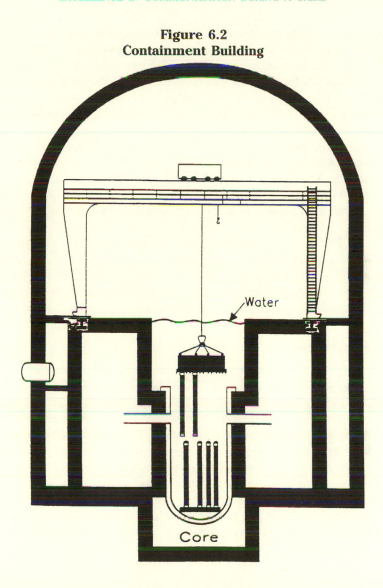

Water

Core

This is a simplified diagram of the IP3 containment building. While only six are shown, there are 193 fuel assemblies. Two of the 193 fuel assemblies were inadvertently lifted during preparations for refueling. Plant staff is studying the problem before resuming the refueling operation.

Source: New York Power Authority.

weren't ringing off the hook and media wasn't pounding down our door. In fact, no media even drove to the plant for pictures, file footage, or to conduct an interview. The event seemed to be a non-event. What mattered to us was that we informed the general public and local officials of what had happened. As far as we were concerned, we did what they had come to expect of us—provide open and honest communication.

In the meantime, plant and Westinghouse staff decided to design and build two nine-foot-tall steel baskets for safely securing the assemblies. Several other teams involved with the retrieval process began developing the retrieval and maintenance procedures, nuclear safety evaluation, and necessary calculations to support the retrieval plan.

On Friday, October 5, the story was reported verbatim in two local newspapers. In both cases, the articles were small and placed with other small news items. Radio broadcasts handled the story in a similar fashion. Unbenounced to us, this would be the beginning of an incredible two-week media frenzy.

The Media Frenzy

On Saturday, October 6 and Sunday, October 7, several more articles appeared that mentioned the fuel assembly incident at the plant. Although most of them depicted the incident as no threat to the general public, the *New York Post* painted a different picture. The headline read, "Accident Shuts Upstate Nuke Plant—100 Flee." At the time of the incident, only twelve workers were in the containment building. Below the picture of the Indian Point site the caption states, "Ticking: Jammed nuclear fuel rods have left this Indian Point nuclear power reactor out of action, threatening to leak radioactivity into the air." To make matters worse, the article depicts the two fuel assemblies as 400 fuel rods dangling dangerously. Although there are 204 fuel rods per assembly, characterizing of this kind can lead the general public to believe that matters are more serious than they actually are. This article would later create a mountain out of a mole hill.

About this time, a team of workers had lowered a small submarine, equipped with a video camera, into the reactor cavity to determine what caused the assemblies to be inadvertently lifted from the core. The problem was caused when guide pins in the upper internals, which align fuel assemblies with the equipment above them, apparently did not disengage from the attached fuel assemblies as designed.

On Monday, October 8 (a holiday in 1990), I received a call at home from my boss, the information officer. He informed me that two television reporters had seen the article in the *New York Post* and wanted to come down to the plant and shoot an interview. I needed to come into work and help make arrangements and provide support. I knew my holiday was over when we finished the conversation.

When I arrived, we gathered to discuss our plan of action. Present at the meeting was myself; my boss, the director of Nuclear Policy and Information; the senior vice president of Media Relations; and our department secretary. The first item we discussed was the fact that a television news reporter was interested in doing a story. And we now had the opportunity to reach thousands of people with our message or this "small event" could become a major news story. The group put together several talking points that the company needed to get across immediately. For example, we needed to inform people that the two stuck fuel assemblies were inside the containment building, a structure designed to protect the public from any release of radioactivity. These talking points were then refined into sound bites for the television crews. A sound bite is an intriguing phrase that gets your point across in about eight seconds or less.

We decided to list the key items we had in place to effectively respond to this event, and what our future actions would be. First, we had an emergency plan and could use it to our advantage during the crisis. We were prepared for a media event like this. Every year we had conducted drills and exercises that allowed us to sharpen our skills in writing press releases, conducting press conferences, and dealing with the media. Second, we were already proactive by having informed the general public, local officials, and the media about the event after it had occurred. This would help maintain our credibility and trust, which would be needed as things progressed. It also demonstrated that we were concerned about the health and safety of the general public. Third, we had a designated spokesperson, the information officer (my boss). He was located at the plant and personally knew the reporters, local officials, and plant personnel. He was able to access timely, accurate, and up-to-date information. Providing the general public, news media, and local and state officials with this information would show our competence, expertise, and openness. The director, senior vice president, and myself would provide backup support, if necessary. Fourth, each of us was always available by pager if media interest became overwhelming.

This allowed us the flexibility to handle several reporters simultaneously with the same message. Fifth, everybody was given a role as part of the media relations team.

My role was to gather information on the event and write shelf statements, briefing papers, and fact sheets as plans to resolve the problem progressed. Also, some of the time I would be stationed in the Technical Support Center (TSC) to obtain progress reports on the event. The TSC was a designated area for technical personnel to gather to support the plant during a nuclear emergency. Although this wasn't an emergency, it needed the expertise of several technical people who knew the workings of the plant well. During this event the TSC had cameras and communication links installed to observe the activities inside the containment building.

Spending Time with Reporters

The television crews were told to meet us at our training center, which was located on the site about a quarter mile from the plant. This would be a neutral territory for both parties and provided a less distracting environment. Located in the lobby of the center were several exhibits on Indian Point 3 and nuclear power in general. This would be an asset for us and would provide the reporters with excellent background footage and information.

All the interviews began in the training center and ended up outside near the plant. Plant schematics and drawings were used to help put the problem in perspective and make it easier for the general public to understand. After the interviews were over, the crews went off-site to interview residents living near the plant for their comments about the incident.

The reporters were obviously aiming for a negative slant, asking questions like, "Could this be another Three Mile Island?" By the time they had left, we felt confident that we had gotten our messages across. The only thing to do now was to wait until the broadcasts aired that evening.

The evening broadcasts all started their stories with the Indian Point 3 fuel assembly story. The slant at first was negative, but as the stories unfolded they became more and more positive. Positive in the sense that the Power Authority had things under control and there was no threat to the general public. Interviews with the Nuclear Regulatory Commission's senior resident inspector, who was stationed at Indian Point 3, also depicted the situation in the same fashion. Neighbors nearby the plant who were interviewed had nothing but positive comments about the plant and its operations. This is where the Power Authority's community outreach efforts truly showed their worth. The time we spent communication with local residents in the communities we served put a "face" on the Power Authority. Through these interactions, residents came to realize that people like you and me worked at the nuclear plant. The plant wasn't just a concrete structure that made electricity.

It was after these broadcasts aired, that the media would soon be at our doorstep in full force.

On Tuesday, October 9, I reported for work as usual at 7:00 A.M. It was only about an hour later when the phones began to ring off the hook with media calls. Most of them had seen the broadcasts the night before and wanted to know more about the incident. The rate of calls was approximately ten per hour and growing. The feeling among the department was that this would probably continue into the night. A decision was made to keep track of all the calls by using a telephone message pad with carbon copies. This way, a reporter's number, time of call, and question could be tracked or referenced later. This would also assist us in being proactive by determining what questions might be asked in the future. This way, answers could be researched and prepared to ensure a timely and accurate response. By the end of the night, we were all tired and worn out, but the adrenaline rush of the day's events kept us upbeat and positive.

On Wednesday, October 10, the Power Authority and Westinghouse staff had developed a plan to move and store the two uranium fuel assemblies that had been inadvertently removed from the reactor. The plan would be submitted to the Nuclear Regulatory Commission for approval before we could take any actions. It involved moving the fuel assemblies over specially designed steel baskets that would be located in a storage area adjacent to the reactor. The assemblies would be lowered into the steel baskets and detached from the upper internals prior to being transferred for safe storage in the plant's spent fuel pool. All the activity would be conducted while the two assemblies, like the 191 others in the reactor, remained submerged underwater. The upper internals would then be placed in their normal storage area, and the fuel assemblies would be inspected.

A second press release, explaining this plan and other relevant information was distributed to the news media. It also included a simple schematic showing the planned movements to safely secure and store the two fuel assemblies (figure 6.3). Once again, media

Figure 6.3
Fuel Assembly Removal Process

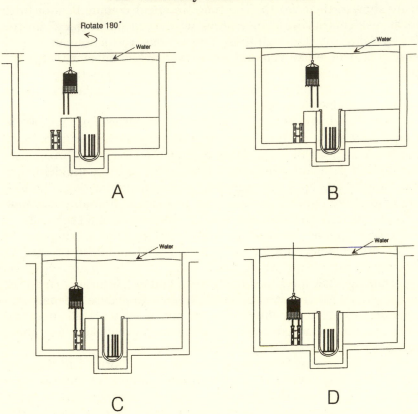

calls flooded the office for more information. With each new press release came new interest from several different radio, television, and print media. Other utilities that operated nuclear plants also called to receive updates and to offer their support. As things got busier in the office, the director and senior vice president came down to lend a hand. The media frenzy was apparent now, and the staff continued to work into the late evening over the next several days.

It is often hard to deal with the general public in a crisis communication situation; however, it is even tougher when that situation is new to everyone. We were prepared for this, and our main goal was to ensure that all communications were timely, accurate, and easily understood.

On Tuesday afternoon, October 16, the Nuclear Regulatory Commission approved the retrieval plan. At 5:00 P.M., the upper internals were moved as planned, about eight feet vertically with the overhead crane to clear the reactor's rim. The equipment was then moved about twenty feet horizontally to the equipment storage area, where the steel baskets had been placed to receive the two fuel assemblies.

At 5:18 P.M., one fuel assembly dropped 10 feet into a steel basket. Workers immediately interrupted the procedure and, as a precaution, left the containment building. Radiation monitoring conducted afterward showed no changes in radiation levels inside containment.

A third press release was distributed on this incident to maintain our communication goal. However, this time would be different. Within a matter of minutes, a reporter called with information he had received from someone inside the plant. Unfortunately for us, the information was wrong and misleading. We now realized that we needed to deal with a new issue—an information leak. However, our preplanning prepared us for such an event. The first thing we had to do was to provide the reporter with the right information. This would prevent the release of incorrect information that could damage our reputation or cause confusion and concern among the public. Our department had to begin monitoring all media for rumors, bad information, or anything out of the ordinary. It would be the only way to keep the general public informed with accurate information. If a trend appeared on a particular matter or issue, it could be eliminated through a press release or press conference. There were no other incidents of this type during the event.

At 8:00 P.M., the remaining assembly was successfully lowered within six inches of the bottom of the steel basket.

At 10:00 P.M., senior management suspended work for the evening to allow workers to rest and regroup. A fourth press release was written and distributed at 10:45 P.M. The calls continued to come in, and were handled immediately by three members of the media relations staff. At this point in the crisis, about 90% of all news stories were balanced and continued to inform the public that things were under control and that there was no danger.

The following day, the remaining fuel assembly was successfully dislodged from the upper internals. The internals were then raised and placed in a support stand on the opposite side of the reactor cavity. A fifth press release was written and distributed to the news media.

As determined through visual inspections, review of previous refueling practices, and engineering analysis, the cause of the event was damage to the guide pins that occurred during the 1989 refueling outage. While moving the upper internals from its stand to the reactor, the internals had not been lifted sufficiently and struck the stand during horizontal movement, damaging several guide pins.

The upper internals were later repaired and the two fuel assemblies were safely secured and stored in the plant's spent fuel pool.

Conclusion

Indian Point 3's communication efforts were successful in keeping the stories balanced, factual, and not sensationalized. The main reason for their success was that trust and credibility were gained at the beginning of the event. Since the window of opportunity for creating trust is very small it must be achieved immediately. The Power Authority accomplished this early by being open and forthcoming with news and by maintaining a continuous flow of information throughout the crisis. Providing accurate and understandable information to the news media in a timely manner made the Power Authority the leading source for information. This proactive action on our part helped to ensure that the news media did not seek out other sources for information, such as: antinuclear groups, local critics, and local officials.

Another advantage the department had was its relationship with local residents, officials, and reporters. Personal contacts throughout the years had created relationships based on open and honest communication. People felt comfortable with asking questions, bringing up concerns, or just discussing plant operations. It is this type of interaction that builds a solid reputation and puts a face on a large company. This could not have been accomplished with one-way communications such as news releases, fact sheets, and brochures.

These friendships build into relationships of mutual trust, honesty, and credibility. Creating these strong ties within the community helped the Power Authority respond effectively during this crisis.

Here are some other helpful hints to effectively deal with crisis communications:

- Have a plan in place and practice it.
- Don't lie.
- Listen, don't be a slave to the question, and have an open mind.
- Use simple language and visuals.
- Prepare key messages.
- If you don't know the answer, say you don't.
- Be prompt in getting information disseminated.
- Distribute a news release for: major events, items of significance, or change in status of the event.

Maynard and Mehrtens (1993) state that businesses of today are being pressured to become a more responsible and multipurpose institution. Companies need the consent and acceptance of the general public in order to survive. Golden (1968) says for a company to obtain that consent they must act in the public interest as the public interprets it at any given time. Fisher (1986) states that "The experts . . . agree that no amount of advertising or ballyhoo will fool anybody if the corporation behind it is trying to throw dust in the public's eye" (p. 60).

The results of our crisis communication plan were in stark contrast to what happened at Three Mile Island (TMI). The problems associated with the communications from TMI caused unnecessary confusion, fear, and concern among the general public. This damaged the reputation of the plant's owner and raised the question of safely producing electricity from nuclear power. In fact, the Harris and Cambridge reports, conducted in the 1970s, showed a decline in the acceptance of nuclear power after the TMI accident.

Bottom line: Don't ever stop communicating just because things are going well. By continuing one's communication with the public, local officials, interest groups, and the media, stereotypes of big business seem to fade. What's left, is mutual trust and respect built on a solid foundation of open and honest communication. Simply put, if the public already knows you, internal resolution of the problem is the only battle left to fight.

References

Bok, S. (1989). *Lying: Moral Choice in Public and Private Life.* New York: Random House.

Cottrell, A. (1981). *How Safe is Nuclear Energy?* Portsmouth, NH: Heinemann.

Ettore, B. (1992). Corporate accountability '90s style: The buck had better stop here. *Management Review,* April, 81:16.

Fisher, A. B. (1986). Spiffing up the corporate image. *Fortune,* July 21, 14:60–72.

Gleick, E. (1996). Does air safety have a price? *Time,* May 27, 147:40–42.

Golden, L. (1968). *Only by Public Consent: American Corporations Search for Favorable Opinion.* New York: Hawthorne.

Gudykunst, W. B., and Nishida, T. (1986). Attributional confidence in low and high context cultures. *Human Communication Research* 12:525–49.

Maynard, H., and Mehrtens, S. (1993). *The Fourth Wave: Business in the 21st Century.* San Francisco: Berrett-Koehler.

NUREG 0654. (1980). *Criteria for Preparation and Evaluation of Radiological Emergency Response Plans and Preparedness in Support of Nuclear Power Plants.* Washington, DC: U.S. Nuclear Regulatory Commission.

Seitel, F. (1994). The ten commandments of corporate communications. *Harvard Business Review,* January, 60:202.

USCEA. (1993). What risk communication research reveals about spokesperson effectiveness. *Exchange,* January/February, 3:3–5.

Wurman, R. (1989). *Information Anxiety.* New York: Doubleday.

7

R&D and Marketing Strategy for Cross-Cultural Cooperation: A Cross-Pacific Study between China and the U.S.

Yanan Ju

Organizational excellence is a game that finds itself forever in the process of creating, negating, then recreating its rules. It's sure a difficult game if its rules keep changing. Cross-cultural organizational excellence can be an impossible game if the two players, each unfamiliar with the other's "traditional" play codes, fail to make a hard enough effort trying to "freeze," so to speak, a minimum set of rules so that they know at least where to start, where to stop, and how to count points. Organizational excellence can be determined by a multiplicity of factors including an organization's integration, coordination, and control systems. Cross-cultural organizational excellence can be compounded by such variables as different cultural value systems, culture-specific organizational practices, needs incompatibility, and lack of linguistic competency of the guest culture.

This chapter supposes that coordination is a key communication process by which to achieve organizational excellence on the assumption that other relevant organizational variables operate at optimal levels facilitating the achieving of organizational excellence. Such coordination can be a challenging task if organizations that are involved in a strategic linkage must overcome barriers created by a continuous negotiation on the definition of each other's tasks, needs, and knowledge and skills requirements, geographic/cultural distances, and different communication code systems and styles. Although a universally applicable theory or model or rules for achieving cross-cultural organizational excellence is not possible, this study has some reference value in a cross-Pacific R&D and marketing interface experiment undertaken by an American company and a Chinese state-controlled enterprise in their joint effort to develop two-wheel electric vehicles and to capture a potentially large market in the most populous nation on earth.

Cross-Cultural Organizational Coordination: Key to Achieving Cross-Cultural Organizational Excellence

Cross-cultural organizational coordination is a process that involves at least two organizations with two distinct national cultural backgrounds located in geographic areas that can be oceans apart physically but seconds away electronically. Cross-cultural organizational coordination is a process of managing organizational interdependence in which each of the two or more firms clearly articulates its needs, concerns, and planned or potential contributions to the joint venture or other forms of cooperation. The universal goal is to forge an appropriate value-added configuration and sustainable competitive advantage to the linkages. An appropriate value-added pattern of linkages among firms is one in which management can integrate, coordinate, and control its firm's needs, concerns, and contributions so that the outcome is mutually satisfying to the units involved and optimizing in value-added activities of the joint venture as a whole.[1]

According to Cushman and King,[2] establishing and maintaining an effective coordination system in a volatile economic environment where an organization's primary and support activities are configured and dispersed throughout the world would be a next-to-impossible task were it not for the development of new information and communication technologies. Electronically, China and the United States are just seconds away; faxes and international phone calls, for example, have become communication routines between cooperating firms on both sides of the Pacific, which greatly helps with coordinating each other's organizational and business activities. Even though various obstacles and barriers remain, the primary communication tool with which to conduct timely exchange of critical organizational and business information is nevertheless there, which may not be a sufficient condition for achieving cross-cultural organizational excellence, but is a necessary prerequisite for it.

Coordinating R&D in the U.S.
and Marketing in China

To avoid any possibility of incurring unintentional damage to the proprietary confidential information regarding the product that two sides have been cooperating on, I will use Company A for the U.S. firm and Company B for the Chinese organization. Company A has been in the business of research, development, and commercialization of electric drive train systems for motorized vehicles, and it enjoys the technical superiority and financial backing to make it a major player in the emerging industry of electric vehicle drive train systems. Company A's technical superiority results from its affiliations with and access to both state and federal high-technology resources. Support from and access to technology at the federal level has been critical to Company A's success. With the end of the Cold War, the United States Congress opened access to qualifying companies to the national laboratories to create jobs and growth through commercialization of their high technologies. The national laboratories were started and dedicated most of their efforts to research and development of military technologies. Company A enjoys a close working relationship with some of these laboratories, and has world-class expertise in batteries, motors, electronic controllers, chargers, and composite materials. Over the years, Company A has committed resources worth millions of dollars to the research and development of electric drive train systems with which to power two-wheel or three-wheel vehicles. Then the question is: Where is the market?

Soon Company A decided that the world's potentially largest market for two-wheel or three-wheel vehicles is in the People's Republic of China. And they found a strategic Chinese partner, Company B, one of the largest state-owned motorscooter manufacturers in the People's Republic. In October 1994, Company A and Company B signed a cooperation and exclusivity agreement in which the two sides agreed to manufacture and sell in China a 50cc motorscooter whose chassis would be made by Company B and whose electric drive train would be provided by Company A. It was also made clear that Company A would be entrusted with R&D and that Company B would take charge on manufacturing and marketing the finished products.

The division of labor between Company A and Company B sounds perfect since Company A's core competency is R&D in the electric drive train system, and Company B sits right on its market, so close to it that it can feel its pulse. But reality does not look as promising as it sounds. Cross-cultural organizational excellence seems as far as the Pacific Ocean that separates Company A and Company B. Besides all the other challenges that lie ahead on the road to excellence, the coordination task between the two companies has been frustratingly difficult, if not impossible. Neither side should take the blame or responsibility for the delay of the program, but each has a lot to learn from and reflect on this cross-Pacific R&D and marketing interface experiment.

The coordination task between Company A and Company B is three-fold: (1) task coordination, (2) "ways of doing things" coordination, and (3) communication coordination.

Task Coordination

Who does what when can be an easy division of labor between two parties that are working on the same product, with one in charge of R&D and the other responsible for marketing. But when the technology keeps changing and the market keeps struggling with government regulations, even a relatively simple task—and its coordination—can prove to be a next-to-impossible venture.

The efficiency of the electric drive train system depends, among other things, on the battery technology, which has been the main hurdle to the development of electric vehicles (EV) across the world. The lead-acid battery is a mature technology and less expensive than other battery technologies, but not advanced enough to be accepted by most EV companies world wide—it is too heavy and too big, and lacks the energy to give an EV the kind of distance range that it needs per charge. Also its life is too short; it would be dead after 200 to 300 cycles of discharge on average, depending on how it is used.

Company A started its test with lead-acid battery on the rationale that it is affordable. This was a pioneering task since no one had ever tried to power a motorscooter with a lead-acid battery. In order to save time, instead of doing the test in the U.S., Company A took everything to Company B and had the Chinese execute the test under the supervision of Company A's technicians. Based on the test results from an intensive three-month test, Company A decided that lead-acid batteries lack the performance capabilities required to commercialize the electric motorscooter either in China or elsewhere in the world. A possible alternative to the lead-acid battery was the nickel-metal-hydride battery. Compared with the lead-acid battery, the nickel-metal-hydride battery has a much higher energy density (i.e., smaller and lighter) and many more recharge cycles (i.e., a longer life). It has the capability to attain a distance of over 100 kilometers, a feature that Chinese motorscooter riders want, according to Company B's market research. The problem is it is unbearably expensive unless it is a very large order. Getting a big order is Company B's task. What Company A needs to do is to redesign the whole electric drive train system to fit with the perfor- mance features of nickel-metal-hydride battery. Again, it sounds perfect and simple. But the reality is not that rosy.

By the time that Company A almost completed the system design for a 50cc size motorscooter, Company B suggested that it might be a more feasible market strategy to introduce, at least at the beginning, a 125cc size one instead of a 50cc size since the cost for the electric drive train system (which consists of battery, a motor, electronic controller, and charger) for both sizes is not a big differ- ence, yet a 125cc scooter can sell for much higher price than a 50cc. Besides, a 125cc scooter can take one passenger, and therefore has a larger market in the populous Chinese market. In other words, the high cost of a nickel-metal-hydride battery can be "digested" or "swallowed" by a 125cc scooter more easily than by a 50cc. Why didn't Company B, from a market perspective, raise the 50cc vs. 125cc issue six months before when the design plan was being worked out? Not to mention that Company A had spent a lot of money on the 50cc project, a six-month time loss can mean millions of dollars if the opportunity to be the first one in the world to hit the market with the product is missed. One reason that Company B did not want to shift from 50cc to 125cc was presumably because all their exiting product lines were 50cc. Besides, the lead-acid battery test was also conducted on the 50cc. It seems that the 50cc had become the mind set for Company B; the law of the market had been vio- lated, ironically, by the one who has been assigned the job. Company B, which has been in charge of market research and marketing, should have done a more thorough marketing job and should have made the 125cc proposal before Company A's work on 50cc started. Company A, which was more knowledgeable about the pricing of the nickel-metal-hydride battery and the whole electric drive train system, should have taken the initiative to provide Com- pany B necessary information to facilitate their rethinking about possible approaches to the unique Chinese market. Lack of coordi- nation between the two not only cost money but also wasted precious time.

"Ways of Doing Things" Coordination

"Ways of Doing Things" coordination can be more challenging than task coordination in effecting cross-cultural organizational excellence since it not only takes a long time to understand another culture's value orientations and behavioral patterns but also requires a new learner to respond appropriately and effectively. Appropriateness means that one must respond in such a way that one will not violate another culture's expectations as well as one's own cultural values. Effectiveness is the degree to which one achieves one's goal relative to one's cost. When two cultures are found on two opposing ends of a cultural values and behaviors continuum, meeting the two criteria of appropriateness and effectiveness is no easy job.

Company A, representing a culture based on capitalism and respect for laws, rules, and regulations, and Company B, whose behaviors are very much dictated by *quanxi* ("connections") and what is called "a socialist market economy with Chinese characteristics," sits right on the opposite ends of the cultural values and behaviors continuum. While both capitalism and *quanxi* have the magic of speeding things up, an obsession with laws, rules, and regulations (or rather, a constantly existing fear of law suits) and "a socialist market economy with Chinese characteristics" have a tendency to slow down action. Company A finds it frustratingly difficult to handle the Chinese concept of *quanxi* and the very much undefined "Chinese characteristics." Company B feels that spending hours, days, weeks, and months negotiating legal documents is a mere waste of time.

Let us take a look at the Chinese concept of *quanxi* and some of the "Chinese characteristics" and see how they can complicate "ways of doing things" coordination between two vastly different cultures. First, *quanxi* is a web of an individual Chinese person's blood and/or social connections which define who s/he is and what s/he is capable of accomplishing without accounting for other resources s/he has available for use. While *quanxi* is practiced in all cultures and societies, it is a way of life in China and among Chinese communities. All Chinese know *quanxi* as a social/business resource is important and thus must be practiced in due course even though one doesn't have to acknowledge it publicly. The understanding is tacitly shared among the Chinese. Second, Chinese *quanxi* must be understood as a system, which requires one to develop a taxonomy. All Chinese have their *quanxiwang,* or network of *quanxi,* which consists of one's blood and social *quanxi.* Blood *quanxi* may include one's family members, relatives, and members from the same clan. Social *quanxi* are all those connections which do not belong to one's blood *quanxi,* such as friends, colleagues, or ex-classmates. Third, the Chinese *quanxi* system is reciprocal in nature. Many Westerners never quite learn the reciprocal nature of *quanxi.* It is never quite enough to say "thank you, my friend, that's very kind of you to have done all this for me, but you must consciously realize you are "in debt" and remember you may have to pay it back one way or another or risk losing this *quanxi* of yours who could be very important to your future business. Fourth, *quanxi* as an individual/business resource should be viewed more as a way of life and practiced as such. Western misunderstanding and, in some cases, resentment of the Chinese practice of *quanxi* is well-understood. In many situations, people practice *quanxi* just because they want to demonstrate their allegiance to and appreciation of their Chineseness, in that practicing *quanxi* makes them an active part of the social fabric, or simply because it's a matter of ritualism.[3]

Because of the defining characteristic of *quanxi,* Chinese tend to view "foreigners" as belonging to out-groups, whose members always find it difficult to gain trust from their Chinese colleagues. It is not impossible for a foreigner to become a member of a Chinese person's network of *quanxi,* but it takes time and lots of interpersonal interactions including, for example, wining and dining. Members of Company A, during their first visit to Company B, felt lost when they had to spend a significant part of their schedule on banquets rather than on formal work meetings. While the Chinese wanted to know their future colleagues and show the visitors their hospitality through informal interactions, the Americans found uncomfortable "wasting" time on activities that did not seem to have a direct bearing on business. Wining and dining, to a typical Chinese businessman, is the lubricant to interpersonal relationships, or *quanxi,* and can have a serious bearing on business. While wining and dining, the hosting president of Company B kept saying to the visiting president of Company A: "When people meet each other the first time, they are strangers; when they meet the second time, they become acquaintances; when they meet the third time, they will be buddies." Chinese believe when people have become buddies, everything will be easy. Therefore, all Company B did during the first visit by Company A was to suggest to the visitors that soon they will become buddies and each other's *quanxi.*

Buddies do not seem to need to spend weeks or months working on an agreement or contract to bind their relationship, which was very much the mentality of Company B. But Company A thought differently. A buddy kind of relationship is good but also risky. It is risky because it may be too "informal" for a business relationship that should be bound by a carefully worked out agreement or contract. To Company A, it didn't matter how much wining and dining had been done; what mattered was the words in the agreement or contract. So Company A never became "intoxicated" during the wining and dining session and kept their impersonal stance at the negotiation table, and their obsession with the precision of linguistic codes at times angered their Chinese counterparts. Even though Company A and Company B very much remained what they were, each came, gradually, to a closer understanding to the other's "ways of doing things," thanks to the willingness to cooperate and the spirit of tenacity on both sides.

Few words can puzzle Westerners more than "a socialist market economy with Chinese characteristics." China's economic reform that Deng Xiaoping launched in late 1978 was designed to transform a Stalinistic planned economy into one based on market mechanisms and macrogovernmental control. It seems that "Chinese characteristics" are implied in the macrogovernmental control at the central, provincial, and local levels. Government has always been heavy since ancient times all the way down to the Mao and Deng eras. No Chinese business entities, state-owned ones in particular, can function without making all the "mothers-in-law" happy.

In traditional China, a married woman would have to subject herself to the absolute authority of her mother-in-law, and mothers-in-law had a reputation for abusing their power and repeating on their daughters-in-law the kind of sufferings they once received from their own mothers-in-law. The Chinese governmental bureaucracies are such mothers-in-law, and millions of Chinese organizations, business and nonbusiness, state-controlled or collectively managed or privately owned, are their daughters-in-law. Deng's economic reforms have not succeeded in reducing Chinese bureaucracies, and there are still too many mothers-in-law standing there and watching how their daughters-in-law run around under their whimsical instructions. The biggest open secret for doing business in China is that you must have the support of the Chinese government at all levels. If an endorsement is lacking from those mothers-in-law, and you still go and do it, sooner or later you would find yourself crying in a corner of the kitchen under the questioning eyes of your mother-in-law. When it comes the second time, you will have learned how to listen and ask for "parental" approval. Having living with your mother-in-law under the same roof for some time, you would behave no matter how rebellious you were once. You would constantly, if not unwillingly, seek instructions from your mother-in-law. The problem for businesses is that you do not just have one mother-in-law in your house, you have a dozen. What if Mother-in-law No. 1 says yes, and Mother-in-law No. 2 says no, and Mother-in-law No. 3 says nothing? Well, that's all your problem; you figure it out.

Company B is a state-owned enterprise and has a dozen of mothers-in-law telling it what to do, which definitely slows things down if one has to listen to all of them. It would routinely take a longer time than expected for Company B to respond to a request made by Company A. Later, Company A learned that a quicker initial response by Company B could be more time-consuming than a delayed response, if the initial response had been made without Company B having first checked with the relevant mothers-in-law. It would usually take more time to start all over again and talk to those mothers-in-law one after another. It is also a routine occurrence for Company B to change a commitment that was previously made. Why? A more powerful mother-in-law, who had not been consulted, could come up with a different opinion. His or her different opinion would, as a rule, rule over a previous decision. Company A was a quick learner and soon learned how to show a better understanding of Company B's otherwise unacceptable behaviors, even though some of its Chinese characteristics have proved much harder to digest than expected from a typical American perspective.

The decision-making process of Company B, which seems more unpredictable than that of Company A, is hierarchically structured, which can either speed up or slow down a decision. When the process starts from the very top, a decision can be made fast. But when the process begins from the bottom and needs to go all the way to the top, even a small decision can take weeks or months. Over time, Company A learned to be patient and understanding; oftentimes, it is not Company B's intention to be slow and fast—the system makes it so.

As mentioned earlier, Company B was not impressed by Company A's obsession with, or rather, fear of legal documentation, whose drafting, negotiating, and signing could take as long as a bureaucratic decision involving a dozen mothers-in-law on the Chinese side. Usually, when the first draft of a legal agreement or contract came from Company B, it tended to be no more than one page. But when it came from Company A, it could be more than ten pages, which the Chinese hate. At the beginning when the two sides barely knew each other, Company A's seriousness with the wording of a contract and its uncompromising stance tended to irritate representatives of Company B, who could be so confused that they interpreted it as Company A's distrust of the Chinese. When the president of Company B said, "when people meet each other the first time, they are strangers; when they meet the second time, they become acquaintances; when they meet the third time, they will be buddies," he meant that buddies do not worry too much about what words are going to be written down on paper. If you continue to show your worry about a legal document even after a third meeting with us, that means you do not trust us. Such interpretation, which seems very natural from the Chinese perspective, led to mutual distrust and communicative defensiveness. But the Chinese learned to understand their American counterparts' ways of doing things as fast as the Americans learned to understand the Chinese, not without, on both sides, paying a price for learning how to improve their "ways of doing things" coordination.

Communication Coordination

Communication coordination between Company A and Company B has presented enormous challenges to both sides. Language remains one of such challenges. When technicians of Company A were working side by side with those of Company B, they could hardly communicate without an interpreter. And more often than not, the interpreter was not that good, which could considerably upset an otherwise harmonious working relationship. In the morning both sides would feel they had some serious conflict going on, but in the afternoon a seemingly explosive problem often turned out to be no problem at all; the morning conflict mysteriously disappeared without either side knowing why. Then the same complication repeated itself the second day. Later, they found the misunderstanding was all caused by bad translation; the translator, who was from Company B, had a very limited knowledge of the English language. Interestingly, many of the misunderstandings were cleared up from the U.S. where Company A used a better translator who would call people from both Company A and Company B who were on the other side of the globe. The monthly international telephone bill for Company A could easily run to four digits.

Thanks to the easy availability of direct-dial international telephone and other forms of electronic communication, Company A and Company B, which are physically oceans apart, feel just a minute away. But the electronic communication is never the same as face-to-face interaction. Electronic communication transmits sound and image, but is unable to create the kind of feel that one gets from face-to-face interaction. Face-to-face interaction has the magic of shortening psychological distance between people and thus creating trust and human closeness. As time progressed, technicians of Company A who were sent to work at Company B in China found it easier to communicate nonverbally than verbally because the translator could make an otherwise simple issue complicated. When the Americans and their Chinese counterparts started to know each other through daily face-to-face interactions, Company A's monthly international telephone bill gradually dropped down. But that doesn't solve the problem of Company A and Company B being oceans apart. It is important to know that instant electronic communication has created a global village only in an electronic way; the physical globe remains to be as large as it has always been, and people who are physically far apart still cannot touch each other the way they do face-to-face. From a practical business point of view, lacking constant face-to-face interactions between Company A and Company B definitely adds to the inefficiency of cross-cultural organizational communication coordination.

Lacking face-to-face interactions, above all, prevents both Company A and Company B from observing and learning each other's culture-specific communication styles, particularly nonverbal communication styles. A fundamental difference between the two cultures' communication styles is that Company A represents a low-context style and Company B is a typical example of high-context style. In simple terms, Company A wants all messages to be clear and as precise as possible, i.e., when you mean no, say no. However, Company B, whose members have been living in a high-context culture, doesn't like to be that way. When they mean no, they may say nothing or even yes with a mysterious smile. Yes doesn't mean that they agree but rather "Yes, I understand" or "Yes, I am listening." They do not say no when they mean no because they feel saying no to a guest can be potentially embarrassing to both sides. It takes time, respect, and willingness to learn to come to a better understanding of each other's high-context versus low-context communication styles. Both Company A and Company B have indeed come closer after $2^1/_2$ years of cooperation, even though their physical separation by the Pacific Ocean seems to have made the task more difficult than if they had had more face-to-face interactions.

Conclusion

Organizational coordination is key to achieving organizational excellence, and logically, cross-cultural organizational coordination is key to achieving cross-cultural organizational excellence. From our brief review of the experiment involving Company A and Company B that are located in two distinctly different cultures separated by the Pacific Ocean, we conclude that cross-cultural organizational coordination, that may involve task coordination, "ways of doing things" coordination, and communication coordination, is a most challenging task. Challenging as it is, it is nevertheless manageable to the extent that firms willing to cooperate are committed to expending the effort necessary to learn each other's rules and coming up with a common framework of reference. Gradually, things may pay off.

Notes

1. See Yanan Ju and Donald Cushman, *Organizational Teamwork in High-Speed Management,* SUNY Press, 1995, pp. 116–17.

2. See Donald Cushman and Sarah King, *Communication and High-Speed Management,* SUNY Press, 1995, pp. 153–54.

3. See Yanan Ju, *Understanding China: Center Stage of the Fourth Power,* SUNY Press, 1996, pp. 48–52.

8

Strategies for Survival in the Global Marketplace: A Study of the Australian Pharmaceutical Industry

Robyn Johnston

The pursuit of excellence has become a prerequisite for organizations and industries striving to achieve or maintain competitive positioning in the increasingly turbulent and globalized marketplace. Conditions are currently evolving which provide a framework for change and the foundation for the pursuit of excellence by Australian organizations. This chapter reports on these changing work context conditions and considers their impact on enterprises from the Australian pharmaceutical manufacturing industry.

Striving for Flexibility in the Workplace

One of the conditions enabling a more effective pursuit of excellence has been the emergence of a climate which has supported the creation of more flexible workplaces. While some have questioned the validity of the flexibility thesis as a basis of the post-Fordist workplace (Foley, 1994), others have strongly argued the need for more flexible workplaces, even suggesting that flexibility may overtake quality as a prime source of competitive advantage (Deloitte and Touche, 1992). Workplace flexibility in Australia has taken different forms. In most situations this increased workplace flexibility has been possible as a result of reform in the industrial relations system (Lansbury and Niland, 1994).

The foundations for a reformed industrial relations system came through a series of accords concerning wage policies negotiated between the peak union body, the ACTU (Australian Council of Trade Unions) and the Australian government between 1986 and 1996.

These accords endorsed and maintained a two-tier wage policy which allowed for a proportion of wage increases to be granted for the achievement of productivity gained through removal of inefficient and restrictive work practices. As part of this approach, collective bargaining for wage increases on the basis of workplace reform and productivity gains could be negotiated at an enterprise rather than at an industry level. This signaled a shift from a centralized industry–based IR system to one driven at the enterprise level.

The ACTU had initially supported the retention of a more centralized wage system, but then shifted its position to become a significant advocate of the more decentralized enterprise–based bargaining approach. It did this despite the proportion argued by many, that an enterprise-bargaining approach was largely incompatible with traditional union methods for doing business (Sloan, 1995) and a deep unease among many workers about the whole union and government–endorsed strategy of replacing industry-wide negotiations on wages and conditions with enterprise level negotiations (Clark, 1996; Foley, 1994).

Union leaders in accepting this more decentralized approach, ensured that their union maintained their influence in the negotiating of enterprise-based agreements and sought to develop more effective enterprise bargaining skills among their memberships during the decade of a Labour government.

The 1996 elections in Australia resulted in a change of government with conservative coalition parties being swept into office. One of the major areas of reform advanced by this government was even further reform in the industrial relations system to allow for increased workplace flexibility. The IR policy of this government established a new system of workplace agreements that enabled employers and workers as individuals greater choice in determining their industrial conditions. This policy also reduced the role of the Industrial Relations Commission in the negotiation of conditions. There has been considerable contestation by the union movement about the fairness of some of these more recent shifts toward an individual, as opposed to an enterprise, bargaining focus. This direction to more individualized arrangements, however, remains attractive to employers on larger unionized sites and to employers in small business (Clark, 1996). Hence, while there is significant contestation about the degree of decentralization of the IR system needed to achieve flexibility, the notion that a more flexible workplace can enhance productivity is not in question.

As a result of the shift to an enterprise bargaining process, many previously established workplace conditions have been reconsidered and new arrangements accepted. These include flexibility in starting and finishing times matched to meet production needs, emergencies, adverse weather, or family circumstances and new salary arrangements, including the introduction of fixed annualized salaries incorporating work on any seven days of the week, shift loading, public holiday payments, annual leave call backs, and annual leave loadings. These elements of enterprise agreements were highlighted in March 1996 by the chairman of a peak Australian employer association, the Australian Chamber of Commerce and Industry (ACCI), as providing workplace flexibility. He announced following a study by the Chamber into the nature of enterprise agreements, that there had been an improvement in the quality of enterprise agreements over the preceding two years with a notable increase in the number of efficiency measures which they had introduced. A later study released in October 1996 not quite so optimistically also indicated that 62% of managers believed that enterprise bargaining had increased the efficiency of Australian workplaces; however, of this 62%, 53% indicated that such agreements had only increased productivity a little. This report also indicated that enterprise bargaining had been associated with increased levels of stress among employees. This report further indicated that it was becoming harder to find areas for more flexibility or efficiency-producing changes in second and third-generation rounds of enterprise bargaining (Murphy, 1996).

Along with more flexible working conditions have come more flexible forms of work organization. Broader job specifications, which have allowed more flexible forms of work design and changing forms of "organizational architecture" have replaced rigid, closely defined job specifications in many industries (Ford, 1995). The most significant broadening of job roles and functions initially took place in many of the blue-collar areas particularly in the manufacturing sector. Findings from a survey conducted by Lansbury and Niland (1994) suggest that such new approaches to work design with broader and flexible definitions of work roles led to the reporting of fewer demarcation disputes. The new structure, however, created new areas of tension between blue and white-collar workers, especially as the scope of blue-collar jobs expanded to absorb tasks previously performed by clerical, supervisory, and even professional staff.

A more flexible workplace design has also seen the emergence of work teams as the fundamental work unit (Shadur et al., 1994;

Ford, 1995; Roberts, 1996; McGhee, 1996). Work teams, pioneered in the manufacturing industry, are now increasingly invading white-collar business with many organizations experimenting with a wide variety of teams. The introduction and use of such teams as a component of best practice is highlighted in the *Leading the Way* study conducted by the Australian Manufacturing Council (1994). The study argued that leading organizations had found that self-managing workteams of cellular workers had delivered the flexibility, participation, and cooperation necessary for competitiveness in today's global market (1994, p. 31).

Changing Management Practices

A second facet of the set of conditions impacting on Australian workplaces which has supported the pursuit of excellence has been an advocacy for changing management practices. There is some evidence that traditional models of management demanding technical skills and command expertise are being replaced. For example, a benchmark study of Management Development in Australian private enterprises commissioned by the National Board for Education, Employment, and Training in 1990 emphasized the importance of the ability to communicate and motivate as the most important factors for progression to senior levels of management in Australia (1990, p. 7). Such findings indicate a recognition of skills not previously seen as paramount in traditional models of best management practices. Similarly, Bagwell (1995) argued that Australian organizations were witnessing the disappearance of "dinosaur" corporate leaders. She stated:

> Taking their place is a new style of corporate leader. He and more recently she eschews the old command and control style of running a business from top down. They flatten hierarchies. They talk to their staff and listen to their responses. . . . They're team leaders who coach talent. But above all they see their workers as valuable human resources, stakeholders in the business.

Similar findings concerning the changing approaches to management by the frontline managers and supervisor are reported by Lansbury and Niland (1994). They posited that with the introduction of flatter organizations and team-based structures the role of supervisor was shifting from a traditional "custodial or policing" function to more of a team leader or facilitator.

While there is some evidence to suggest this changing approach to management is impacting through restructured workplaces, newly designed job roles, team working, and to some extent implementation of Total Quality Management approaches, there is also competing evidence to suggest that further change is required and that such practices are not universal (Gittens, 1995). A government-commissioned report about Australian management practice, *Enterprising Nation,* argued that in 1995 while there were examples of management matching world best standards in Australia, new approaches to management education were required. The report argued that Australian managers needed to develop skills in the area of entrepreneurship, global orientation, soft skills, and strategic skills as well as needing to improve their teamwork skills, including the coordination of a more diverse workforce and being prepared to take responsibility for outcomes (Industry Task Force on Leadership and Management Skills, 1995).

Thus, arguably, while there is evidence of more consultative, participative models of management and supervision practices in Australian organizations, there is room for further development in this area of workplace functioning. This need, however, is being recognized and hence conditions exist that are more conducive for the changes that will promote the organizational excellence being sought.

Fostering New Learning

A further dimension on the set of conditions facilitating the achievement of organizational excellence is the increased focus on the processes of individual skill formation and a more collective form of organizational learning. In recent years government, employers, and employee organizations have been committed to significant reform in vocational education and employee upskilling. The union movement in supporting workplace reform, has striven to have workplace training requirements embedded in industrial agreements to ensure their members are provided with skills to allow them to operate in reformed workplaces. Australian governments since the mid-1980s have initiated policies directed toward the process of skill formation and the nurturing of workplace learning. A key element of initiatives in this direction was the establishment of a national competency standards–based system of training and development. In adopting this competency-based approach to skill formation, a broad concept of competency was adopted with all aspects of work performance (task skill, task management skills, contingency management, and job role environment skills) being included in the developed competency standards.

Other dimensions of this new focus on workplace learning have allowed for increase articulation between qualifications; the recognition of previous learning of employees; accreditation of training, which in the past had not been accredited; the opening up of the training market to allow private providers including employers to deliver accredited training; and new vocational learning opportunities after the compulsory years of schooling. This new attention to learning has also resulted in increased systematic employee development and some growth in average training expenditure by employees across the whole economy.

Accompanying the emphasis on employee upskilling, there has been an attempt to develop learning as opposed to providing training in a number of organizations. This has included attempts in some organizations to foster a form of organizational learning that extends beyond individual learning and is part of a trend that is obvious in leading organizations in other developed countries.

The notion of organizational learning, or establishing an enterprise as a learning organization, varies among its devotees. In some organizations it has been predominantly superficial involving little more than the change of the nomenclature of the training and development function to include the word *learning*. In more developed forms organizational learning is seen more as an ideal to be pursued and is associated with the establishment of structures and cultures that encourage employees to critically challenge their existing frameworks and mindsets about the way they work, solve problems, and resolve issues (Ford, 1995; Field, 1995; Limerick and Cunnington, 1993). As such, organizational learning integrates traditional human resource development approaches with organizational work design, process design, reward and communication frameworks. Field (1995) argues that in the ideal learning organization there is a convergence between skills, training and learning, technology and information, work organization, and employee relations, with each element synthesizing in an integrated fashion to enhance the capacity for greater productivity. More recently the notion of fostering organizational learning has been linked with new forms of managerial practice and innovative knowledge management practices.

Ford (1995) and Field (1995) cite numerous examples of organizations in Australia where learning has become embedded in all functions of the organization. They see as an outcome that organizational leadership is happening at all levels in such organizations, continuous improvement-based on learning is extensive, and work organization and workplace design are altered to include continuous learning opportunities. Ford (1995, p. 25) describes one example where a learning center has evolved to support workplace reform by improving opportunities for people and teams to learn how to reform their workplace.

Thus there has been significant upskilling in the Australian workforce over the past decade to better equip industry to compete in a more competitive economy. At the same time, there has been a move in lighthouse organizations, a move to create organizational learning through holistic integrated approaches to learning and improvement. At such sites learning is no longer seen as doing more of the same but about encouraging employees to focus on new ways of doing.

It could therefore be argued that, within Australia, these conditions have provided both a framework for changing workplace practices and also support the pursuit of organizational excellence. Dimensions of this framework comprise the acceptance that greater flexibility is required for workplace functioning, and this shift is reflected in the changing approaches to industrial relations and working conditions. Other dimensions include the new orientation to what constitutes good management practice. This is leading to the emergence of more consultative, cooperative workplaces with leaders and supervisors in best-practice organizations, adopting rules that involve coaching rather than command. A third interrelated dimension of the framework is a recognition and support for workplace training and learning. This has involved technical upskilling for groups often previously unskilled and insufficiently skilled in using newer technologies, as well as upskilling for organizational problem-solving and decision-making. These dimensions of general change have formed a foundation for the pursuit of organizational excellence that can be seen throughout Australian industry generally and certainly within leading enterprises in the Australian Pharmaceutical Manufacturing industry, as detailed in the next section.

Pharmaceutical Manufacturing Industry in Australia

The pharmaceutical manufacturing industry in Australia is responsible for the manufacturing, packaging, and distribution of pharmaceutical and proprietary medicines for both Australian and overseas markets. It comprises more than two hundred organizations and currently employs 13,000 workers, with a prediction that this number of employees will increase to 29,000 by the year 2006. Employees in this industry are represented by a range of unions, with most blue-collar workers being represented by the Australian Workers Union (AWU-FIME) the National Union of Workers (NUW), and the Shop and Distributive Allied Employees (in the stores areas).

Most pharmaceutical manufacturing enterprises in Australia are operating as subsidiaries of multinational companies. In the last decade the industry, worldwide, has witnessed significant rationalization both between and within companies by way of take-overs, mergers, and joint ventures with greater classification of core business. These changes have resulted from the pressures of competition and the high costs of technological change and R&D initiatives. At a global level, it is a dynamic industry working within what has become an increasingly volatile marketplace. Activities at the global level impact on Australian manufacturing as a certain freedom in local planning is curtailed. Decisions about viability of both product manufacture and plant are often made in the U.K. Switzerland, or the U.S. For example, in recent years decisions to discontinue production in Australia have been made by parent companies including CIBA Geigy, Sandoz, and Bootes. The multinational relationship, however, does provide the potential for benchmarking corporate facilities worldwide, and as a result, effective performance in Australia has led to the increased development of manufacturing investment to supply global markets.

To support this industry in attaining and maintaining a competitive position in a global market, the previous government targeted pharmaceutical manufacturing as a growth industry recognizing that this was an industry that had some competitive advantage in the region. Such advantages arose from the willingness of this industry to invest in the education and training for its workforce and a medical infrastructure that often provided world-first breakthroughs. The government therefore established the Pharmaceutical Industry Development Program, which was designed to encourage pharmaceutical manufacturers make a significant commitment to increased internationally competitive production and research and development. In return for meeting increased export and R&D targets, pharmaceutical manufacturers were offered higher prices for some of their products listed on the Pharmaceutical Benefits Scheme. While there has been some dispute about the efficacy of the approach between competing enterprises in the industry since the commencement of the scheme, the international companies and local companies which have participated have made significant growth in R&D as well as in exports and capital investments (Pharmaceutical Industry Draft Report, 1995).

As of late 1995, the industry in Australia was still being hailed as a growth industry with commitments to 1999 of $725 million in R&D of $4.36 billion in exports, of $5 billion in value-added production and of $770 million in capital investment (Pharmaceuticals, *The Australian* 1996, p. 20).

Other government-funded programs have also provided the industry with assistance. These have included funding for programs which have upskilled employees (Schwenke, 1996) as well as a workplace reform program which was an industry-level cooperative project designed to encourage employers and employees to work together for the promotion of widespread reform in the industry. This program involved an industry-wide program to further the enterprise-bargaining process in this industry, to establish consistent skills levels across the industry, and an initiative to upskill women employees at the shop floor level who make up the majority of employees in the manufacturing area.

This is an industry that is striving for excellence in order to maintain its level of competitiveness in global markets. In so doing, from analyses of activities of leading enterprises from within the industry, the influence of the workplace climate change discussed in the preceding section can be seen. The remaining section identifies aspects of these changing workplace conditions which can be seen impacting on this industry as revealed through various reports and interviews with key personnel.

Flexibility in the Pharmaceutical Manufacturing Industry

Much of the increased flexibility gained by this industry has been achieved through the readiness of enterprises within this industry to establish enterprise-based industrial agreements as a basis for achieving workplace efficiency. Such agreements, according to McDermott (1995), were becoming the primary basis for conditions of employment in this industry, with more than 64% of enterprises either operating with or negotiating such agreements by 1995. Annualized salaries, twelve-hour shifts, less rigidly defined job roles particularly at shop floor levels, 24-hour production, and employee involvement programs were among the array of changed working conditions established by such agreements. This increased flexibility achieved thereby has been significant as this industry was once restricted by very highly structured job roles rigidly defined by role task and trade. One commentator with broad experience in this industry reflected on the magnitude of change stating:

> The job functions (in this industry) were so broken down by union and task that it made it really impossible to operate. Added to that you had the situation that you could not even hire temporary labour without getting union permission. . . . The situation has changed and the introduction of more flexible job design created through the existence of enterprise agreements. This change has not resulted in mass sackings of permanent staff, even though some permanent positions have become temporary as staff resigned and there has been incremental growth. (McDermott, 1995, p. 6)

The increase in flexible working conditions is also reflected in the comment of another manager from this industry. In describing the major changes that took place at his site, he argued:

> With job design principles we have gone from a control model where you are talking about individuals limited to confined jobs, to a system made up of a series of skills which people are asked to carry out. We have done away with fixed job definitions and gone to flexible definitions. These are definitions based on skills not on boundaries. We have gone from rules and procedures to shared goals and values and have moved from the adversarial scene to joint problem solving. (McDermott, 1995, p. 7)

Such changes in the workplace climate have allowed for better utilization of staff which has increased profitability through increasing unit production at lower costs. At the same time there has been a broadening of job roles partly made possible by the simplification of technology and the upskilling of previously unskilled workers.

The industry has also gained flexibility as a result of changing organizational structures. One of the major forms of structural change in this industry has been the creation of work teams. At some sites the move to more team-based structures was introduced with the update of technology and site layout accompanied by a process improvement approach. While the nature of teaming has varied across the industry a survey conducted as part of the Pharmaceutical Manufacturing Reform project has shown that more than half of the companies surveyed reported implementing new structures that involved creating work teams (McDermott, 1995). The report claims:

> The typical structure for such enterprises has involved the absorption of supervisory foreperson layer into a team structure with a team facilitator position being created. The most successful examples of fully functioning workteams have team facilitators who have been internally trained and appointed from the shop floor. (p. 18)

A further dimension of the move to a team structure that has become common in the industry has been the integration of tradespeople, offline functions (documentation, finance, quality control, and auditing), and staff into manufacturing teams. One enterprise from this industry which has achieved flexibility and workplace reform through the introduction of team structures is ICI. In describing the move to team structure a manager from this organization stated:

> We wanted to get the concept of self managing teams. By self managing we meant that we removed, in most cases, the first line of supervision and devolved those accountabilities back to the workgroup. There has been a major cultural change in moving from a control to a commitment driven organisation. (Groves and Mealor, 1990, p. 6)

This process, however, has not been without problems in all pharmaceutical manufacturing organizations. One manager interviewed as part of the research for this chapter reported that some pharmaceutical manufacturing sites using this approach have found that tradespeople have resisted such a move, feeling a sense of isolation from their skills base as a result of the move to team structures. At least two major pharmaceutical manufacturers are developing a more matrix type of reporting structure to overcome this problem while retaining the team approach. A further problem resulting from the movement in organizational architecture to a much more empowered team type structure has been the sense of derailing felt by those previously in junior management positions.

New Styles of Management in the Pharmaceutical Industry

This climate which is fostering a more participative management approach in Australian industry generally is also impacting on this

industry. Middle to senior management in this industry is comparatively highly educated, with most positions having postgraduate
qualifications and requiring extensive experience from both within
and outside the industry. The Building Bridges survey (McDermott,
1995) reported that there were poor to average management skills
in professional technical officers across the industry. There is certainly evidence, however, that this industry is fostering an empowerment approach to management through the development of
leadership and management skills in its employees. For example, at
the Parke Davis plant in NSW the concept of employee as problem
solver has been well-established. To support employees learning
what were once seen as managerial skills, there has been a con-
certed effort to provide in-house managerial skills training in the
processes associated with systematic problem-solving and statisti-
cal analysis for all staff. Other organizations have appointed workplace change facilitators from shop-floor employees to improve the
formal communication flow. These workplace change facilitators see
their role as being that of a conduit taking information from the
shop floor to management and as assisting in decision-making,
thereby helping to eliminate the command and control model of
management. Team facilitators at some other sites have been primarily appointed as coaches and team developers, although there is
some evidence that those holding these positions can revert to more
supervisory behaviour when pressure for product becomes intense.
A spokesperson for the industry (unidentified) argued:

> In recent years the focus on people management and the how to
> do this has become much more prevalent for managers within
> the industry as employees take over more responsibility for the
> technical management of the manufacturing process.

While more common in some of the larger pharmaceutical
manufacturing organizations, there is evidence of a more consensual form of management in some smaller pharmaceutical manufacturing companies as well. Alexander Yuille, managing director of
Cenovis Australia, highlighted the importance of adopting a management style based on trust of team members to make their own
decision. She stated:

> Developing trust is part of the workplace revolution that we're
> experiencing. . . . In previous times a control style of manage-
> ment was required. Now managers need to provide people with
> an opportunity to flourish. (Gordon, 1995, p. 5)

Most companies in the industry have a strong commitment to involving employees at all levels in the reform process. Approximately two-thirds of the organizations within this industry have established a collaborative strategy that includes an elected and formal consultative committees. These groups typically deal with issues including production scheduling, training performance indicators, improvements in cost, quality and delivery, safety issues, and communication of information (McDermott, 1995). This change in mindset is evident in the comments of one manager from the pharmaceutical manufacturing industry when he stated:

> In the past management we would have developed vision for the future, worked up a series of actions and tried to inform the workforce on a need to know basis. . . . This time we operated very differently. We said "We have a vision for the future. Here are the assumptions it is based on, here are the financial, structural, organizational and all the other issues that are going to support this vision." We took it to the workforce and got their feedback and we asked "Do you agree with these assumptions for the future?" We asked them to challenge the assumptions that had been made and to contribute to the fleshing out some of these assumptions. (Groves and Mealor, 1990, p. 5)

Other enterprises have paid close attention to the role of communication with and feedback from employees. Regular site meetings are common as are meetings along functional lines to disseminate organizational and divisional progress and comment on workplace issues.

Learning-Based Initiatives in the Pharmaceutical Manufacturing Industry

The industry has also embraced the new focus on learning described earlier. In larger enterprises, training for blue-collar operatives has moved from an unplanned buddy system in which information and instruction were provided on a need to know basis. The training reform agenda, the introduction of new technology, and the need for enterprises to achieve accreditation under the therapeutic goods administration of 150,900 quality standards provided an impetus for change in the industry. In 1993, Pharmaceutical Manufacturing Production competency standards were endorsed by the National Training Board, and they were subsequently used as a basis for a certificate in Pharmaceutical Manufacturing to be offered by the Technical and Further Education sector for blue-collar workers of this industry. At least one enterprise has negotiated customized development program for its more senior staff members with an Australian university. Another significant change leading to the delivery of more systematic training within enterprises has been the appointment of training officers to many pharmaceutical manufacturing enterprises to oversee the training of manufacturing personnel. Some leading enterprises have upskilled their workers through Good Manufacturing Programs and literacy programs. Others have focused on problem-solving and computer literacy programs. Schwenke (1996), reporting on the integrated training approach adopted by Merck Sharp and Dohme, reports:

> The changed approach to training was initially met with some scepticism, however this soon disappeared as positive changes were perceived, particularly changes that afforded flexibility in job description. (p. 71)

Some hesitancy on the part of women to embrace learning and upskilling opportunities was identified in the Workplace Reform Project (McDermott, 1995). As a result, a government-funded industry-specific program was designed to assist in developing more confidence in women in the pharmaceutical manufacturing industry and to thereby allow them to embrace some of the potential benefits of workplace reform and new workplace learning opportunities. The expectation that learning should be part of the work experience has become strong in leading pharmaceutical manufacturing organizations. A trainer from one organization stated:

> One of the most significant changes in the pharmaceutical industry, particularly at my site is the acceptance of learning and training associated with work. There are a lot more expectations from employees that the employer should be providing learning experiences and training and rotation opportunities to allow them to undertake more interesting work.

Conclusion

The changing climate in Australian workplaces has provided a foundation for change in the Australian pharmaceutical manufacturing industry. Workplaces of this industry have responded to the new flexibility within the industrial relations system and adopted work-place practices, which in turn, have increased the flexibility of their organizational operations. New approaches to management are apparent in many of the enterprises of this industry, particularly in relation to the management of blue-collar workers. Workplaces have become more collaborative and consensual. The new focus on learning has also impacted on this industry. Many enterprises have adopted programs for upskilling their blue-collar workers to maximize the flexibility allowed under the new system of industrial relations; some have attempted to establish a more integrated holistic approach to learning and linked upskilling of workers to include problem-solving and decision-making skills. While further research involving extensive examination of specific practices being implemented within the pharmaceutical manufacturing industry may provide a clearer picture of what practices are contributing to organizational excellence in the industry, there is certainly evidence that shows the dimensions of the changed workplace climate impacting on Australian workplaces generally are providing a foundation for change and the ongoing pursuit of excellence in this industry. They are also contributing to the predictions that the industry has a positive future, as signaled in the words of the then minister for Industry and Science and Technology when he stated at the Annual Conference of the Australian Pharmaceutical Association:

> The industry typifies Australia's innovative strengths. Not just research and development strength but also excellence in areas such as skills development, design, quality management and best practice cultures (Pharmaceuticals, *The Australian,* 1995).

References

Australian Manufacturing Council. (1994). *Leading the Way: A Study in Best Manufacturing Practices in Australia and New Zealand.* Melbourne.

Bagwell, S. (1995). Death of the Macho Male Manager. *Australian Financial Review,* September 29.

Clark, D. (1996) Behind Industrial Relations Reform. *Australian Financial Review,* April 3.

Deloitte and Touche. (1992). Winning the Global Markets: A Survey of US and Japanese Manufacturing. A research report by Deloitte and Touche Manufacturing Consulting Services.

Dunphy, D., and Stace, D. (1990). *Under New Management, Australian Organizations in Transition.* Sydney: McGraw-Hill.

Field, L. (1995). *Managing Organizational Learning: from Rhetoric to Reality.* Melbourne: Longmans.

Foley, G. (1994). Adult Education and Capitalist Reorganization, *Studies in the Education of Adults* 26(2).

Ford, B. (1995). Integrating people, process and place—the workplace of the future. Paper presented at the Australian Council for Quality Eighth National Quality Management Conference, Sydney.

Gittens, R. (1995). Enterprises Can't Cope with Change. *Sydney Morning Herald,* September 8.

Gordon, C. (1995). Management Skills for the Next Millennium. *Magazine of the Australian Institute of Management,* March.

Groves, D., and Mealor, T. (1990). Award Restructuring at the Workplace— the ICI Botany example. *Work and People* 13(3).

The Pharmaceutical Industry Draft Report. Australian Industry Commission. (1995). Canberra.

Pharmaceuticals, a Special Advertising Report. (1996). *The Australian,* September 22, pp. 20–21.

Industry Task Force on Leadership and Management Skills (Karpin). (1995). *Enterprising Nation Renewing Australia's Managers to Meet the Challenges of the Asia Pacific Century.* Australian Government Publishing Service.

Lansbury, R. D., and Niland, J. (1994). Trends in Industrial Relations and Human Resource Policies and Practice: Australian Experiences. *International Journal of Human Resources Management* 5(3).

Limerick, D., and Cuimington, B. (1993). *Managing the New Organisation: A Blue Print for Network and Strategic Alliances.* NSW Australia, Business and Professional Publishing.

McDermott, H. (1995). *Building Bridges.* Findings and project recommendations presented to the Pharmaceutical Industry Workplace Reform Steering Committee.

McGhee, K. (1996). The New Team Spirit—Why Working in Groups Lifts Performance and Productivity. *Sydney Morning Herald,* March 16.

Mitchell, J. (1995). A Worrying Mix of Too Little and Too Much. *Australian Financial Review,* March 24.

Murphy, K. (1996). Doubts over Bargaining. *The Australian,* October 10.

National Board of Employment, Education and Training. (1990). *Interim Report on the Benchmark Study of Management Development in Australian Private Enterprises, Commissioned Report No. 5.* Canberra: Australian Government Publishing Service.

Roberts, P. (1996). Team Playing—It's Easier in Theory, *Australian Financial Review,* March 28.

Schwenke, C. (1996). Merck Sharp and Dohme (Australia) Pty Ltd: An Integrated Approach to Work-based Training. In J. Moy (ed.), *Workbased Training.* Adelaide: NCVER.

Shadur, M. A., Rodwellj, Simmons, D., and Bamber, G. (1994). International Best Practice, Quality Management and High Performance: Inferences from the Australian Automotive Sector. *International Journal of Human Resource Management* 5(3).

Sloan, J. (1995). Rights of Workers and Union Not Necessarily the Same. *The Australian,* November 10.

9

Beyond Benchmarking Institutional Advancement: Jump-Start to Fund-Raising Excellence

Rod Miller

Cooperation and Common Vision

The cooperative effort of colleagues, especially organizational leadership, the volunteer board, and development staff, is widely accepted as the only powerful team to advance the mission of the service enterprise. Initially, this requires the board, chief executive officer (CEO), and chief development professional to evolve a strong working relationship. As any player of team sport knows, when the team works with a common vision and cooperation, quick follow-through is possible, thereby increasing the successes. Exceptional achievement, or excellence, is seen in many places: the ballet company whose principal dancer leads it to a higher plane; the sales force achieving the impossible; the rowing crew whose elegant, polished-wood shell lifts so the water sings along the side—we can all think of poignant personal experiences which exemplify virtuosity. Although the core advancement team in any enterprise will consist of the board, CEO, and chief development professional, the progressive enlistment of volunteers, externally and internally as "champions" of resource development and institutional advancement, is necessary for true success.

Enterprises using excellent advancement practices characteristically perform with implicit understanding of the differences and linkages among fund-raising, development, and institutional advancement. Briefly, distinctions should be drawn between "fund-raising" which is producing money required by an institution and "development" which connotes a well-organized program to include annual giving, big gift solicitation, foundation and corporation solicitation, public grants and planned gifts, all at a more sophisticated level. "Institutional advancement" includes both of these activities integrated with strategic planning that prioritizes community needs, fund-raising, publications, volunteer activities and public relations—all coordinated to generate understanding and support of the enterprise served. Truly effective institutional advancement becomes possible when resource development is keyed to the strategically planned development of the enterprise. Excellence in institutional advancement is then achieved by exploiting the media relations and market positioning of the enterprise. For the progressive improvement of this pivotal relationship among the board, overall enterprise leader, and development professional, one cannot overcommunicate. With rapid change as the norm, each of these colleagues struggles to find a common understanding of the institutional priorities and practices that prove effective to develop the resources of the enterprise.

Evolution of a common vision within a team occurs best by planned and reviewed actions that encourage innovation and initiative-taking. Both traditional and less usual practices are employed at successful institutions to struggle with the joint creation of a common vision. When institutional planning is tackled through a classic top-down and bottom-up process, this tends to increase both the quality of the refinement of objectives and the level of ownership of the final plan with all levels of staff.

Strategic Plan

Key elements of a plan can be derived in an issues management approach, with senior management examining the issues that pertain to further the institution's goals. For effective outreach, it must first be accepted that the institution will be willing to extend its consultative communication framework, respecting professional integrity of program staff while facilitating informed decision-making, effective planning, and full accountability. Any planning activity must ensure that staff, volunteers, and even clients are enticed to help advance the potential of the institution.

In the strongest enterprises. Leadership resolves to

- maintain the enterprise's distinctiveness by communicating its "real world" role, while developing a community leadership and change agent role

- value and respond effectively to clients

- respond to the changing character and role of information systems

- build international perspectives into activities.

Organizational communication needs to be confirmed as key to the enterprise's performance. Interaction among staff and clients will increasingly be informal in the future. Staff will be expected to be even more available, including on weekends and vacations (partly facilitated via the mobility offered by wireless communications) and will increasingly take an active role in the enterprise's planning process. Already senior managers who fail to negotiate such interchange with staff are being recognized as ineffective dinosaurs.

Productive Operations

Implicitly and explicitly, the plan should encourage consultative interaction with clients as the paradigm for all operations, including resource development. Any resource development goal presupposes building relationships with prominent constituents, including community leaders, to support priority areas of the enterprise for the benefit of the community. With resource development so intrinsically dependent on bringing people of influence and means close to the enterprise's leadership, the climate to put the enterprise's vision into operation requires the

- development of trust among colleagues and clients

- mutual agreement of "stretch" targets and processes for delivery

- support for and measurement of achievement.

Persistently, the demands and bases for improvement in all three areas will be found by keeping focus on the improvement of the pertinence and timeliness of all actions.

Trust

The soundest evolution and maintenance of trust occurs through the achievement of previously agreed goals and targets. Reciprocally, whether board member, senior manager, other colleague or external client, the delivery of the goal to bring people closer requires foremost, the evolution of trust. The four specific factors influencing trust and credibility are perceptions of

- caring and empathy
- competence and expertise
- honesty and openness
- dedication and commitment. (Sheldon, 1996, p 18)

Such fragile perceptions flourish in the development team of the board, CEO, and development professional when the role that each confidently accepts includes keeping a current awareness of services and contact with the clients of the enterprise, advocacy of the enterprise in the community, and inviting investment in the enterprise. In "start-up" enterprises, the founder and his or her advisors will commit to these responsibilities. As the enterprise grows, it often happens that the original spirit becomes lost—even in the founder who might still sit in a reified position on the board or be a very active staff person.

The effort to engage board members as part-time volunteers who further the enterprise's plan works best by seeking a very sound relationship among the group and with the enterprise's leadership and all development staff. Each board member is best teamed with a staff member, and the expertise of each, in resource development, is grown together. Each new board member is asked to suggest peers of influence and means whom s/he will invite to a hosted briefing, usually at one of the enterprise's main operating locations, and will undertake follow-up visits after the gathering.

To maintain the relevance of these briefings to colleagues and clients, the strategic plan is used to key priority areas for presentation at the briefing and to give direction on the interests expressed for follow-up discussions. In the enterprise that is committed to service through real-world partnerships, the strategic plan becomes a filtering device. The plan will reflect only opportunities to which the institution would best respond and only the specific programs or projects designed to address the priorities important to the institution and its clients for the foreseeable future. For example, if the CEO were to take the initiative to provide a permanent endowment to fund ongoing needs, the plan can give focus to the briefings and

the follow-up discussions about this initiative. Although the enthusiasm to find external funds often lags general enthusiasm for such
strategic moves, the CEO can offer financial commitment to the
scheme, such as by matching external funds raised with internal
resources, and thereby enhance the enterprise's reputation as a
relevant "doer" in tune with key clients' concerns.

By deciding on specific initiatives of importance to the enterprise's future, the ideal board/staff relationship of mutual trust can
evolve, providing a basis for each part of the enterprise to understand the functions and responsibilities of the other. These working
relationships are more fluid and productive than relying solely on
the often-advocated job descriptions for board members or planning retreats of board and staff together. Successful actions to implement planned activity are most effective in building a trusting
relationship among colleagues and clients.

Client confidence also improves best through regular contact
that assists the delivery of planned results. Specifically, people who
have money are tired of being asked to give to organizations that do
not demonstrate sound management of activities that make a difference in the community. The only way to overcome such a deficiency
is to craft a powerful development team which seeks funds as an
investment to extend the delivery of benefits to the enterprise's
clients. Development staff should work closely in the shadow of the
CEO to strengthen the relationships of CEO and the board with people
of influence and means who are invited to invest in the community
through the funding of the enterprise.

In this way, even community leaders who might initially know
little of an enterprise can receive information, express their interest,
become involved, and invest in the enterprise with a sound understanding of the quality of their investment. Persistently improving
this process has seen the annual fund-raising of some organizations
double or better in less than five years while dramatically increasing
the number of donors.

Although the wave of enthusiasm for quality processes has waned
on some lecture circuits, many organizations in the private and public
sectors rightly continue to encourage coordinated quality assurance.
The few enterprises that have lightly integrated processes for quality
development processes and outputs are reaping continued benefit.
The development function should both stimulate and monitor interpersonal contacts, written proposals and the implementation of agreements for donations and coordinate an enterprise's fund-raising.
Although line management remains responsible for the performance

of areas receiving funds, the development function must ensure regular reporting to donors for accountability on the use of those funds, and this will require at times the CEO's authority to ensure timely performance of program heads. In addition, the development function coordinates the quality of the enterprise's interaction with donors and the wider constituency.

Trust is further strengthened when clients are asked what more the enterprise could be doing and how the services of the enterprise might be improved. In one university, following a survey which showed the purpose of fund-raising was still not sufficiently understood or accepted, the development staff commenced a program to improve the understanding of the division of responsibilities for fund-raising. Some initiatives that proved useful in this organization are:

- senior managers participating in sessions about effective fund-raising (facilitated by a fund-raising specialist)

- development liaison officers allocated to program areas with the highest fund-raising potential

- focus groups with internal clients on development opportunities

- development staff attending the executive meetings of programs, and in turn, the program staff attending the staff meetings of the development office.

At the same university, the development manager requested an independent audit of the development operations by two experienced, vice presidents of fund-raising. This resulted in suggestions for substantial refinement of fund-raising processes, including better involvement of senior management in fund-raising and the subsequent establishment of an external relations unit. Subsequently, a survey of internal and external clients who used the development function in the preceding year was conducted to determine satisfaction levels and expectations. Forty-five donors and fifty-one staff responded to the survey, with 84% of responses rating performance at the excellent or good levels. As a result of specific responses, program heads and development liaison officers were able to improve the processes to request funds and interact with donors, such as through a task group to improve service delivery under agreements for externally funded positions.

Results from these self-evaluations and improvements assist the continued building of excellence by the proactive development of trust through shared success. This institution completed a five-year major gifts campaign successfully. In addition to securing its largest donation at that time of $2 million, the face-to-face briefings that the institution's leaders provided for investors/prospects and alumni were increased, linking contacts to priority areas of the university.

It is reasonable to expect that during a five-year period in which the formative development office is given further focus, as income doubles, the cost of the fund-raising function may be cut by a third, resulting in expenditures below 20 cents to attract $1 from individuals and organizations. This is compared with the accepted standard of 25 cents for the "gift" dollar, cited by pertinent professional bodies for an organization at a similar stage of evolution. The development function was also benchmarked against two international universities (McGill University in Canada and Strathclyde University in Scotland). These strategic alliances stimulated a greater leadership role within the university, exemplified in the development of a detailed procedure for academic staff to follow, for example, when negotiating industry partnerships for funded professional chairs (with the aim of providing better client service). This quality initiative helped to close the previously substantial time lag between when the external source agreed to fund a professorial chair and the date on which the appointment was taken up at the university.

As a support to the self-evaluation processes established to improve the enterprise culture of this university, the development function completed ISO9000 certification to help keep purposeful focus on client service and satisfaction. Once the quality processes were fully documented and independent certification completed, development staff were positioned to improve service delivery continuously to clients by reviewing and improving the fit between actions and the documented processes and systems in an ongoing quality improvement process. Implicit and explicit to implementing these processes were targeted expectations agreed among colleagues who now sought substantial, rather than incremental growth.

"Stretch" Targets and Processes

For the substantial growth needed to bring real development to an enterprise, the commitment needed by the complete development team is great. For a board member, CEO, or development staff member to feel most comfortable asking another to invest in an organization, it is essential for the "asker" to make a "stretch" investment first. A "stretch" investment is one that others consider is a generous investment, from what is known of the person's financial means.

Boards often consist of people who bring either expertise or means or both, together with people who are on the board because they are representative of another group or organization, or are elected, nominated, or invited. Opinions vary considerably on what is the most desirable balance for the board, but one point is beyond dispute. For an enterprise to be effective in resource development, it is essential to build a board in which every board member is prepared to invest and get others to invest at substantial levels. This critical process of securing and increasing board members' investments must be uppermost when benchmarking development operations.

How the CEO and development staff work together to build and then maintain a board of such caliber remains the single greatest challenge facing service enterprises worldwide. Where stretch targets are agreed by the development team (including the board and CEO), systems to engage community and enterprise leaders in seeking ambitious, though achievable, targets are able to be emphasized throughout a five-year development plan. This was certainly the case for the evolution of the development plan at one university.

Five-year Targets. By setting targets five years earlier to achieve the goal of building relationships with prominent alumni and community leaders to support priority areas of the university for the benefit of the community, the development function aimed to secure:

1. partnerships with 200 leading organizations and a further 500 prominent individuals

2. annual fund-raising income of $5 million and a substantial endowed investment fund

3. personal involvement of all graduating students and 10% of total alumni.

The development staff were committed to be accountable to the community by ensuring easy access to people and program information, timeliness of action, pertinence of contact and information, and clear reporting arrangements. Internally, through the university's planning process and regular contact with the development function, heads of program identified priority areas that required improved relationships and/or resources to meet emerging needs or to further existing areas of strength.

Monitoring and Improvement Processes

The chief development professional monitored the achievement of targets monthly. The lead development volunteer reported on results to the alumni affairs and development committee. Client surveys were conducted at least annually and development staff improved the resource and alumni development processes by self-critically reviewing performance against benchmarks, regularly holding problem-solving sessions, and meeting weekly to set priorities and review priority actions. While strengthening the university's position within existing sectors, the university also established more relationships with nationally and internationally based corporations, alumni, and nonalumni individuals (including financial commitments through bequests in wills and other planned gifts).

The achievement of a working consensus about targets and processes in each of these areas required the CEO and the board to be available to the development staff to consider realistic but stretch targets to which all members of the team would commit. Resource development staff should meet with the CEO and board to scrutinize the information needed to set targets. As an example, whether for a $25 million or a $250 million campaign target, the main question to answer is who is a lead prospect (not suspect) who has the ability, as well as being sufficiently interested and linked to the enterprise, to give better than 10% of the goal. Four to five prospects, not one, per investment at this level will be needed, and a sobering exercise is to ask target setters to progress down the gift-range chart putting real names against each of the investments needed. The cold realization of the effects of a failed campaign usually dawns. This is also an opportunity to recommend the closer involvement of more people with the influence and means to help the organization advance.

With a board too busy or reluctant to use their influence to secure funds for the development of the enterprise, the cooperation of the CEO to provide induction or reinduction programs is often successful. Some enterprises develop systematic programs to involve the board in the lifeblood of the organization. These programs often include:

- VIP tours into parts of the enterprise that are of interest

- The use of "visiting experts" to conduct board leadership or focused strategic planning sessions, particularly addressing resource development.

Such opportunities to see the core operations of the enterprise as more than what appears in the board's meeting papers often prove effective to lift the sights of the board and the development staff. Both groups also come to appreciate the scale of opportunity in working together to implement ambitious plans.

Whatever challenges emerge in the board-staff relationships to encourage stretch targets, the board is the single most important resource for fund-raising and institutional advancement. Where the board is not productively engaged in fund-raising, the board chair, CEO, and development staff are equally responsible for initiating change. As members of the development team, everyone shares the responsibility to devise methods for making resource development succeed. People have to live with inconsistencies, but nothing is more demanding and satisfying than working to achieve even greater investment from committed individuals both inside and outside the enterprise. Time and expertise are only two of the prerequisites to board membership—part of the entry qualifications for the satisfying experiences that such involvement with the enterprise brings. The third, stated earlier, is the ability and willingness to give and to identify, involve, and ask others, and it is this which continues to be the most challenging and most powerful element in seeking virtuosity in resource development.

Achievement Beyond Benchmarking

Service enterprises are not entitled to charity. When people are asked for money to save an organization from crisis, naturally the first response may be relief that should disaster take the organization down, this would mean one less drain on the community. Harsh as it might seem, the first test of the extent to which funds will be invested is whether or not an organization is necessary—in the community's eyes. The second, and equally important test is how significant is the achievement of the enterprise in serving a community need. The organization committed to excellence steps beyond benchmarking and is able to state what difference the enterprise is making in the community. While there needs to be a market for the services, the services provided must be what the community needs and the services must also be marketed.

A well-known story from Peter Drucker illustrates this point. He described one hospital that stood out from two others with a similar quality of medical services in the same community because of the quality of its communication with former patients. Two weeks after leaving the hospital someone called to find out how patients are. If patients were not doing well, they were called again three weeks later. Then at the end of the year all patients were sent a calendar as a memento of the relationship established (Drucker, 1990). Nonverbally, what was communicated was that the people at this hospital cared about their patients. This organization marketed its product well.

Too often the mission of an enterprise (i.e., why it exists) is confused with its goals (i.e., what it aims to do). A well-positioned enterprise is one that first identifies clearly the community need it serves. It is then positioned to outline the sum total of all the reasons why someone should support it. One agency delivering food to the homeless commences its case statement simply, "Hunger hurts." With the community need so powerfully stated, the enterprise is then positioned to indicate what strategy is most effective in meeting this need and to follow this up with the track record of the enterprise.

The case for securing investment is the substantive base for benchmarking how well the organization achieves the addition of value to the community. It is a powerful statement of the impact of the enterprise, the mission, the goals, the objectives, the programs, the finances, the staff, the facilities, and even the history of the enterprise. When all these case components are accessible in a single place and they are being translated regularly into both the public relations and fund-raising programs, the case is well-defined. If community needs lead the resource development priorities of the enterprise and drive the marketing strategy, the addition of value to the community can be substantial. Where the enterprise is concerned primarily with the development of strategic partnerships in order to extend its community service, rather than being preoccupied with slogans and self-image, the case for resource development is measurable. Any externally funded initiatives, whether community-based programs, clinical services, a professorial chair, scholarships or applied research, must make an appreciable difference in the community in a predetermined time period. Each agreement to fund such initiatives implies a contract of care that, in turn, requires clarification of understanding and expectation in writing and constant face-to-face and written reporting or adjustment of arrangements to ensure that preset milestones are being exceeded.

When a program is agreed upon with a community partner, the enterprise should confirm the operation of the initiative through a confirming proposal, letter of agreement, or memorandum of understanding. This confirmation might, where appropriate, invite the partner to be involved in the selection of any staff related to the initiative and must outline reporting and accountability measures. For substantial programs or any (including senior staff) appointments, a strategic advisory committee, including representatives of the community partners, is recommended to monitor the performance against expectations. The committee should consider and approve milestones developed by a program leader that are forwarded to the funding source through the enterprise's leadership. Throughout the term of the initiative and to secure a renewed or preferably upgraded commitment, a quality process will document improvements based on the information exchange between clients and the enterprise.

Even when the information exchange between clients and the enterprise is regular, the level of influence and means, as well as the number of influential investors must be reviewed constantly. While the main reason for failed fund-raising campaigns is that not enough "asks" are made, an equally important reason is that there are insufficient prospects at the levels of giving needed to assure success. Only by involving enough people of sufficient means in the special role that the institution has to play are campaigns able to succeed.

Long ago, St. Augustine suggested that people "work for results." Leadership identifies what results are possible in resource development, which requires a clear understanding of how to do better what is already done well. Other capacities, such as the ability to capture both planned and unexpected successes, are pivotal to build the strategic teams so necessary for effective resource development.

One organization concerned with offering a variety of services to young people might have the vision of "delivering the country's future through our youth"—a challenging prospect. Yet to articulate this vision, leadership needs to recognize what the organization must become to meet the needs. Leadership must be able to say what the constituents want the organization to become.

Some enterprises take a long vision of their development function, even designing services intended to bring return very much later. One university CEO in the 1920s, as Drucker relates, set about establishing local businesses and running them for a couple of years until they broke even. Then he gave the businesses to the most promising new graduates of the university's business school, together with $10,000 in cash—a substantial sum at that time. The only request to the new entrepreneurs was expressed as follows: "You build the business and, if successful, don't repay us. Remember us." (Drucker, 1990.) Understandably, that university today enjoys a very substantial and still-growing endowment. This is vision in two senses of the word. The ultimate tests for any organization are centered upon how well it articulates and delivers its vision and whether this vision is shared.

Integrating Enterprise and Campaign Vision

To help bring an enterprise's fund-raising and external relations to levels of scope, quality, and effectiveness characteristic of the best programs, it is important to build on the successes of the development program to date. It is normally necessary to involve leading clients such as patients or alumni, as well as corporate and foundation leaders even more closely in the enterprise. Preparation for a campaign to raise an additional "stretch" of resource support can provide a valuable opportunity to energize further the development efforts.

At the heart of campaigns are relationships: especially stronger relationships with people who are able to make leadership gifts (of at least $100,000 and greater) to the enterprise's mission. The insights, energy, and drive of clients (for some enterprises, patients or alumni) and other leaders of corporations and foundations are important to bring to the benefit of the enterprise. By engaging people more closely in the life of the enterprise, the development effort can progressively achieve new levels of giving. For people to make substantial gifts, the enterprise must become core to the emotional life of each prospective lead investor. As an example, the following proposes an integrated plan for one enterprise to jump-start its development effort to levels of excellence in institutional advancement. To achieve this goal quickly, the enterprise first had to reach out to key constituents and respond to individuals' varying levels of involvement. To establish and strengthen the effort, early decisions were needed from leadership about the development vision to be used to identify and involve key constituents, build their commitment, personalize communications and strengthen the stewardship of existing investors.

With the CEO, the chief development professional and three other development professionals in place, the following set a timetable for the initial six months of preparation to jump-start the enterprise's previously existing development effort, to seek progressively the commitment of enterprise and volunteer leadership and development staff to appropriate actions. To decide the most appropriate actions, the CEO and chief development professional need to work closely together and preferably review at least monthly detailed progress reports.

Define Enterprise Needs and Priorities

Determine what are the main community needs that the enterprise seeks to meet in the future, initially drawing on the ideas and comments of influential and affluent constituents (including clients such as patients, alumni, and friends). Firstly, convene gatherings hosted by the CEO and/or board members at locations where the concentrations of wealthy investors and friends are greatest. These gatherings are opportunities to update lead gift prospects about the enterprise and learn more about invitees' interests and accomplishments. The format should allow primary focus on:

- what issues are expected to confront clients served by the enterprise, say 25 years hence

- what understandings and skills will clients need to be able to access via the enterprise

- how the enterprise can make a difference to the daily lives of people.

By distilling themes from ideas and comments offered at these gatherings, enterprise leaders and volunteers become better equipped to determine the vision for the long-term future of the enterprise. This advancement vision needs to be agreed upon to encourage people to help provide the substantial resources proposed to ensure excellence and value in the enterprise's services.

Targets

- Identify at least sixty prospective lead donors, of whom at least about ten are potential key volunteer leaders (of whom a maximum of ten in total are already involved in the enterprise).

- Draft a development strategy to address pertinent community needs to help determine the enterprise's needs and priorities, for the consideration of the CEO and the board.

Prepare a Written Campaign Plan Outline

Essential to the detailed development of the campaign plan is its integration with the strategic planning for longer-term development, as previously indicated. The campaign outline presents the case for supporting the enterprise. It becomes the prime focus for communications, highlighting how staff and volunteers strive for excellence to deliver added value, by emphasizing activities at the enterprise. For example, a college might emphasize:

- *The magic that occurs when a client and staff member work together*—a bright student and faculty member will pursue excellence and, in doing so, add value by exploring new ideas or putting knowledge to work. The case statement will celebrate the variety of how students make use of what they learn, in the classroom or laboratory, through internships, performances, cooperative education opportunities, as well as in community projects or competitions in which they participate successfully. What characterizes students at the college will be the focus, since people mainly give to students—believing that students provide the promise of a better future;

- *The accomplishments of clients that results from the value added by the college*—alumni who have built well-rounded, successful lives by striving for excellence to add value locally nationally, or internationally in the arts, sciences, business, the professions, or through public service.

- *New major initiatives and plans of the board, staff, or friends* that add value to the services offered; the purpose should be to strengthen the belief that everyone can contribute to college development

Target

- Draft campaign outline needs to be presented as an appendix to the development strategy.

Intensify Donor Research and Evaluation

Identify at least 400 individuals or organizations who have the ability, with appropriate involvement, to make leadership gifts (from

$100,000 to preferably at least 10% of the campaign goal) to the enterprise:

- Set face-to-face sessions with leadership volunteers to locate high-achieving former clients and friends of the enterprise.

- Establish "desk research" using Internet search engines and research services such as Investment and a service known as "PIN" to profile the wealth, record of philanthropy, interests, and linkages for prospective lead donors.

Targets

- Ensure at least five detailed and five brief profiles of prospective lead donors are completed per week.

- Establish scanning of news report and stock/financial information on lead prospects for weekly summaries.

Increase the Number of Face-to-Face Communications with Wealthy Individuals

Build up individual and team visits to the lead and major gift prospects/donors, to enhance stewardship of gifts and/or match interests to the enterprise's activities and plans. As appropriate, ask for initial gifts and renew or upgrade the level of giving.

Target

- Average of four visits per week per enterprise representative (CEO, chief of development, other professional staff, or volunteers).

Review Processes of Annual Fund

- Analyze year-to-date results by donor groups in relation to communication practices used.

- Assess opportunities to use new approaches to engage groupings of enterprise constituents, improve telephone caller training, and strengthen the emotional impact of communications and mailing packets and other areas to determine needed adjustments.

Targets

- Make any needed adjustments to achieve results set for the current fiscal year.

- Agree on processes to achieve increased targets to be set for the next fiscal year.

Personalize Communications

Review development invitations, correspondence, phone protocol, publications, and Internet pages and, where needed, increase personalization and/or complete outstanding projects:

- Coordinate telephone thank you and conversations about the enterprise to all current donors, in preparation for solicitation in the next fiscal year.

- Coordinate handwritten notes or e-mails to any donors not reached by phone for thanks and subsequent solicitation.

- Personalize communications between program leaders and donors or program funds.

- Identify and engage one to two donors or friends who might be prepared to be advocates of the enterprise, initially at ten strategically important potential funding organizations.

- Tailor acknowledgment letters to donors of larger gifts—for all gifts ensure receipts and acknowledgments are mailed within twenty-four hours of gifts being received.

- Establish mixers and other opportunities for regular interaction between investors and program professionals.

- Engage appropriate investors in planning and implementing regular telephone calling to other investors to invite attendance at selected enterprise events.

- Conduct internal/external client survey in collaboration with the enterprise's public relations staff.

Targets

- Reach at least 1,000 donors/prospects for telephone "chats."

- Complete personal notes to all other donors.

- Coordinate progress reports from each program leader to each donor.

- Engage at least ten people as advocates of the enterprise within potential funding organizations and agree on a program for continued interaction.

- Ensure donor acknowledgment standards are met.

- Hold two investor mixers per year.

- Pilot telephone outreach to fellow investors, initially to support established events.

- Establish baselines for measuring the interaction of constituents with the enterprise and the levels of satisfaction with contacts, particularly development communications.

Increase Recognition of Client Accomplishment

In addition to giving public recognition to accomplished constituents in the enterprise's publications, it is important to stimulate personalized, congratulatory notes from the CEO for close constituents who receive community or professional honors. Where possible, similar notes should be elicited from former program professionals who have dealt with the person.

The range of opportunities for an enterprise to recognize clients and former clients include:

- highlighting accomplishments at conferences and meetings

- distinguished achiever awards

- leadership seminars that permit sharing of expertise

- systematically inviting clients to make guest lecture at community workshops

- Seeking input on planning and marketing for the further development of community involvement in the enterprise's publicly available programs.

Initially, the enterprise and volunteer leadership need to decide what opportunities are most suited to the enterprise and recruit further key constituents to champion particular programs in partnership with senior staff and volunteers.

Targets

- Identify further opportunities to highlight client accomplishments at schedules events.

- Present a client achievement award each month and two distinguished client awards for each program area each year.

- Build up to two client leadership seminars per month during each half-year.

- Each program area should invite at least one outstanding client to present (initially) to a community group each half-year.

- Each program area should suggest opportunities for a community project brief each half-year.

- Recruit "champions" from the friends' association to recommend marketing opportunities to increase community attendance and involvement at enterprise events.

Review of Records and Database Support

Assess the accuracy and responsiveness of development record-keeping, including database entry, checking, and reporting processes. Review the capacity of the information system to be used for relationship marketing.

Target

- Agree on best practices for records and database entry and a schedule of reports.

Benchmarking

Such targets must be appropriate to the capabilities of the people and other resources available to achieve them and should be arrived at carefully. To set such targets and related processes to share the enterprise's vision through face-to-face communication in a way that can be measured, an enterprise needs first to set internal benchmarks and then should agree with one or two world leaders to benchmark development processes with an ongoing exchange of information. The aim of the exchange is to provide a framework for substantial improvement of the development processes of participating enterprises, initially through focus on the involvement of key prospects and their solicitation for major gifts. The benefits of the program include the sharing of results achieved against agreed upon benchmarks, detailed processes that prove successful, and information about reward systems for development professionals who support productivity improvements.

Focus is on how closely key individuals are being drawn to the enterprise with the assistance of the enterprise/community champions of development. A "champion" is a staff member or external community leader who is committed to developing priority areas for the enterprise's advancement. Champions work closely with development staff as advisers and contacts to prospective investors. External champions have a linkage and/or interest in the enterprise and may be prominent former clients, community leaders and/or interest in the enterprise and may be prominent former clients, community leaders and/or philanthropists. Internal champions are usually members of the enterprise's executive leadership responsible for areas that are prospective or are already gaining strong community support and funds.

Internal Benchmarks

Typical internal benchmarks that might be established include:

1. Common to fund-raising and external relations

   - External champions hosting functions of peers to show-case the enterprise's priorities

   - Face-to-face briefings by champions with investors/prospects (functions hosted by enterprise leaders; briefing visits with investors/prospects; functions including honorary awards, conferences, outstanding service recognition, former board information sharing, CEO breakfasts)

   - Client satisfaction with the speed and importance of the service

2. Fund-raising

   - 20% annual growth in gross income

   - Cut revenue to cost ratio (by an agreed percent of costs for each dollar raised)

- New three to five-year written pledges at major investment level

- Targeted income for CEOs discretionary use on priorities

3. External relations

   - Additional constituents volunteering to assist the enterprise in specific leadership roles

   - Prominent constituents organized to meet the enterprise's leaders, and, in the case of an educational institution:

      - 100% increase of alumni sending information to be published in keep-in-touch notes

      - Increased number of accurate alumni records

Process Documentation

Each of the core development processes should be briefly documented from the identification of the initiative, through prospect identification, through "asks" to acknowledgments and recognition.

1. *Initiative identification.* When a resource development initiative is identified in consultation with a program leader as a priority area, the development staff member responsible for liaison works with the specific area leaders to prepare an outline statement.

2. *Prospect identification research.* The development officer should add to prospect identification research by drawing upon the knowledge and contacts of external champions in the first instance. Prospect identification research is conducted through

   - peer contacts or external champions, especially CEO or board-level peers

   - public records and information services, such as Investnet, newspapers, magazines, databases, and reference sources, and market research services in order to discover the wealth and interest areas of potential prospects.

   - internal contacts, i.e., the internal champion may already know of an organization or individual with specific funding interests.

Once a prospect is approved, the development officer arranges meetings between the prospect and the staff and nominated champion(s).

3. *Ask.* Within three months, the development officer is responsible for organizing the timing for an ask. The development officer comprehensively briefs a champion who will normally make the ask. All contact is noted immediately after each contact on a file note, preferably directly in the computerized development database and file.

4. *Acknowledgment.* When an ask is successful and a level of gift is agreed upon with the prospect, a development officer provides the leader of development written terms of the gift signed by the investor, prior to signature by the appropriate enterprise leader.

5. *Recognition.* Depending on the amount or nature of the investment, appropriate personalized recognition is planned. If, for example, the gift is at a level designated as important strategically to the growth of further investment, the investor should be formally recognized at a recognition ceremony and presented with an appropriate certificate or plaque. All investors are to be acknowledged with an appropriate thank-you letter within 24 hours.

Internal Communication Program

To supplement and support these processes, best practice requires a program of pertinent activities to help make all the enterprise's staff more aware of the success of colleagues working with the development function. Whether or not staff of the development area initiates a contact that leads to a gift, emphasis should remain on the acknowledgment of fellow staff and looking for ways to do better, while communicating the success that has already been achieved. Emphasis is particularly to be placed on face-to-face communication, when one major accomplishment of the development area is mentioned and credit is to be given to the nondevelopment staff member responsible, at every function, meeting, or social event attended. An open house should be regularly held to give the opportunity to meet staff and find out more about how development staff can work with program colleagues. Functions are to be regularly held to which donors, volunteers, and colleagues are invited to thank them for supporting particular resource development initiatives.

In addition to normal business contacts, each development staff member is encouraged to find an excuse to telephone three nondevelopment staff members each week and use the opportunity to mention one achievement of program colleagues working with development. Print media are also to be used to show the success of program colleagues in getting funding by working with development staff. Typically, development staff reports monthly against a range of objectives that provide recognition for a well-rounded range of actions—not confined only to "getting the dollars."

Conclusion

Where better than three-quarters of the conditions described herein pertain, the organization has evolved a system for achieving excellence in institutional advancement. Where better than two-thirds of the conditions are in place, it has some capacity for excellence in institutional advancement, but has much yet to do. Anything less than this and the best course in considering whether to launch a major campaign is to wait and work.

The result of failed campaigns can be as much as five years of cynicism and major future blockages to effective relationships in this area among colleagues, clients, and investors, which might even lead to the end of the enterprise. The benefits of excellent resource development, in addition to achieving the dollar goals, include an increased capacity to meet the community need which the enterprise serves, the greater involvement of leadership from the community, and the advancement of the long-term development strategy of the enterprise.

References

Carbone, Robert F. (1989). *Fund Raising as a Profession.* Clearinghouse for Research on Fund Raising. College Park: University of Maryland.

Drucker, P. F. (1990). *Managing the Non-Profit Organization: Practices and Principles.* Oxford: Butterworth-Heinemann.

Rosso, H. A. (1991). *Achieving Excellence in Fund Raising: A Comprehensive Guide to Principles, Strategies, and Methods.* San Francisco: Jossey-Bass.

Sheldon, K. (1996). Credibility is Risky Business: An Interview with Vincent T. Covell. *Communication World,* April, pp. 16–19.

Thayer, L. (In press). *Making High-Performance Organizations: The Logic of Virtuosity.*

Worth, Michael J., and Asp III, James W. (1994). *The Development Officer in Higher Education: Toward an Understanding of the Role.* Clearinghouse on Higher Education. Washington, DC: George Washington University.

10

Intuition and Metacommunication Strategies in Times of Change

Ernest F. Martin Jr.

In today's high-speed, empirical, volatile world of business, the old-fashioned "hunch" continues to be an important managerial tool. Some people call it intuition. Some people know it as a flash of inspiration or a strong gut feeling, while others think of it as a little voice that whispers to them. It is part of what we as multidimensional human beings do—unconsciously and sometimes consciously. Intuition, inspiration, creative thought, and psychic ability are all part of an infinite—and infinitely useful—process called metacommunication.

Metacommunication portrays the communication process and the multidimensional participants as pure energy. If we are beings of energy, then it follows that we can be affected by energy. Even orthodox medicine has begun its evolutionary progression toward the development of energy treatment. Communicators are also beginning the evolutionary progression. This paper provides a new synthesis of understanding in a field that needs some type of theoretical foundation for further thinking and testing of approaches to communication. Certainly, this is transitional, waiting to be expanded upon, changed, and reshaped by newly acquired experimental evidence.

From Communication to Metacommunication

The communication process involves the sending and receiving of a message through some channel—with a resulting response. The communication process takes place in a variety of contexts, including mass communication with television and radio, interpersonal or group communication with a few people or another single individual, and intrapersonal where people talk to themselves as they think, feel, and respond to stimuli.

163

In the field of communication studies, conceptualization of how individuals operate within a variety of communication contexts and ways to enhance the effectiveness of the situation form the core knowledge of the field. In an attempt to help the field of communication incorporate research and theory from other areas, the process of communication is enlarged to include the new developments, a process termed metacommunication. Metacommunication incorporates aspects of consciousness that have been referred to in the past as intuition and intrapersonal communication as well as telepathy, precognition, remote viewing, and/or ESP.

The need for this additional conceptualization of communications is necessitated by developments in our overall view of the world, especially in physics, biology, medicine, philosophy, sociology, and psychology. It is also necessitated by business changes in the world.

High-Speed Business Marketing Environment

It is typhoon season for business. Winds of change are barreling in from all directions—east, west, north, and south. Technological changes are incessant. Competition is tougher than ever and coming from the least expected places. The customer is more sophisticated and demanding. Government regulations are tougher. Everyone is restructuring, reorganizing, reinvesting, downsizing, outsourcing—all at an ultrasonic pace. The typhoon of change is not a storm to wait out because the winds are unrelenting. The long-term weather report is for more of the same.

King and Cushman (1995), plotting the typhoon's course, point to three trends converging in the late 1980s and continuing in the 1990s and propose High-Speed Management theory, the first communication-based management theory. Information and communication technologies dramatically alter how research and development, manufacturing, marketing, and management work. Dramatic increases in world trade, the emergence of a global economy, and the development of three large core markets have been facilitated by the information and communication revolution. The technological breakthroughs and increase in world trade have made success in business difficult because of the volatile business climate characterized by rapidly changing technology, quick market saturation, shrinking product life cycles, and unexpected competition (Cushman and King, 1993). Martin (1996a; 1996b; 1997) argues that cultural differences play a critical role in business operations in business operations in this global, competitive environment. The cultural differences across markets and within markets require sophisticated communication strategies within the traditional communication model (Martin, 1995). However, traditional communication models, sophisticated in their own right, do not extend to the meta-communicative possibilities of multidimensional consumers and employees, which open up worlds of possibilities in management and marketing strategies.

In the high-speed environment, change, and successful adaptation to change, is imperative. Kriegel and Brandt (1996) propose an exercise to gauge the speed of change on the job. They ask workshop participants to look back on their job three years ago, remembering what they used to do, how they did it, whom they worked with, who were the competitors, what technologies were used, how the organization was structured, the size of the workload. On a scale of 1 to 10, over 80 percent of the people rate change at work between 7 and 10 during this short time. Now if projecting into the future, how would the person rate the changes they think will occur in the next three years? Future changes will be bigger and come faster because the rate of change grows exponentially, not incrementally. The typhoon season, especially blowing in from Asia, has just begun.

Intuition and Business

Successful management of on-going change requires a variety of personal and organizational keys. Emery (1994) argues that businesses over the past decade have begun to realize that analytical thinking arrives too late for a twenty-four hour global marketplace. Naisbett and Aburdene (1985) point to both intuition and vision transforming society. They point out intuition has long been accepted in sports but is only now being recognized as a powerful management tool. Dr. Weston Agor (1984), former professor of management at the University of Texas, set up a Global Intuition Network in the 1980s with continuing research and conferences on intuition and business. Apollo 14 astronaut Edgar Mitchell founded the Institute of Noetic Science in 1973 for the study of "intuitive knowing" (Nadel, 1996).

Intuition, creativity, and innovation are linked. Fostering intuition and creativity by the right environment, and by specialized training in the case of creativity, has been in U.S. business for several decades. By the mid-1980s, many blue-chip companies—General Electric, IBM, AT&T, were holding workshops to remove mental blocks that dampen natural creative thought. In the early 1990s a spirit of intellectual conservatism caused the quantum leap approaches to lose popularity, not surprising in the light of resource scarcity and personal hardship caused by downsizing. Human resources personnel have simply been too busy with outplacement for casualties and "mourning" and morale boosting for survivors. As redundancy and attrition run their course, intuition and creativity enhancement has resurfaced, precisely because of the effects of downsizing. Two-day workshops are replaced, however, with businesses building creativity into their processes, to make it systemic. Creativity in itself is not useful from a corporate perspective, regardless of how interesting it is to the individual, unless it can be applied in the workplace. Whatever skills are developed, the environment must be conducive to change (Thackray, 1995).

Intuition allows for correct decisions, even before all the facts in. Richard DeVos, the cofounder of Amway Corporation, observes that total dependence of facts limits the adventurous spirit that is crucial to the process of innovation and discovery. He believes facts alone often end up being why an idea will not work. He argues companies only advance when intuition is integrated and used along with facts and logic in the decision-making process (Barker, 1992). Kotite (1994) argues entrepreneurs will find their best counsel from "gut reaction." Emery (1994) relates visionaries in business to their use of intuition—the vision emanating from the intuitive mind allows him or her to "see."

Highly profitable hunches or intuition is legendary in business. Most decisions are made on the basis of incomplete information. Facts may not be available or there may not be sufficient time or staff assistance to uncover them. Some executives throughout history have a reputation for making the right decision without apparent evidence. Conrad Hilton, a legendary hotel business intuitive, wrote in "Be My Guest" that after he has done everything he can to figure out a problem, he keeps listening "in sort of inside silence until something clicks," and he feels a right answer. Inventor Art Fry of 3M was singing in a choir and needed bookmarks that would not fall out of his hymnal when he got the idea for Post-It Notes, the ubiquitous memos with a sticky strip on the back. Ross Perot's decision to start ED.S after being at EBM, Walt Disney's decision to build Disney World in Florida, and Ray Kroc's decision to buy U.S. franchise rights from Richard and Maurice McDonald are some of the many successful intuitive decisions (Rowan, 1986; Dean and Mihalasky, 1974).

Fast-changing situations in business today demand greater use of intuitive faculties. Pelton, Sackmann, and Boguslaw (1990) categorize business decisions on a "type 1" or "type 2" continuum. Type 1 situations are simple or analyzable; solutions are foreseeable, predictable, or programmable; A leads to B, and may occur routinely; similar to *XYZ*; planning helps. Type 2 situations are complex or unanalyzable; solutions are unforeseeable, unpredictable or unprogrammable; A may or may not lead to B, and are never routine; not like anything; planning is not possible. Because of accelerating social, political, and technological change, type 2 situations are increasing and confronting more managers on all levels. They state their empirical evidence leads them to believe there is a strong correlation between intuitive capacity and effectiveness in the face of type 2 situations—in other words, intuition is critical within the high-speed business environment. Actors and musicians, for example, have been found to have demonstrable intuitive skills (Harvey, 1994).

Intuition and Metacommunication

Intuition is a wonderful word because it means so many different things to different people. It has a long tradition of use in philosophy, mathematics, business, psychology, engineering, linguistics, music, literature, religion, and science, particularly with reference to the creative process.

Some of the many definitions and understandings of intuition are mutually inconsistent. According to the *Random House Dictionary of the English Language,* intuition is "direct perception of truth, fact, etc., independent of any reasoning process; immediate apprehension." Another definition from the same dictionary refers to intuition as "a keen and quick insight." Intuition comes from the Latin verb *intueri,* which means "looking or knowing from within." Intuition is knowledge that comes from some stratum of awareness just below the conscious level. It is knowing directly, without mediation by a conscious or deliberate rational process (Goldberg, 1983). It explores the unknown and senses implications and possibilities that may not be readily apparent (Jung, 1923). Other definitions stress that the intuitive process is itself unconscious. Intuition, again, is "knowing without knowing how you know." Metacommunication involves the processing of messages (including those that yield intuition) which happen within a multidimensional individual. In short, intuition is knowing, meta-communication is how the intuition develops.

Many business leaders will readily admit that s/he might indeed possess certain intuitive powers that are of real assistance in generating ideas, choosing alternative courses of action, and picking people. Business people interviewed by Emery (1994) describe intuition as "clear knowing without being able to explain how one knows," "knowing without conscious awareness," and "hunches or random thoughts moving to conviction." Intuition is nonrational, nonlinear, insightful, nondata-based, and an extension of the five basic senses. Intuition is not logical, rational, commonsensical, an emotional state, or based on experience.

Naturally, attempts have been made to reduce the intuitive process to something less mysterious. Norman Simon (1989), the Nobel laureate economist and cognitive scientist, has suggested that intuition is nothing more than the brain's capacity for subliminal computation. Frances Vaughn (1979), a transpersonal psychologist, describes intuition as a way of knowing—recognizing the possibilities of any situation. Some social scientists view intuition as learned habits and social conditioning. Others believe that intuition is predicated upon biological instinct, for example, the intuition of a salmon in locating its spawning ground. The fabric of intuition may well include these threads, as well as others.

Goldberg (1983) categorizes many "faces" of intuition. Discovery intuition or detection supplies answers to a specific problem. Creativity or generative intuition supplies alternatives, options, or possibilities. Evaluation intuition is a binary function of yes or no, go or don't go. Operation intuition prompts us where to go and what to do. Prediction intuition has an element of prophecy (in most instances of intuition). Illumination intuition is a type of transcendence—knowing but without an object of knowing.

Cappon (1994) provides, to date, the most complete classification of intuition, based on instincts coalescing into intuition, the capacity for which is stored deep in the brain. His belief is that in the millions of years preceding the development of speech, intuition ruled everyday life. Speech evolved some 250,000 years ago, yet *Pithecanthropus erectus* dates back some 4.5 million years. During that period, survival from predators and other daily decisions had to be instantaneous, instinctual, and intuitive. Intuition was likely the only form of organized preverbal intelligence. The original instincts and intuition were probably based on a rapid access system, separate from conscious thought, unencumbered by hesitation and doubt.

Since the development of speech, however, intuition has gradually lost dominion to "informed thinking." With the transfer of information made possible by speech development, the brain began its rapid expansion and evolved the ten-billion-cell neocortex. Logical, speech-promoted intelligence took over at the expense of experiential-based instinct. Cappon argues that the mind developed barriers to access, specifically levels below consciousness. Furthermore, in the centuries since the Enlightenment, the role of intuition has been degraded to the point it is often depicted as mystical and psychic. From this, Cappon postulates a classification of twenty hierarchically stacked intuitive skills, from basic, perceptual, and cognitive to higher levels of knowing.

While we can learn more about intuition by examining instances of its operation in daily life, we are in the ironic position of being unable to identify times in which intuition is not operating. Philosophers such as Immanual Kant, for example, maintain that it is through intuition that we construct and maintain the basic elements of our world—our sense of space and time, our sense of identity, our sense of the truth of things, our sense of beauty and goodness. Intuition, derived from the very structure or essence of our minds, is viewed in philosophy as being prior to all perception and all *(a priori)* reasoning. In linguistics, intuition is understood as the process by which listeners recognize the meaning of words and sentences, and speakers form words and sentences to create meaning. From these perspectives, our intuitions serve as providing continuity and meaning in our lives, moment by moment.

In other contexts, intuition requires, and then adds to, years of experience and training filled with thoughtful reasoning and social conditioning. An inventor, Lynn Charlson, who made his fortune in the field of hydraulics, cultivated a daily habit of spending thirty minutes every night before going to sleep in visualization and contemplation of specific technical problems. It was this process that led him to develop the first hydraulic power steering unit and other fundamental patents in the area of hydraulic motors. It is of significance that Charlson, in retrospect, has come to view his intuitions as having a connection with higher spiritual sources. This is a viewpoint shared by other inventors, such as Chester Carlson (inventor of the Xerox process) and Arthur M. Young (inventor of the Bell Helicopter)—who have also made significant financial contributions to intuition and parapsychology research and related fields.

These inventors join the company of Henry Ford and Thomas Alva Edison in having a deep and abiding interest in the subject of a universal spirit and reincarnation. From here, we enter into a realm that, in modern times, has been relegated to metaphysics—beyond all possible verification. In fact, reported intuitions of spiritual dimensions constitute an enormous area of study. The ancient literature includes the Egyptian Book of the Dead, the Old and New Testaments, the Talmud, the Kabala, the Tibetan Book of the Dead.

All of these converging insights and methodologies from a variety of fields relating to intuition suggest that we have the potential to evolve the process—metacommunication—to allow useful training and further research.

Background for Metacommunication

The human body is an energy system. Both the modern scientist and the ancients agree that everything in life is formed of vibration. Vibration exists in objects, in animals, in people, and in the atmosphere around us. The vibrational frequencies of animate life are more active, vibrant, and variant than that of inanimate matter, but vibration exists in all. Vibration is the movement of energy passing. Ideas create thought forms; thought forms create pictures. The wavelength of frequency determines substance, sound, color, and form. The frequency of energy determines its density and volume. Therefore, vibration is part of consciousness at every level of awareness and growth (Wendell, Wendell, and Willis, 1988).

This understanding has developed slowly. In the past Western medical and communication practice considered living organisms to operate mechanically, based upon a model of the world as an intricate mechanism, with the body as a type of grand machine which is controlled by the brain and peripheral nervous system. When an organism was not functioning properly, the cause was ascribed to structural defects in the system arising out of chemical imbalances. A growing awareness has occurred, not only of the interactions between chemical states and electromagnetic fields (e.g., DC currents enhance fracture healing) but also mental effects. For example, hypnosis, meditation, visualization, biofeedback, and other techniques demonstrate that the directed mind can control autonomic body functions such as skin temperature, blood pressure, breathing, pain, as well as repair of the body and chemical balances. Professor William Tiller of Stanford University (Gerber, 1988) points out other fields, not yet clearly discriminated, also are part of the chain reaction. He labels them "subtle energy fields." Human beings are networks of complex energy fields that interface with physical/cellular systems.

The recognition that all matter is energy forms the foundation for understanding how human beings are dynamic energy systems. Quantum physics for many decades has treated atoms as waves of vibrating possibilities and frozen particles of actuality when observed. An atom is a wave of oscillating possibilities as long as it is not observed; the atom stops vibrating and objectifies one of its many possibilities ("frozen") whenever it is looked at (Herbert, 1993). The unseen connection between the physical body energy forces and the subtle energy forces holds the key to understanding the inner relationship between matter and energy (Gerber, 1988).

Metacommunication portrays the communication process and the multidimensional participants as pure energy. If we are beings of energy, then it follows that we can be affected by energy. We are in the midst of a massive paradigm shift from the older mechanical worldview of the Newtonian pragmatists to the new perspective of an interconnected holistic universe as envisioned by the Einsteinian thinkers. The more advanced quantum physicists are now coming to the same conclusion about the underlying unity of humanity and nature that ancient Chinese and Indian philosophers described in their writings that depict subtle human relationships with the cosmos (Capra, 1984; Pribram, 1984; Gerber, 1988).

Holograms and Metacommunication/Multidimensional Source/Receiver

Humans communicate through a variety of frequency domains. The distinction of the physical nature of matter becomes lost on a subatomic level since matter as a substance is composed of particles which are themselves points of frozen light, with particular frequency characteristics. Matter is composed of highly complex, infinitely orchestrated energy fields (Gerber, 1988).

To better understand how metacommunication works, we can use a working knowledge of light—specifically laser light and holography. Laser light is very special; it is called coherent light because of all its waves are extremely orderly, with all of its waves moving in step like soldiers marching in a parade. There are many applications, from laser eye surgery to videodisks, fiber optic telecommunication, and holography. The hologram is a special three-dimensional picture made by sending a single laser beam through an optical beam splitter to create two laser beams that originate from the same source. One of the beams (designated "the reference beam") passes through a diffusing lens that spreads it from orderly pencil-thin rays into a flashlight-like beacon. The reference beam is directed by mirrors to an unexposed photographic plate. Meanwhile, the second beam (designated "the working beam") is passed through a second diffusing lens. The difference between the two beams is that light from the working beam is used to illuminate the object being photographed. The light from the working beam bounces off the object, and then falls upon the photographic plate.

What happens at the photographic plate is the basis for a new way of understanding the universe. When the pure unaffected reference beam meets with the reflected light of the working beam, an interference pattern is created—waves of one beam mixing and interacting with the other waves. The interference pattern causes a three-dimensional hologram. By shining a pure beam of laser light similar to the reference beam through the hologram, one can view the three dimensions of the object recorded by the working (reflected) beam. If a small piece of the holographic film is cut away and held to a laser light, the entire, intact, three-dimensional image of the photographed object is there. The reason for this is the face that the hologram is an energy interference pattern. Within this pattern, every piece contains the whole (Gerber, 1988).

The holographic model gives us new ways of understanding the communication process. We have energy fields at various frequencies able to occupy the same "space" simultaneously. Eastern esoteric literature often referred to "etheric," or subtle, matter which is less dense than physical (e.g., of a higher frequency nature). Gerber (1988) refers to the etheric body as a subtle counterpart to what we call the physical body, an energy interference pattern with the characteristics of a hologram, made up of matter of higher frequencies. He carries this concept further, postulating, along with Nobel prize–winning physicist David Bohm, the "implicate order" of a holographic universe with higher levels of order and information holographically enfolded in the fabric of space and matter/energy, with every piece containing the whole (Bohm, 1982; Briggs and Peat, 1984). If such a cosmic hologram exists, Gerber (1988) argues it is, unlike the static hologram a dynamically moving system that changes constantly. Furthermore, "because what happens in just a small fragment of the holographic energy interference pattern affects the entire structure simultaneously, there is a tremendous connectivity relationship between all parts of the holographic universe" (Gerber, 1988, p 61).

The cosmic hologram is likely to be composed of overlapping energy interference patterns of many different frequencies. Each frequency-specific holographic pattern would carry information of a unique nature relative to the characteristics of that frequency domain.

Multidimensional Energy Systems

Since matter is a kind of frozen light, it must have particular frequency characteristics. The difference between physical matter/energy and subtle energy/matter is only a difference of frequency. It is acknowledged within physics that energy of different frequencies can exist within the same space without destructive interaction. This principle is demonstrated daily by the bombardment by radio and TV broadcasts that pass through our homes and bodies. This electromagnetic energy is invisible to our eyes and ears because it exists at a threshold of energy beyond the frequency sensitivity of our physical organs of perception. If a TV set is turned on, however, these normally invisible energies become encoded into energies of visible light and audible sound, which are within perceptual range of sensitivity. When we turn on the TV set we do not see channel 2's image mixed with Channel 7's. Because the energies are of slightly different frequencies, they can exist within the same space without interfering with each other. It is only because of the interaction of our TV set as an extension of our senses that we can even tell that these energies are present.

This principle of energies of different frequencies occupying the same space, nondestructively, has theoretical implications for matter of different frequencies. Because of their differing inherent frequencies, physical and subtle matter can coexist in the same space, just as radio and TV waves can pass through the same space without interference. Gerber (1988) argues that the holographic energy field template is superimposed on the structure of the physical framework. Yet all of the energetic frequencies are interconnected and in dynamic equilibrium.

One energy system has been explored and is now widely accepted—the acupuncture meridian system. Acupuncture has been used in China for several thousands years. The procedure has its roots in the ancient philosophy of Taoism, a belief that people are one with the universe and that all life is permeated with the life-giving energy of *chi*. Part of this belief is that all of our experiences have opposites, such as hot and cold, day and night. Yin and yang merge and compliment one another throughout life, creating a balance. When the forces are in balance, a person is in good health. When the forces are not in balance, disease may occur. Acupuncture is a method used to restore the balance in life. Although it is often thought of as alternative medicine, it has been surprisingly successful in the treatment of many ailments where more conventional methods have not been successful.

In the 1960s Kim Bong Han is Korea demonstrated meridians of rabbits and other animals by way of microautoradiography, following the path of radioactive isotopes. He demonstrated through many experiments that the meridian system is not only interlinked within itself but also appears to interconnect with all cell nuclei of the tissues, yet the meridian system is independent of the vascular network. Additionally, in embryonic chicks, the meridian ducts were formed within fifteen hours of conception, even before the formation of the most rudimentary organs. Kim's findings suggest some type of information flows through the meridian to the DNA control centers of the cells (Russell, 1971). Gerber (1988) argues the meridian system forms an interface between the physical body and the subtle energy forms. Bioenergetic information and vital *chi* energy move from the subtle body to the cellular level of the physical body via this specialized meridian network. The implication that energies are communicated through the acupuncture points of the meridian system is supported by measurements of electrical skin resistance in and around the acupoints. Quantitative measurements by various researchers have demonstrated that there occurs approximately a twenty-fold drop in electrical resistance at the acupoints (Gerber, 1988). Electronographic body scans have found that changes in brightness of the acupuncture points precede the changes of physical illness in the body (Dumitrescu and Kenyon, 1983).

The meridian system is not the only link between our physical body and our subtle energetic systems. Various ancient texts of Indian yogic literature describe an energy system with seven centers. These energy centers, referred to as *chakras,* are said to resemble whirling vortices of subtle energy (Leadbeater, 1927). The *chakras* are connected to each other and to portions of the physical-cellular structure via fine subtle energetic channels known as *nadis.* The *nadis* are formed by fine threads of subtle energetic matter, different from the meridians, which parallel the bodily nerves in abundance. Various sources have described seven major, five alta major, and 348 minor *chakras* with up to 72,000 *nadis* in the subtle anatomy of human beings (Ryerson, 1983). Experimental findings that tend to confirm the presence of the *chakra* system in human beings have been carried out by Dr. Hiroshi Motoyana in Japan and Hunt at UCLA (Motoyama and Brown, 1978).

Problems of Awareness

Human energy systems are used in the metacommunication process. A person may not be aware of what is happening. Metacommunication, like all awareness, depends on one's state of consciousness, one's attitude, motivations, level of relaxation, and other psychological or mental aspects. Because we are bombarded by stimuli from all directions, we need filters to block out all but the most essential items from our conscious awareness, called filter theory. Unfortunately, the pressures of living in a city, with millions of others and all their thoughts and emotions, has desensitized us to block out all but the most immediate perceptions. With the blocks we are not even aware of what close friends and family are feeling, let alone whether or not some distant relative is in need of help.

The process of increasing awareness, working with metacommunication, is called, by some people, "becoming aware of the subconscious," since it is only in conscious awareness we are blocked (Mishlove, 1994). We can work with all of the frequency channels of the multidimensional human as communication channels.

Conscious experience is a very limited channel. We can be conscious of only about seven things at any one time, yet there are 10,000 million neurons and 100,000 million synapses in the brain (Hubel, 1979). Nobody really understands what is happening when we become conscious, or aware, of something—a thought, a feeling, another person. Part of metacommunication is the ever-present information, constantly monitored and responded to by various energy systems of the human at an unconscious level, that occasionally break into consciousness. Signal Detection Theory (SDT) is a psychological theory in which the concept of a threshold as a fixed point of transition in sensory events is rejected, on the grounds that theoretically ALL signals contribute to the continuum of sensory activities on which decisions and behavior are based. Theoretically, therefore, one is stimulated by everything in the universe. As this is impossible to cope with, the barriers blocking such awareness have to be proportionately stronger. The process of metacommunication, as well as modalities of meditation, hypnosis, shamans, healers, and mediums, allows a concentration (focusing) of awareness rather than a diffusion throughout the universe, allowing awareness of different frequency bands of sensory input. According to SDT, responding to an external stimuli is a two-stage process: the first is sensing and the second is deciding on the appropriate response. Instantaneous information with no consideration of time and space is not physically possible—it is possible, however, at a quantum mechanical level.

Techniques for Enhancing Metacommunication: Tapping into the Cosmic Hologram

Ordinary light from incandescent light bulbs is known as incoherent light, with light waves traveling randomly—chaotically—in all directions. One might think of average human thought as random and incoherent. Conversely, laser or coherent light is highly focused, with all light waves traveling in step similar to soldiers in a parade. If the energy produced by an incandescent bulb were to be made coherent, the resulting focused laser beam can burn a hole through a steel plate. One can extend the analogy to the production of coherent thought activity—increased brain wave coherence. Coherent light also codes and decodes holograms. There is some evidence to suggest that increased coherence of brain wave activity (altered states) may be associated with human remote viewing, psychokinesis, and psychic activity. Long-term mediators attempting psychic feats (also known as *siddhis*) were found to have brain wave patterns of increased energetic coherence during psychic events. Other researchers have found a shift in brain wave frequencies toward the theta/delta range (1–7) cycles/second, along with increased hemispheric synchronization during human psychic functioning (Whitton, 1974; Cade and Coxhead, 1979).

The key principle is that coherent consciousness may display properties that go beyond ordinary waking consciousness. When a person goes from incoherent random thought to coherent consciousness, it may be as powerful as transforming incandescent light to the brilliant energy of a laser beam. By achieving this highly focused level of awareness, we may be able to selectively tune to specific frequency bands of energetic input, similar to tuning the station dial on a radio.

Physicists have now computer-modeled how rudimentary rules of behavior applied to self-propelled particles moving chaotically can lead to synchronized activity (Herbert, 1993). In the model, a given area is sprinkled with a certain number of particles. Each particle moves at the same speed, but in a random direction. Start-

ing with this configuration, the computer calculates particle veloci-
ties at subsequent times according to a simple rule: With each time
step, every particle assumes the average direction of motion of the
particles in its immediate neighborhood, modified by a small random perturbation. Computer simulations reveal that the type of
movement observed depends on the number of particles packed
into a given area and on the level of random perturbation, or noise.
Remarkably, at high densities and low noise, all of the particles end
up moving in the same spontaneously selected direction. The possible clustering and migration may have significant insight into the
way that a person goes from incoherent random thought to coherent consciousness in altered states.

The Training Process for Metacommunication: Coherent Waves in Altered States

Ways of exploring coherent consciousness and training for effective
metacommunication include (but are not limited to) ways to bring
the brain wave to an altered state. It is somewhat like developing a
method of knocking some kind of hole in the barrier between the
conscious and the unconscious levels of mind and opening this door
on demand and at will.

Hypnosis is a particular altered state of selective hypersuggesti-
bility brought about in an individual by the use of a combination of
relaxation, fixation of attention, and suggestion. Hypnosis, either self-
hypnosis or guided to trance by another person, allows an altered
state of consciousness in which to learn and practice metacommunication. Actually, almost everyone is already familiar with hypnosis, although not realizing it perhaps because it is such a natural
state of mind. For example, most people while driving along a familiar expressway, at some point in time, have driven past the desired
exit, being "wide awake" in activity but the mind was elsewhere. At
this point, the person had drifted into an altered state of consciousness. Here is why. A person's subconscious stores everything learned,
including how to drive. As one moves to a consistent speed on the
highway, the conscious mind is free. Because the knowledge required
for driving now exists in the subconscious, conscious mind drifts
off, allowing subconscious to become more active. When attention
is needed to change lanes, avoid something in the road or slow for
an off ramp, the conscious mind comes into play again. Sometimes
a person may even arrive and wonder how it was so quick. Driving
is only one automatic activity. Altered states with automatic activities,

many times allowing daydreaming while drifting from an alert state into a different level of consciousness, include taking a shower, mowing the lawn, dining alone, and exercising. Brain wave activity is different as these states change.

In an alert state (beta), there is normal intellectual functioning and normal reflexive and motor response. In light trance or day-dreaming state (beta-alpha), there is relaxation of the body, slowed breathing and pulse, withdrawal into self, direction of attention to imagined activity, dialogue, or event. In moderate trance (alpha-theta), there is loss of awareness of surroundings, closed eyes, increased awareness of internal heartbeat and/or breathing, increased receptivity of senses, intensified imagery, literal interpretation of speech. In deep trance (lower theta-upper delta), there is further reduction of activity and energy output, limpness or stiffness of limbs, narrowing of attention, increased suggestibility, illusions of senses possible, loss of auditory receptivity and environmental awareness, heightened function of creative process. In full to deep sleep (lower delta), there is suspension of voluntary exercise and severe reduction or absence of conscious thought.

Through appropriate techniques anyone can achieve a trance level. The hypnotic process is very delicate, however, requiring a mixture a high patient motivation, trust, and confidence and a good measure of hypnotizability. Once an individual overcomes initial apprehension through understanding the truth about hypnosis, it is an easy experience—one in which the patient will awaken feeling more relaxed, at ease and positively motivated than before going into hypnosis.

Meditation. Meditation is a process of clearing the mind of conscious thought that allows higher information to be processed through the individual's consciousness. Meditation allows all mental activity to settle down and often results in the mind to become more peaceful, calm, and focused. In essence, meditation allows the awareness to become "rejuvenated." Meditation can be considered a technique or practice. It usually involves concentrating on an object, such as a flower, a candle, a sound or word, or the breath. Over time, the number of random thoughts occurring diminishes. More importantly, attachment to these thoughts progressively becomes less. The mediator may get caught up in a thought pattern, but once s/he becomes aware of this, attention is gently brought back to the object of concentration. Meditation can also be objectless, for example, consisting of just sitting. Experiences during meditation probably vary significantly from one individual to another, or at least if different techniques are involved. Relaxation, increased awareness, mental focus and clarity, and a sense of peace are the most common byproducts of meditation. While much has been written about the benefits of meditation, the best attitude is not to have any expectations when practicing. Having a sense of expectation of (positive) results is likely to create unnecessary strain in the practice.

Biofeedback.   Biofeedback is a method for learned control of physiological responses of the body. These responses can be either in the voluntary system, such as skeletal musculature, or in the involuntary, or autonomic, nervous system, such as heart rate, vascular responses (frequently indirectly measured as temperature), and sympathetic discharges (measured by the electrical skin response). The experimental data to support the feasibility of such learned controls first appeared in the 1950s with the work of psychologists such as Neal E. Miller. They increased in the 1960s, mostly through animal studies, although some experiments with humans were also performed. Next came a joint endeavor between experimental psychology and physiology. It became clear that certain dramatic gains could be achieved by using psychological techniques on patients with medical problems (Richter-Heinrich and Miller, 1983; Basmajian, 1989; Olton and Noonberg, 1980).

     Biofeedback can be used to control certain biological responses that cause health problems, such as headaches, chronically taut muscles from accidents or sports injuries, asthma, high blood pressure, and heart arrhythmias. It is often used instead of, or as a complement to, drugs in pain control. Biofeedback can be done with back-amplified breathing sounds, heart beat sounds, or tones generated from body activity. Green and Green (1977) demonstrated the many physical benefits of biofeedback at the Mayo Clinic. In learning to control body functions we are starting a whole process of self-development and self-awareness which generalizes from the specific to the normally unconscious activities. Our minds can control our body processes.

Other Altered-State Approaches to Coherent Thought Waves

Trance Dancing.   Trance is a technique of achieving an altered state by dancing, drumming, and/or chanting. As a shamanic practice, trance dancing alters our consciousness to enter nonordinary reality. Through ancient breath patterns, movement and rhythms which impact the brain, the trance dancer begins to see with their senses rather than their eyes. While the body dances, tremendous energy is awakened and spontaneous healing occurs; some are filled with visions of power animals, spirit guides, and nature. Altered state trance dancing is not a new social custom. The ancients have been doing it for centuries. The mid-1980s hippies of Goa used Euro-techno-beats to the same affect. Then it was Amsterdam, Tokyo, London, Melbourne, and major cities in the US, using frequencies and beats that transport the dancer into a trance state.

Ganzfeld. *Ganzfeld,* German for "total field," is a process to take a person into a hypnogogic state by listening to white noise or serene sounds of nature while covering the eyes with translucent goggles with a red bulb so that only a homogenous red glow is seen. In the *Ganzfeld,* first, all senses are stripped away, then, the conscious mind, so fantasies, imagery, memories, daydreams, and other expressions of the subliminal mind come into play. Recent *Ganzfeld* studies indicate telepathic communication possibilities—especially after subject training in altered state techniques (Roach, 1995; Bem and Honorton, 1994; Harvey, 1994).

Historically, Arctic explorers were the first people to describe the *Ganzfeld* effect. After they gazed into a frosty field of snowy white, they reported experiencing a form of snow blindness. Upon further research in the 1930s, it was discovered that when people gazed into a featureless field of vision (a *Ganzfeld*), they quickly and consistently entered a profoundly altered state. When someone is exposed to a *Ganzfeld,* they often experience a progression of effects that can be described as follows: (1) all color drains from your field of vision; (2) the size of your field of vision oscillates; (3) you "see" a swirling kaleidoscope of colors; (4) with practice the mind can be used in an extremely focused way.

Neurotechnology (Mind Machines). Neurotechnology refers to devices capable of producing changes in the electrical activity of the user's brain. When these occur, people may experience deep, stress-relieving relaxation, increased receptivity to information (with the ability to process and recall it), and automatic changes in dysfunctional thoughts, feelings, and behaviors. At times people enter a creative reverie with fertile ideas and solutions to problems. Every thought, feeling, sensation, and level of awareness has a corresponding brain wave pattern. Mind machines, through flickering lights and precisely controlled rhythmic tones, stimulate and synchronize the hemispheres of the brain while entraining the brain wave frequencies into desirable states of consciousness. In the 1930s, researchers found that repetitive light stimulation (strobing) caused brain waves to follow and pulse at the same frequency (entrainment). Today's mind machines have lights in glasses that pulse at predetermined frequencies, generally from 1 to 40 cycles per second (Hz). Most programs start out in the beta frequency range (13 to 40 Hz) and gradually slow (ramp) to the target range.

Reiki. *Reiki* (ray-key) is a Japanese word for "universal life force" and a system of natural healing that channels *Reiki* through the hands. *Reiki* accesses the source of life to heal the self and others on spiritual, mental, emotional, and physical levels. Reiki allows the source of well-being to enhance and balance natural life forces through nonintrusive therapeutic touch. Health maintenance, pain relief, mental quietude, and healing result from its application. In addition to health benefits, *Reiki* can open creative channels. Creative energy is the essence of all healing. In the late 1800s a specific formula for accessing universal life force was discovered in some Sanskrit sutras found in a Kyoto zendo by a scholar seeking knowledge of what the Buddha taught about healing. Mikao Usui was contemplating what he had learned when he received a transcendental initiation, the results of which were the abilities of healing by laying on of the hands and of sending healing over distance. Much later he realized that the experience of God is more essential to fulfillment of the purpose of life than the power of healing. Since *Reiki* is multidimensional it can be a catalytic factor in personal evolution no matter what beliefs are held. The innate ability to channel healing energy though the hands is awakened through a series of direct transmission initiations that attune and align energy centers in the body and hands. The *Reiki* energy can be a valuable way of achieving a trance level.

The Training Process for Metacommunication: Conscious States

While in conscious states, metacommunication processes to enhance intuition involve a variety of skills. Three are briefly highlighted here: lateral thinking, mind maps, and journal writing.

Lateral Thinking. Lateral thinking is the ability to arrive at an inspirational conclusion by using an "insight switch" in thinking to a different track. It is the ability to add a slight twist to the pattern of logical thinking to produce an unexpected answer. Lateral-inspirational thinking is a sudden leap from one line of logical thinking to another. The secret to the whole conscious process, as Edward

DeBono (1990) discovered, is a magic trigger, which creates a leap into an alterative logical thought pattern by introducing discontinuity.

As an example using "PO" as a triggering factor, in lateral thinking seminars Edward DeBono, gives a graphic demonstration. He hands one of the seminar attendees a dictionary and tells her to shut her eyes, open the dictionary, run her finger down the page and stop anywhere. She was then told to open her eyes and tell us the main heading word nearest her finger. The word, in this case, is *incubate*. The problem DeBono set will be solved with the use of this "trigger" word.

You are driving down town in your car and you suddenly realize that you need some milk. You see a corner store up ahead, pull up in front of this shop, and go inside to buy a carton. You leave your car running and the keys in the ignition. You are in the shop less than 60 seconds but as you come out, you find your car has been stolen. You report this to the police but realize you may never see your car again. However, a week later, you are walking down a side street in another part of town and you see your car, parked in front of a sleazy bar. You hastily glance into your car and see that it is locked. You are in an isolated part of town and you are naturally reluctant to go into the bar in search of the thief. You figure that by the time you find a phone and the police arrive, the car could have gone again. So, what to do?

This is the problem and we have a trigger word—*incubate*. Now concepts are developed around this word. For example: to hatch; to grow from nothing; egg—round object—stationary; inert object—capable of later life; to nurture under controlled conditions; addition of special conditions to make it function as intended; etc. There are often as many as forty such suggestions, but the ones mentioned are selected as the most likely key trigger concepts. Work around the concepts. The concept "inert object—capable of later life" evolves into the statement that the car is inert until the key is inserted and the engine starts. Someone else suggests that if the incubator was not switched on, the process could not complete itself. A logical train of thought from here suggests the fact that if the key could not be inserted into the ignition, the engine could not be started. If the door key were prevented from opening the door from the outside, the same effect could be achieved. Ah ha! It suggests that the door locks be jammed with bits of slit matchsticks in the keyholes, so that the key cannot be inserted into the car door. To further make the "incubator" inert, two tires can be let down. With only one spare tire available, the car cannot be made mobile quickly. Obviously, all this is not very practical if you are standing in front of your stolen car, but as you get more and more into the use of lateral thinking, then these "lateral" solutions pop into your mind spontaneously. A "random" word can trigger a lateral movement in ordinary thinking. By attaching one of these to your problem, a lateral influence is exerted by forcing you to think along a totally different track—a track that you would normally not consider. Any word will suffice. Some words, however, seem to give the best results. Here are some words that have worked well: ridiculous, invert, reverse, escape, kamikaze, deity, impossible, container, window, and time. In logical vertical thinking, we concentrate on what is relevant and ignore the rest. In lateral thinking we concentrate temporarily on something which is irrelevant and ignore the rest in the meantime.

Mind Mapping.   A mind map consists of a central word or concept; around the central word you draw the five to ten main ideas that relate to that word. You then take those words and again draw five to ten main ideas that relate to each of them. In this way an exponential number of related ideas can quickly be produced (Buzan, 1993). Mind mapping can be important in releasing intuition consciously. Originality is fostered with the technique. For example, two people draw mini mind maps around the idea *shoe*. (A mini mind map only goes one level deep—it only has words that are directly related to the central idea). If each person comes up with seven related words, how many do you think would be duplicates between the two people? The average is one word in common, and anything above two is unusual.

Journal Writing.   Journal writing is a way of getting in touch with creativity and intuition. Our minds help us think through and understand things up to a certain point, and writing can help us focus the mind to do this. But there's a deeper source of wisdom, creativity, and insight inside us that we're normally not used to being in touch with because we rely on the surface mind so much. The basic technique of journal writing, which is to simply make yourself open and to write down whatever comes to mind, to listen to your inner self and write what comes, provides a simple way to begin getting in touch with this deeper source of intelligence and inspiration. Journal writing is a process of asking questions and listening for answers. It helps us focus our mind to think through something, but it also helps us tap deeper resources than the mind. It's also a process of learning to be honest with ourselves, to find what is true for us.

References

Agor, W. (1984). *Intuitive Management: Integrating Left and Right Brain Management Skills.* Englewood Cliffs, NJ: Prentice Hall.

Barker, J. (1992). *Future Edge.* New York: William Morrow.

Basmajian, J. V. (1989). *Biofeedback: Principles and Practice for Clinicians,* 3rd ed. Baltimore: Williams and Wilkins.

Bem, D. J. and Honorton, C. (1994). Does Psi Exist? Replicable Evidence for an Anomalous Process of Information Transfer. *Psychological Bulletin* 15:4–18.

Bohm, D. (1982). *Wholeness and the Implicate Order.* New York: Routledge and Paul Kegan.

Briggs, J., and Peat, F. (1984). *Looking Glass Universe: The Emerging Science of Wholeness.* New York: Simon and Schuster.

Buzan, T. (1993). *The Mind Map Book.* New York: Plume.

Cade, M., and Coxhead, N. (1979). *The Awakened Mind.* New York: Delacorte Press.

Cappon, D. (1994). *Intuition and Management: Research and Application.* Westport, CT: Quorum Books.

Capra, F. (1984). The New Vision of Reality: Toward a Synthesis of Eastern Wisdom and Western Science. In S. Grof (ed.), *Ancient Wisdom and Modern Science.* Albany: SUNY Press, pp. 167–79.

Cushman, D. P., and King, S. S. (1993). Visions of Order: High-Speed Management in the Private Sector of the Global Marketplace. In A. Kozminski and D. P. Cushman (eds.), *Organizational Communication and Management.* Albany: SUNY Press.

Dean, D., and Mihalasky, J. (1974). *Executive ESP.* Englewood Cliffs, NJ: Prentice Hall.

DeBono, E. (1990). *Po: Beyond Yes and No.* Larchmont, NY: International Center of Creative Thinking.

Dumitrescu, I., and Kenyon, J. (1983). *Electrographic Imaging in Medicine and Biology: Imaging the Aura Using New Techniques.* Essex: Spearman.

Emery, M. (1994). *Intuition Workbook.* Englewood Cliffs, NJ: Prentice Hall.

Gerber, R. (1988). *Vibrational Medicine: New Choices for Healing Ourselves.* Santa Fe, NM: Bear and Company.

Goldberg, P. (1983). *The Intuitive Edge: Understanding and Developing Intuition.* Los Angeles: Jeremy P. Tarcher.

Green, E. and Green, A. (1977). *Beyond Biofeedback.* New York: Delacorte Press.

Harvey, L. (1994). Mental Telepathy in the Lab: Tests Show Psychic Ability Among Actors and Musicians. *Omni,* November, p. 20.

Herbert, N. (1993). *Elemental Mind: Human Consciousness and the New Physics.* New York: Penguin.

Hubel, D. H. (1979). *The Brain.* Scientific American, September, pp. 38, 188.

Jung, C. (1923). *Psychological Types.* San Diego, CA: Harcourt Brace.

King, S. S. and Cushman, D. P. (1995). Leading Organizational Change: A High-Speed Management Perspective. In *Communicating Organizational Change: A Management Perspective,* pp. 35–64.

Kotite, E. (1994). Gut Reaction: When Your Intuition Talks, Listen. It May Be the Best Advice You Get. *Entrepreneur,* April, p. 152.

Kriegel, R., and Brandt, D. (1996). *Sacred Cows Make the Best Burgers.* New York: Warner Books.

Leadbeater, C. W. (1927; reprinted 1977). *The Chakras.* Wheaton, IL: Theosophical Publishing House.

Martin, E. (1995). Communication in Asian Job Interviews. In D. P. Cushman and S. S. King (eds.), *Communicating Organizational Change: A Management Perspective.* Albany: SUNY Press, pp. 277–311.

Martin, E. (1996a). Cultural Blinders and Binders: Paradoxical Self Reference Criteria when Dealing with News Media. In A. Gutschelhofer and J. Scheff (eds.), *Paradoxical Management: Contradictions in Management— A Management of Contradictions.* Vienna: Linde Verlag, pp. 431–46.

Martin, E. (1996b). Hong Kong Advertising. In K. Frith (ed.), *Advertising in Asia: Communication, Culture and Consumption.* Ames: Iowa State University Press.

Martin E. (1997). Lessons in Marketing Strategies During Recession: From High Speed Management to Sun Tzu's *Art of War.* In D. P. Cushman and S. S. King (eds.), *Lessons from the Recession: A Management and Communication Perspective.* Albany: SUNY Press.

Mishlove, J. (1994). Intuition: The Source of True Knowing. *Noetic Sciences Review,* Spring, pp. 31–36.

Motoyama, H., and Brown, R. (1978). *Science and the Evolution of Consciousness: Chakras, Ki, and Psi.* Brookline, MA: Autumn Press.

Nadel, L. (1996). *Sixth Sense: How to Unlock Your Intuitive Brain.* London: Prion.

Naisbett, J. and Aburdene, P. (1985). *Re-Inventing the Corporation.* New York: Warner Books.

Olton, D. and Noonberg, A. (1980). *Biofeedback: Clinical Applications in Behavioral Medicine.* Englewood Cliffs, NJ: Prentice Hall.

Pelton, W. J., Sackmann, S., and Boguslaw, R. (1990). *Touch Choices: The Decision-Making Styles of America's Top 50 CEOs.* Homewood, IL: Dow Jones–Irwin.

Pribram, K. (1984). The Holographic Hypothesis of Brain Function: A Meeting of the Minds. In S. Grof (ed.), *Ancient Wisdom and Modern Science.* Albany: SUNY Press, pp. 167–79.

Richter-Heinrich, E., and Miller, N. E. (1983). *Biofeedback: Basic Problems in Clinical Applications.* New York: Elsevier.

Roach, M. (1995). A Postcard from the Twilight Zone, *Health,* July–August, pp. 42–43.

Rowan, R. (1986). *The Intuitive Manager.* New York: Little, Brown and Co.

Russell, E. (1971). *Design for Destiny.* New York: Ballantine Books.

Ryerson, K. (1983). *Flower Essences and Vibrational Healing.* Albuquerque, NM: Brotherhood of Life.

Simon, N. (1989). Making Management Decisions: The Role of Intuition and Emotions. In W. Agor (ed.), *Intuition in Organizations.* Newbury Park, CA: Sage Publications.

Thackray, J. (1995). That Vital Spark. *Management Today,* July, p. 56.

Vaughn, F. (1979). *Awakening Intuition.* Garden City, NY: Anchor.

Wendell, M. D., Wendell, G. W., and Willis, M. B. (1988). *Creative Color: An Analysis and Synthesis of Useful Color Knowledge.* Phoenix, AZ: EFP.

Whitton, J. (1974). Ramp Functions in EEG Power Spectra During Actual or Attempted Paranormal Events, *New Horizons* 1:174–83.

11

The Strategic Impact of Affect on Decision-Making

John Penhallurick

The whole Western philosophical tradition has been based on a clear distinction between emotion and reason. The common approach to emotion in the managerial literature is to see it as the antithesis of reason; as a contaminant that managers should seek to avoid in pursuit of organizational excellence. And certainly, most managers express such a view when asked for their opinion. As an unnamed manager stated, in response to the question, Emotion and reason, are they separate things for you? replied:

> Quite different, quite different. How I feel about something is quite different from a logical reasoning process to come to a conclusion. I can feel good or bad about a decision I've made, but the process that I go through, the reasoning is quite different from the feelings at the end. The best decisions are the ones that I make when I think through very logically and reasonably, keeping my feelings to one side. (Health Report, 1996)

Psychology, too has until recently seen emotion as of peripheral interest:

> most empirical research in psychology has proceeded on the implicit assumption that behavior, cognition, and emotion can be studied as separate, independent faculties. . . . Of the two paradigms that have dominated our discipline so far, neither behaviorism nor the more recent cognitivist approach have paid much attention to the study of affect. (Forgas, 1995, 41)

However, we believe that theories should deal with people as they are, not as we might like them to be. For example, most of the published literature on causal reasoning assumes managers utilize covariation information. Salancik and Porac (1986), however, suggest that in complex situations, such a procedure is beyond human information processing capabilities, and propose that "individuals derive much of their knowledge of causal importance by abstracting from snapshots of the associational structure existing in the environment as a whole" (p. 87).

We wish to argue that affect plays an integral role in human information processing and behavior, and hence that any adequate theory of organizational communication must take affect into account. Since organizations have their being and are continuously restructured through communication, it follows that organizational communication practices are fundamental to organizational excellence. And since affect plays a key role in communication, any theory that seeks to characterize how to obtain organizational excellence must also take affect into account.

The period since about 1980 has seen an increase in the number of studies dealing with affect. However, the dominant view remains that individuals participate in rational, logical, and sequential behavior when making decisions or performing other cognitive functions. According to Sypher, Donohew, and Higgins (1988):

> From a psychological perspective, it is agreed that stimulation of the brain and energy for the body is needed by the human system. Arousal is fundamental to human behavior, and more than one third of the brain's volume involves pleasure centers seeking continuous stimulation. However, whilst the importance of emotion has been recognised, and more recently has increasingly been the focus of research, it has also suffered years of inattention from many disciplinary discourses. (p. 2)

A knowledge of human information processing suggests that the idea that reason is the antithesis of affect is fallacious, just as the notion of absolute objectivity is an illusion. On the latter point, the social construction of reality necessarily involves a set of values, beliefs, and assumptions—in short, an ideological position.[1] Affect so permeates our thinking that that notion of affect-free cognition is an illusion. Rather than an absolute opposition between the two, we must think in terms of gradient phenomena, in terms of the degree and kind of affectual influence on cognition.

An important part of the traditional reluctance to deal with affect is surely the definitional difficulties attending any discussion of affect. There are issues of the boundaries of affect, of cortical versus limbic dimensions, linguistic issues, issues of duration, and

of directedness. Hence, it is necessary to spend some time characterizing the terms and systems we are dealing wit. We will follow
Park, Sims, and Motowidlo (1986) in using the term *affect* as the
most broad and encompassing term. We will reserve the term *emotion* for the more cognitive dimensions of affect.

Let us turn first, then, to the cognitive dimensions of affect.
Here we encounter our knowledge of emotions, sometimes referred
to as "cold" emotion. We can discuss fear, anger, and joy without
significantly experiencing the corresponding feelings. The precise
nature of schematic representations of emotions is an interesting
question because of a potential conflict between the universal aspects of affect and obvious differences in the way different languages
provide words for affect.

One of the best discussions of this topic is the study by Ortony,
Clore, and Collins (1990), *The Cognitive Structure of Emotions.* They
define emotions as "valenced reactions to events, agents or objects,
with their particular nature being determined by the way in which
the eliciting situation is construed" (p. 13). The fact that emotions
are valenced is what distinguishes them from other states, such as
cognitive states (e.g., "surprise," or "interest") and body states (e.g.,
"sleepy" or "droopy"). The definition by Ortony et al. also refers to
eliciting conditions, which are part of the universal basis of emotions. In chapter 3, they distinguish three major ingredients of appraisal: goals, standards, and attitudes, which constitute, respectively,
the criteria for evaluating events, the actions of agents, and objects.
The other basis for some universal features of emotions is the common physiological endowment of the limbic system, which is discussed below.[2]

Ortony and colleagues (1990) define emotion *types,* as opposed
to what they call "the multitude of discriminable emotional states"
(p. 15). First, they classify emotions as *valenced reactions to consequences of events* (which involve the types "pleased" or "displeased"),
actions of agents ("approving" and "disapproving"), and *aspects of
objects* ("liking" or "disliking"). In the case of *consequences of events,*
these are further subdivided into *consequences for others* versus
consequences for self. Consequence for others, in turn, is divided into
desirable for others (with the types "happy for" and "resentment") or
undesirable for others (with the types "gloating" and "pity"). *Consequences of events* focussing on *consequences for self* is subdivided
into *prospects relevant* (with the types "hope" and "fear") in turn
subdivided by *confirmed* ("satisfaction" and "fears confirmed") and
disconfirmed ("relief" and "disappointment") and *prospects irrelevant*

("joy" and "distress") in the domain of *well-being. Valenced reactions to actions of agents* focus on *self agent* (leading to "pride" or "shame") or *other agent* ("admiration" and "reproach") in the domain of *attribution*. The domains of *well-being* and *attribution* lead to the joint domain of *well-being/attribution* compounds ("gratification," "remorse," "gratitude," and "anger"). Finally, under *valenced reactions to aspects of objects,* we have the domain of *attraction,* involving "love" and "hate" (cf. Ortony, Clore and Collins, 1990, p. 19).

The concept of emotion types should be distinguished from words referring to emotions in different languages. Different words may relate to different degrees of intensity of a basic emotion type, as in the case of English "concerned," "frightened," and "petrified," which manifest different degrees of the type *fear.* Varying numbers of words in one language relate to each type, from many words to one type (as with *fear*), to only one word (e.g., English "relief" for *pleased about the disconfirmation of the prospect of an undesirable event*), to in some cases, no one lexical item (e.g., at least in English, for *displeased about the confirmation of the prospect of an undesirable event*).

Affect also plays an important role in other schemas. Schemas, which structure semantic memory, are largely derived from generalizing across our memories of specific events, stored in episodic memory. These memories of specific events include our affective response(s) to the event, and clearly, we generalize across those affective responses as well as across more objective features of events. So it is likely that our script schema for a visit to the dentist will include a feeling of apprehension, while our script schema for a visit to a favorite restaurant would include feelings of pleasurable anticipation.

There is clear evidence that these emotional tags serve as a powerful organizing principle for cognition. According to Bower's (1981) network model, affective states have a "specific node of unit in memory that . . . is also linked with propositions describing events from one's life during which that emotion was aroused. . . . Activation of an emotion node also spreads activation throughout the memory structures to which it is connected" (p. 135). Evidence from this comes from the well-known mood congruity effect (cf. Bower 1981), namely, that events conveying an emotional tone which matches an individual's current mood are attended to most closely and learned best. One can also cite mood state–dependent retention; that is, things can be better recalled from memory when the mood state at the time of the formation of the memory matches the mood state at the time of recall. If you are feeling sad, it is easier to recall other sad memories than it is happy ones.

The other dimension of affect centers on the limbic system. This "gut" level of affect centers on the hypothalamus, but it also involves other brain structures, including the amygdala, hippocampus, and limbic cortex. The limbic system is not simply an evolutionary relic on the way to the triumph of the cerebral cortex; it is fundamentally involved in thinking. Discussing the nature of thoughts and consciousness, Guyton (1991) states: "Each thought almost certainly involves simultaneous signals in many portions of the cerebral cortex, thalamus, limbic system and reticular formation of the brain stem" (p. 643). He continues:

> Therefore we might formulate a definition of a thought in terms of neural activity as follows: A thought results when the "pattern" of stimulation of many different parts of the nervous system at the same time and in definite sequence, probably involving most importantly the cerebral cortex, the thalamus, the limbic system, and the upper reticular formation of the brain stem. This is called the "holistic" theory of thoughts. The stimulated areas of the limbic system, thalamus and reticular formation are believed to determine the general nature of thought, giving it such qualities as pleasure, displeasure, pain, comfort, crude modalities of sensation, localization to gross areas of the body, and other general characteristics. On the other hand, the stimulated areas of the cerebral cortex determine the discrete characteristics of the thought. (p. 643)

Most communication research on the limbic system has been done in the context of mass communication effects: specifically, possible effects of violent or sexually arousing material. Such research is particularly associated with the work of Dolf Zillman. Zillman (1982, p. 54) distinguishes between cortical and limbic arousal but tends to treat the latter in a "black box" fashion. In fact, his emphasis on the "non-specificity of arousal," which is important for his theory of "Transfer of Excitation,"[3] treats the limbic dimension of affect as undifferentiated: "the bulk of the evidence shows that more or less all emotions are fed by elevated sympathetic activity in the autonomic nervous system. . . . For all practical purposes any feedback of an arousal state is non-specific and only indexes its intensity" (p. 59).

This is a somewhat oversimplified view of the functions of the limbic system. Until recently, one could not expect any familiarity with the anatomy and functions of the limbic system except with specialist audiences. With the rise to the best-seller list of Goleman's

(1996) *Emotional Intelligence,* I am sure that well-read Americans discuss the intricacies of the amygdala and hippocampi over martinis.[4] However, in a discussion of affect, it is important to have at least a general understanding how the limbic system contributes to affect, and to cognition in general.

A key structure in the limbic system is the hypothalamus, which controls most of the vegetative and endocrine functions of the body, as well as many aspects of emotional behavior. We are all surely aware of the physical symptoms that accompany strong arousal, including elevated heart rate and an increase in perspiration. However, we will say no more about those vegetative and endocrine aspects and focus on the contributions to affect. As Guyton (1991) notes: "several limbic structures, including the hypothalamus, are particularly concerned with the *affective* nature of sensory sensations—that is, whether the sensations are *pleasant* or *unpleasant*" (p. 652). Specifically, stimulation of the lateral hypothalamus can lead to overt rage and fighting; stimulation of the ventromedical nucleus can cause satiety and tranquility; stimulation of a thin zone of the periventricular nucleus, and also of the central gray area of the mesencephalon, usually leads to fear and punishment. Guyton (1991) stresses the importance of reward and punishment in behavior:

> Almost everything we do is related in some way to reward and punishment. If we are doing something that is rewarding, we continue to do it; if it is punishing, we cease to do it. Therefore the reward and punishment centers undoubtedly constitute one of the most important of all the controllers of bodily activities, our drives, our aversions, our motivations.[5] (p. 655)

Other parts of the limbic system play an important role in thinking and feeling. The amygdala "is believed to help pattern the person's behavioral response so that it is appropriate for each occasion" (657). According to Guyton, "The amygdala receives neuronal signals from all portions of the limbic cortex as well as from the neocortex of the temporal, parietal, and occipital lobes, especially from the auditory and visual association areas. Because of these multiple connections, the amygdala has been called the 'window' through which the limbic system sees the place of the person in the world" (p. 656). In addition, stimulation of the amygdala can "cause a pattern of rage, escape, punishment and fear similar to the rage pattern elicited from the hypothalamus as described earlier. And stimulation of other nuclei can give reactions of reward and pleasure" (ibid.).[6]

The hippocampus appears to be even more involved in information processing, as well as affective responses:

> reward and punishment play a major role in determining the importance of information and especially whether or not the information will be stored in memory. A person rapidly becomes habituated to indifferent stimuli but learns assiduously any sensory experience that causes either pleasure or punishment. Yet what is the mechanism by which this occurs? It has been suggested that the hippocampus provides the drive that causes translation of immediate memory into secondary memory—that is, it transmits some type of signal or signals that seems to make the mind rehearse over and over the new information until permanent storage takes place. Whatever the mechanism, without the hippocampi *consolidation* of long-term memories of verbal or symbolic types do not take place.[7] (Guyton, 1991:657)

Finally, among the structures of the limbic system, the limbic cortex plays a major role in affect and cognition. As Goleman (1996) notes: "The brain's damper switch for the amygdala surges appears to lie . . . in the prefrontal lobes" (p. 24). He continues:

> Ordinarily the prefrontal areas govern our emotional reactions from the start. The largest projection of sensory information from the thalamus . . . goes not to the amygdala, but to the neocortex and its many centers for taking in and making sense of what is being perceived; that information and our response to it is coordinated by the prefrontal lobes, the seat of planning and organising actions toward a goal, including emotional ones.[8] (p. 25)

From what we have said, it makes little sense to ask whether affect causes cognition or vice versa. Rather, the two strands are continual processes that are interwoven in complex ways. We prefer the conceptualization of Lewis et al. (1984, pp. 285–86), which places cognition, and emotion in a behavioral sequence (figure 11.1).

Figure 11.1

Emotional behavior	E---------E--E------------E--E--------E--E
Cognitive behavior	--------C--------C--C------------C-------C
Time	
	t_1 t_2 t_n
Sampling window	____ w_1 _____ w_2 _____ w_n ____

In this figure, E represents emotional behavior and C cognitive behavior as they occur over time. If behavior is sampled between times t_1 and t_2 an observer would see emotion following cognition. If the behavior is sampled between t_2 and t_3, an observer would see emotion preceding cognition. In fact, a wider time scale would reveal the continuous interplay between emotion and cognition.

To summarize the preceding discussion: affect involves a complex set of structures and activities both in the cortical and the limbic system. The limbic system is not simply an undifferentiated "engine," but itself discriminates to some extent between different kinds and degrees of affect. Aspects of the limbic system are also fundamentally involved in all information processing. The cortical system contains a classification of emotions, but affectual memory units play an important organizing role in memory. Although the cortical and limbic systems are distinct, they closely interact. "Feelings," as opposed to simple knowledge of emotions, necessarily involves limbic arousal. "Feelings" may be present as *mood,* in which case we are dealing with "low-intensity, diffuse and relatively enduring affective states without a salient antecedent cause and therefore little cognitive content (e.g., feeling good or feeling bad)" or as *differentiated affective responses* which "are more intense, short-lived and usually have a definite cause and clear cognitive content" (Forgas, 1992, p. 230). One is forced to conclude that it is impossible to separate affect and cognition, or "rational" thought, because the idea of the purely rational, purely analytical manager is a myth.

There are a number of accounts on the role of affect in managerial roles. To mention a few: Park et al. (1986, pp. 223–31) summarize the role of affect in performance appraisal tasks and find significant influence from affect as a result of both mood and differentiated affective responses. Ellsworth and Smith (1988) and Kellner, Ellsworth, and Edwards (1993) demonstrate the role of affect in judgmental outcomes. A recent valuable addition to theories on the role of affect on managerial behavior is Forgas (1995).

Forgas identifies two main models of the role of affect in judgmental tasks. The first is "Affect-as-information," which "suggests that rather than computing a judgment on the basis of recalled features of a target, individuals may ask themselves: 'How do I feel about it' and in doing so, they may mistake feelings due to a pre-existing state as a reaction to the target" (Schwarz, 1990, p. 529, cited in Forgas, 1995, p. 43). The other main contender is "Affect-Priming Mechanisms," a theory which suggests that "affect can indirectly inform social judgments by facilitating access to related cognitive categories" (Forgas,

1995, p. 44). The Affect-Priming Mechanism can explain a good deal in relation to selective attention, selective encoding, selective retrieval, and patterns of association and interpretation. However, Forgas points out that both fail in certain cases.

In their place, Forgas (1995) proposes a multiprocess Affect Infusion Model (AIM). According to the AIM, "different processing strategies imply different kinds of mood effects on judgments, including the possibility of no mood effects or mood incongruence" (p. 47). The AIM is said to involve two major assumptions. The first is Process Mediation, that is, that the nature and extent of mood effects on judgments largely depends on what kind of processing strategy is adopted by a judge.[9] The second is that of Effort Minimalization, that is, "social actors are effort-minimising information processors inclined to adapt the simplest and least effortful processing strategy as long as it satisfies the minimal contextual requirements" (Forgas, 1995, p. 46). The amount of effort that a judge should be prepared to extend should depend on a limited range of variables: features of the target, of the judge, and of the situation.

In place of the single strategy of classical information processing, Forgas (1995) proposes four kinds of strategies. The first two, Direct Access and Motivated Strategy, "involve relatively closed information research processes offering little opportunity for affect infusion to occur"[10] (p. 46). Direct Access involves the rapid retrieval of rich, preexisting stored evaluation. Since it involves "little or no constructive elaboration and the strongly cued retrieval of an existing crystallised judgment," it is likely to be quite robust and resistant to affective distortions. Motivated Strategy is likely to involve low affect infusion because "the pattern of information search and the outcome of the judgment are guided by a prior motivational goal" (p. 47).

The second two, the Heuristic Strategy and the Substantive Strategy, are High Affect Infusion Strategies. Heuristic processing is said to be most likely when "the target is simple or highly typical, the personal relevance of the judgment is low, there are no specific motivational objectives, the judge has limited cognitive capacity, and the situation does not demand accuracy or detailed consideration" (Forgas, 1995, p. 47). In these circumstances, judgments may be influenced by irrelevant associations stemming from mood. The Substantive Strategy "requires a subject to learn and interpret novel information about a target and relate this information to preexisting knowledge structures. . . . This strategy . . . is more likely when the target is complex or atypical and the judge has no specific motivation to pursue, has adequate cognitive capacity, and is motivated to be accurate" (p. 47). According to Forgas, the AIM predicts that affective influences on judgments should be greater the more extensive and constructive the processing used. He notes "This counterintuitive prediction has received empirical support in recent years" (p. 47).

Forgas's research further illuminates the rich interplay between affect and cognition. Our discussion of the role of affect in information processing and behavior leads naturally into the idea of emotional intelligence, which supplies the title of Goleman's (1966) book. Goleman draws on two seminal studies of the affectual dimensions of intelligence. One is the work of Howard Gardiner on multiple intelligences, summarized in Gardner (1993). Gardiner rejects the idea implicit in most IQ tests of restricting "intelligence" to the ability to answer items on such tests. He defines intelligence as entailing "the ability to solve problems or fashion products that are of consequence in a particular cultural setting" (p. 15). He proposes seven types of intelligence: musical, bodily-kinesthetic, logico-mathematical, linguistic, spatial, interpersonal, and intrapersonal (pp. 17–24). It is the last two kinds of intelligence which relate most clearly to the emotional dimensions of thought and behavior, and which form the focus of other seminal papers.

Drawing on Thorndike and Stein's (1937) concept of "social intelligence," as the "ability to understand and manage people" (p. 275), Salovey and Mayer (1990) define emotional intelligence as "a subset of social intelligence that involves the ability to monitor one's own and others' feelings and emotions, to discriminate among them and to use this information to guide one's thinking and actions" (p. 189). They continue: "We posit that life tasks such as those described by Cantor and her colleagues[11] and constructive thinking are laden with affective information, that this affective information must be processed . . . and that individuals may differ in the skill with which they do so" (p. 189). Salovey and Mayer's conceptualization of emotional intelligence (see p. 190) analysis emotional intelligence in terms of

1. *Appraisal and expression of emotion,* which may be in the *self,* and hence *verbal* or *nonverbal,* or in *others,* and hence involve *nonverbal perception* or *empathy*

2. *Regulation of emotion,* either in the *self* or in *others*

3. *Utilization of emotion,* which may involve *flexible planning, creative thinking, redirected attention,* or *motivation.*

Goleman argues, we believe correctly, that emotional intelligence is an essential ability for managers, which brings us directly back to the question of organizational excellence. In chapter 10, "Managing with Heart," Goleman (1996, p. 150) applies emotional intelligence to three areas: being able to air grievances as helpful critiques, creating an atmosphere in which diversity is valued rather than a source of friction, and networking effectively.

In conclusion, I would like to focus on the significance of the affectual dimension of organizational communication on what is probably the greatest issue in organizations throughout the Western world at present: the massive wave of layoffs, and the stress caused by that trend. A cover story in *Business Review Weekly* (March 11, 1996) summarized the situation:

> The restructuring of corporate America has carried enormous social costs. Nitiu Nohira, a professor at the Harvard business school, tracked the changes that engulfed 100 of America's largest companies . . . from 1978 to the present. He found that on a net basis, 22% of the workforce of these companies, or 3 million workers, was laid off during the period, and 77% of all layoffs involved white-collar workers.

Nor is this trend restricted to the United States. In a book of immense importance, Lester Thurow (1996) points out that the downsizing trend has spread to Europe and Japan. He points out that in the first four months of 1994, 180,000 downsizings were announced in Germany, and that Germany expects to lose 500,000 jobs in major sectors such as the automobile, machine tool, electrical, and chemical industries.

The causes of this trend are complex, and we do not suggest that companies can, or should, return to the days of life-long job security. And there is no denying the U.S. economy's impressive performance in relation to generating new jobs, a low unemployment rate, a striking improvement in productivity, and low inflation. However, the American Stock Exchange's initially favorable reaction to massive layoffs does not necessarily amount to the last word on best management practice.

There are at least two questions here. First, are massive layoffs a good thing for the company? And second, if it is necessary to lay off staff, what is the best way to do it? Although in many cases some layoffs may be unavoidable, there is increasing evidence that the way of the ax may not be best. In an article by John Connolly (1996), Peter Drucker is critical of CEOs such as Al Dunlap, famous for his downsizing of Scott Paper: "This edition [January 15, 1996] of *Business Week* has a scathing review of Dunlap."

> When you look at the results of down-sizing they're very disappointing. In the first year, the stock goes through the roof. In the second year, they're doing as badly as before. Sure many companies are overstaffed, particularly in middle management, but the meat axe isn't the answer. . . . A lot of downsizing is amputating before the diagnosis. The executives are doing what the security analysts want. They take action and the markets applaud. There is no one who knows less about business than security analysts. They think business is about finance. I know. I was one. (p. 145)

There is also evidence that firms who had not laid off workers, but who had concentrated on growth showed greater profitability than those who savagely cut their workforce. *Business Week*'s Keith Hammonds (1996) wrote:

> The new paradigm says that layoffs are not inevitable. Rather stability is more effective and easier for society to take. . . . The old way: Wells Fargo Co. makes a hostile bid for First Interstate Banking Corp., threatening 8,000 jobs and enraging Californians. The new way: Steel producer Nucor Corp. manages down-turns by gearing down to four-day workweeks; employees lose pay but keep their jobs. Southwest Airlines Co. avoids job cuts by sticking to its low cost strategy through good times and bad; workforce stability, it thinks, gives it an edge over rivals. (p. 38)

It is easy to understand the negative effects of savage layoffs in terms of the affectual results with the remaining employees. The result will inevitably be fear, resentment, and anger. As Allan Sloan (1996) observed in a *Newsweek* article: "You can practically smell the fear and anger in white-collar America, because no-one in CEO-land seems to care" (p. 69). Such emotion do not lead to high productivity. If they did, prison workshops would set world benchmarks for productivity.

As Karen Pennar (1996) of *Business Week* states, quoting Shoshana Zuboff, a Harvard business school professor and author of *The Age of the Smart Machine,* "only a handful of companies have committed the resources to help their workforces develop new skills" (p. 34). The article continues:

> The only way they can beat out their competitors is by enabling their larger asset—their workforce—to be more innovative in using the technology to create new products and new services that sell well. Instead, throughout its decade-long restructuring, Corporate America has primarily viewed workers as liabilities rather than assets.

Lester Thurow (1996) describes a world where the classical notion of competitive advantage has lost its meaning. The traditional sources of competitive advantage, such as availability of raw materials and capital, have been nullified by the new global economy. The key to success in the highly fluid world which Thurow (1996) depicts is knowledge and brainpower. "Today knowledge and skills now stand alone as the only source of comparative advantage. They have become the key ingredient in the late twentieth century's location of economic activity. Silicon Valley and Route 128 are where they are simply because that is where the brainpower is. They have nothing else going for them" (p. 68).

But just when key knowledge workers are more important than ever, the worldwide downsizing trend means that such workers have no reason to be committed to the company. With downsizing, companies are unwilling to invest in training. The net result of this trend, as Thurow points out is "less skills investment at exactly the time that more skills investment is needed. The system evolves toward less commitment and less investment just as it should be evolving in the opposite direction" (p. 288).

The second question raised above relates to the manner in which layoffs are done. Keith Hammons (1996) describes the "middle path" that is emerging: It "concedes, too, that employers bear an obligation to help workers through transitions. And it attempts to align the interests of investors, managers, and employees, aiming to share both the risks and the rewards of doing business" (p. 37). He continues: "Why should employers buy into this? Certainly the profit motive remains as relevant as ever: companies that can't compete are the ones that shed jobs and abandon communities." Some examples of the middle way in action: "At Starbucks Corp, which provides all employees—even part-time store clerks—with health insurance, stock options, and training and career counselling, worker turnover is less than 60% annually, well below the 300% restaurant industry average. When Pinnacle Brands Inc. lost $40 million of trading-card business to the 1994 baseball strike, it challenged workers to come up with new products and cost-cutting ideas; they did, and sales jumped 80% in two years. No jobs lost" (p. 37).

Such actions reflect emotional intelligence in action. We have moved from a theoretical demonstration that affect is important in thinking and behavior, to a practical demonstration of the values of emotional intelligence in management. We have tried to demonstrate that affect is complex, and that is closely involved with cognition and judgment and decision-making. We have presented the idea of emotional intelligence and related it to management practices. In conclusion, affect matters!

Notes

1. I hasten to add that this does not commit me to the postmodernist view in which all interpretations are equally valid. I agree with the view advanced by Thomas Sowell (1991, p. 46) that "the historic sharing of cultural advances, until they became the common inheritance of the human race, implied much more than cultural diversity. It implied that some cultural features were not only different from others but *better* than others."

2. Color displays a similar combination of common physiological universals, common universal real-world phenomena (lightwaves of different frequencies), and language-specific terms. In terms of the common physiological basis of feelings described below, it would be surprising if the basic distinctions of Ortony et al.'s scheme are not lexicalized in all human languages.

3. "Because of the comparatively slow decay of autonomic arousal . . . and the individual's capacity to re-cognize stimulus changes and to select an appropriate response quasi-instantaneously . . . , residues of excitation from a preceding affective reaction will combine with excitation produced by a subsequent affective stimulation and thereby causes an *overly intense* affective reaction to the subsequent stimulus" (Zillman 1982, p. 59).

4. Goleman's account in chapter 2, drawing on the work of the neuroscientist J. LeDoux, describes how in crises, sensory signals can cause the amygdala to respond before the neocortex, triggering a near-instantaneous fight-or-flight response. See LeDoux (1992, 1993, 1994). However the emotional dimensions of organization life do not, as a rule, trigger such dramatic responses.

5. The fact that certain feelings are "hard-wired" in the amygdala suggests a possible alternative basis for a universal theory of emotions. We might start with these hard-wired feelings instead of Ortony et al.'s (1990) analysis of the perceived world.

6. However, Guyton describes such reactions as "rare." Presumably, they are involved with the extreme crisis response described in chapter 2 of Goleman's (1996) book.

7. Recent neurophysiological research using magnetic resonance imaging and positron emission tomography has revealed that information which is going to be stored in long-term memory is first stored in the hippocampus. At night, when the person is in deep sleep, the hippocampus fires, and there is an answering pattern of firing in the neocortex, indicating the transfer of the information to long-term memory.

8. Goleman (1996) further notes: "One way the prefrontal cortex acts as an efficient manager of emotion . . . is by dampening the signals for activation sent out by the amygdala and other limbic centers. . . . The key "off" switch for distressing emotion seems to be the left prefrontal lobe. Neuropsychologists studying moods in patients with injuries to parts of the frontal lobs have determined that one of the tasks of the left frontal lobe is to act as a neural thermostat, regulating unpleasant emotions. The right prefrontal lobes are a seat of negative feelings like fear and aggression, while the left lobes keep those raw emotions in check, probably by inhibiting the right lobe" (p. 26).

9. Contrast this with the "single-process assumptions implied by classical information-processing models in cognitive research: these models assumed robust, universal and relatively context-insensitive mechanisms" (Forgas, 1995, p. 46).

10. Forgas (1995) notes: "Although direct access judgments should not be infused by current mood, this need not mean they are devoid of affective quality: accessing a past affective experience can be an important component of many stored, crystallized judgments" (p. 46).

11. Specifically, filling individual personality styles in social situations. See Cantor et al. (1987).

References

Bower, G. H. (1981). Mood and Memory. *American Psychologist* 36:120–48.

———— and Cohen, P. R. (1982). Emotional Influences in Memory and Thinking: Data and Theory. M. S. Clark and S. T. Fiske (eds.), *Affect and Cognition*. Hillsdale, NJ: Erlbaum, pp. 291–332.

———— and Weiner, B. (1984). Affective Consequences of Ability Versus Effort Ascriptions: Controversies, Resolutions and Quandaries. *Journal of Educational Psychology* 76:148–58.

Cantor, N., Norem, J. K., Niedanthal, P. M., Langston, C. A., and Brower, A. M. (1987). Life Tasks, Self-Concept Ideals, and Cognitive Strategies in a Life Transition. *Journal of Personality and Social Psychology* 53:1178–91.

Connolly, J. (1996). The Old Man and the Sea-Change. *The Bulletin,* January 23–30, pp. 144–45.

Ellsworth, P. C. and Smith, C. A. (1988). From Appraisal to Emotion: Differences among Unpleasant Feelings. *Motivation and Emotion,* 12:271–302.

Forgas, J. P. (1992). Affect in Social Judgments and Decisions: A Multiprocess Model. In M. Zanna (ed.), *Advances in Experimental Social Psychology,* vol. 25, San Diego: Academic Press, pp. 227–75.

———. (1995). Mood and Judgment: The Affect Infusion Model (AIM). *Psychological Bulletin* 117:39–66.

Gardner, H. (1993). *Multiple Intelligences: The Theory in Practice.* New York: Basic Books.

Goleman, D. (1996). *Emotional Intelligence.* London: Bloomsbury.

Guyton, A. C. (1991). *Textbook of Medical Physiology,* 8th ed. Philadelphia: W. B. Saunders.

Hammonds, K. H. (1996). Writing a new social contract. *Business Week,* March 11, pp. 37–38.

Health Report. (1996). Radio National, Australian Broadcasting Corporation, April 22.

Kellner, D., Ellsworth, P. C. and Edwards, K. (1993). Beyond Simple Pessimism: Effects of Anger and Sadness on Social Perception. *Journal of Personality and Social Psychology* 64:740–52.

LeDoux, J. (1992). Emotions and the Limbic System Concept. *Concepts in Neuroscience* 2.

———. (1993). Emotional Memory Systems in the Brain. *Behavioral Brain Research* 58.

———. (1994). Emotion, Memory and the Brain. *Scientific American,* June.

Ortony, A., Clore, G. L., and Collins, A. (1990). *The Cognitive Structure of Emotions.* Cambridge: Cambridge University Press.

Park, O. S., Sims, H. P., and Motowidlo, S. J. (1986). Affect in Organizations. In M. P. Sims and D. A. Gioia (eds.). *The Thinking Organization.* San Francisco: Jossey-Bass, pp. 215–37.

Pennar, K. (1996). Economic Anxiety. *Business Week,* March 11, pp. 33–34.

Salancik, G. R., and Porac, J. F. (1986). Distilled Ideologies: Values Derived from Causal Reasoning in Complex Environments. In M. P. Sims and D. A. Gioia (eds.), *The Thinking Organization.* San Francisco: Jossey-Bass, pp. 75–101.

Schwarz, N. (1990). Feeling as Information: Informational and Motivational Functions of Affective States. In E. T. Higgins and R. Sorrentino (eds.),

Handbook of Motivation and Cognition: Foundations of Social Behavior: Foundations of Social Behavior, vol. 2. New York: Guildford Press, pp. 527–61.

Sims, M. P., and Gioia, D. A. (eds.) (1986). *The Thinking of Organization.* San Francisco: Jossey-Bass.

Sloan, A. (1996). The Hit Men. *Newsweek* in *The Bulletin,* March 11, p. 69.

Sowell, T. (1991). Cultural Diversity: A World View. *American Enterprise,* pp. 44–55.

Thorndike, R. L., and Stein S. (1937). An Evaluation of Attempts to Measure Social Intelligence. *Psychological Bulletin* 34:275–84.

Thurow, L. C. (1996). *The Future of Capitalism: How Today's Economic Forces Shape Tomorrow's World.* New York: Morrow.

12

Training Strategies for Excellence: Selecting the Appropriate Models for the Specific Task

Susanne R. Morris and Robert C. Morris

Amid the turbulence of change confronting organizations in the twenty-first century, a great deal has been written about the need of organizations to resize, refocus, and regroup. Substantial literature has appeared which details how this is being done by successful and less successful organizations. We have learned about the strategies and tactics of reengineering, downsizing, merging, and continuous improvement, to list but a few responses or organizations to these pressures.

Underlying many of these responses has been a drive for excellence: better customer service, better use of information, greater market share, meeting global competition, greater profitability, enhanced flexibility, greater adaptability, faster response, shorter total cycle time, and more effectiveness and economy. There are no doubt other motivating factors as well.

Within this context, relatively less has been written about the implications of these changes for training. The opportunity to contribute to a new collection of essays focusing on excellence in communicating organizational strategy is especially timely for reflection on the substantial changes occurring in public and private-sector organizations as they affect training. The purpose of this chapter is to document some of our observations and experiences and reflect on the trends we see unfolding and their implications.

This topic is of interest not only because we are involved in the training profession. In the increased globalizing of organizational productivity and excellence, there is a fundamental link between global competition and the need for training. According to one expert, training is an essential option because "companies are scrambling to look at every possible way they can make themselves more competitive" (Albert Vicere of Pennsylvania State University, quoted in Hoffman, 1996).

There is also a link between the drive for excellence and more knowledgeable manpower. Lester Thurow (1996) of MIT's Sloan School of Management says that the rapid growth industries of the 1990s (microelectronics, biotech, telecommunications, material science industries, civilian aircraft manufacturing, machine tools, and robotics and computers are all brain power industries, and "where they take root and flourish depends on who organizes that brainpower... and educates toward that objective best." Thurow goes on to say that "knowledge has become the only source of long-run sustainable competitive advantage. Recent studies show that rates of return for industries that invest in knowledge and skill are more than twice those of industries that concentrate on plant and equipment."

According to consultants at Towers Perrin, the New York–based consulting firm specializing in human relations services, for example, success in building more flexibility and adaptability and speed of response will be determined more by enhancing the adaptability of the workforce in the near future than by superior technology or deep pockets. Indeed, moving—or transiting—to excellence can require a serious engagement with training.

Training has been burdened with differing definitions. In some cultures, one does not use this term at all. Training is what one does with animals. Humans are "capacitated." Others dislike the term because it implies static, nonreflective skill acquisition. They prefer "learning" instead. Our working definition: training is a "deliberate activity to enhance human capacity through the development of skills and the ability to acquire and apply pertinent knowledge."

Two critical considerations in determining how organizations respond to the urge to provide more knowledgeable manpower are time considerations and needs. These may even be the most fundamental variables. Cushman and King (1995, p. 21) suggest that, increasingly, time is emerging as the most critical, most fundamental variable organizations have to deal with in responding to change (not dollars, personnel, or information). Perception of needs, nevertheless, is the engine which drives most human activity (see, e.g., Maslow, 1954) and organizations are, after all, clusters of human activity. In any case, organizational training is usually rationalized in terms of need as derived from a needs assessment or some kind of discrepancy analysis of the difference between desired condition and current status.

Two Critical Variables: Needs and Time

Needs

We assume we are dealing with real needs. The problem is to decide what type of need to pursue, and those perceiving a need will have to decide whether training is a valid response. Communication audits reported by Slovacek (1994), for example, showed that other responses such as installation of improved technology or coordination and communication systems sometimes solved problems without necessitating organized training.

Where training is deemed to be part of the organizational response, however, the training need can be conceptualized in various ways. Indeed, describing the training need is fundamental to most training designs, i.e., doing a needs assessment is usually the first stage.

For this analysis, the training need is characterized in two dimensions, i.e., known where training outcomes can be readily specified, and unknown, where training outcomes cannot be readily specified.

At this stage, a caveat is in order. When we are referring to needs, we mean specific needs: known and unknown in a targeted area. We recognize that one could claim a broad enough need, e.g., better health or economy, and state that the need is known. That is too general for this discussion—more like a goal. This characterization of need refers to those that relate to reaching a particular objective with its corollary problem identification, evidence of skills, conditions evident in the organization and its environment (e.g., mission, resources, culture, and politics), and evidence of possible approaches to resolution.

Those who have finally come to terms (or were raised) with the behavioral revolution in social science may ask whether any organization worthy of survival would support training whose outcomes cannot be readily specified. Certainly, one of the first skills learned by the training practitioner is to be able to write a sound behavioral objective clearly related to a needs assessment. We are suggesting, however, that there are conditions in which organizations find themselves in which the objective is becoming harder to craft because the organization's needs are becoming less predictable. A television executive engineer recently observed that deciding which training to invest in for his operations was becoming increasingly problematic because the technology is changing rapidly and he does not know which innovations will make the most sense to his corporate directors. Television is highly technology-driven and may be an extreme example, but we believe that the dilemma of training for unknown needs is confronting more and more organizations.

Defining needs is critical. Our discussion relates to those organizational needs that, to a greater or lesser degree, are properly subject to resolution, in part or wholly, by training initiatives.

Time

When we consider time, we are referring to the amount of time available before the results of training are to be applied. This may or may not coincide with the amount of time available for training, but often is. For example, training on how to turn a valve might meet an immediate need, while training in hydraulics may meet future needs for specific needs not yet envisioned.

The time variable also can be conceptualized in alternate ways, but for this analysis, will be characterized in two dimensions: unconstrained to constrained. Truly unlimited, or unconstrained, time before training application probably does not exist (except in the minds of conceptualizers). What we are speaking of is *relatively* unlimited or unconstrained time. This tends to be found less in modern organizations, given the need to respond to increasing rapidity of change. It still may be appropriate and necessary when the end product is highly valuable or there is strong public consensus that anything less is unworthy. Training for astronauts, religious figures, certain medical specialists, and other scientists comes to mind. Training for the old masters like Michelangelo, which involved lengthy apprenticeships, could be viewed in the same way.

Constrained or limited time before training application is increasingly the case now. This is not merely because many organizations have less resources to invest in training than they had, for example, a decade ago. In some cases, reduced training time is simply more appropriate. The international development agencies with which we work have found that past success in particular projects in concert with the broader efforts of the developing countries in which they work, have made longer-term training less necessary. There are now local and national alternatives available to provide it. Building on a broader and higher skill base, these organizations now find that supporting the shorter-term training for particular skills is what is needed.

There are additional reasons why limited time is now more the case: People cannot, or do not want to, be away from their work for extended periods. Skills have a shorter self-life than ever before. Training may be available only at a specific time even though application is not anticipated to be immediate.

If we join the variables in a matrix, we begin to see some interesting relationships emerge regarding training models or approaches, as summarized in table 12.1.

The Training Models

General Competence

This model features training for general knowledge and awareness of facts and processes, such as problem-solving and interpersonal skills. It is primarily activities-based, i.e., the knowledge content is conveyed through descriptive material, exercises, and projects chosen by the trainer for a generic type of trainee. Typically, this training takes place in the classroom, although more is beginning to appear via computer. Because the training is general and designed to be widely applicable, its utility for any particular trainee is less predictable. This kind of training may need mediating measures to ensure recognition, such as certification by external authorities. The cost tends to be midrange but depends on use of media and associated development costs.

Because of the longer term horizon before training is to be applied and because the needs to which the training could be applied are not known with any precision, the focus must necessarily be on general awareness and fundamentals. Because the future is unknown, what worked in the past becomes the reservoir for content. Selecting training content which is still useful and relevant can be a challenge. Because of this, training programs organized in this model are sometimes accused of being out of touch or, worse, a waste of resources.

Yet there is still a need for these programs. New employees may lack fundamental skills. This reasoning has led some organizations, such as Motorola, to establish their own "universities." In the era following adoption of the affirmative action politics in the United States, some organizations found they could enhance their competitive status for government contracts by supporting general degree

Table 12.1
Time

Characteristics	Unconstrained	Constrained
	General Competence	**Packaged/Handbook Training**
Focus	More on general knowledge and awareness of facts and processes, e.g., problem solving, creativity, and interpersonal skills	Awareness and skills for generalized or specific techniques; not necessarily organizationally unique for application
Structure	Activities-based, classroom locale, some media-based	Activities and/or results-based; classroom and worksite locale; more amenable to a packaging, e.g., CBT
Outcomes	Less predictable, widely applicable, may need mediating measures of accomplishments, e.g., certification by external authorities	More predictable but highly dependent on fit of material to need, trainer interpretation; can be internally validated
Cost Tendency	Midrange, depending on media development costs	Usually low, but multimedia development may raise cost substantially
Examples	• Classroom professional training • Academic degree training • General workshops	• On-the-job (internally serviced) • Technical procedures
	Professional/Specialist	**Just-in-Time**
Focus	Awareness and skills for specific clusters of competencies; development of expert systems	On specific processes and results; organizationally-based problems
Structure	Activities and results-based, classroom and worksite locale, some media-based	Specific organizational groups, often actual teams; classroom with on-site facilitation; media-based
Outcomes	Applicability more limited, more predictable, usually requires external validation	More predictable given strong support from organizational management; more narrowly applicable; internally (organizationally) validated
Cost Tendency	Usually high	Mid to high range, depending on amount of on-site facilitation use of media; self-amortizing
Examples	• Guild-type • Internships, Residencies • Refresher certification • Speciality workshops • Shadowing	• Specific business processes • Hands-on coaching • Need to know

training for minorities. Although the current economy has led some to reduce support for general competence training based on this rationale, this model of training is actually gaining increasing support and respect. Some organizations, e.g., GE still invest in this model of training for their fast-track employees, while limiting the training of all others to need-to-know (see later section, "Just-in-Time").

The reason for choosing to implement general competence training has changed somewhat. In the past, such training, which emphasized processes in addition to awareness, was usually more attractive. This accounts, in part, for the spectacular success enjoyed by the field of communication within the broader spectrum of the social sciences.

Now the process which undergirds renewed interest in this model of training is the learning process itself. Learning how to learn, or continuous learning, is now becoming the flagship for general competence training. More about this trend will be discussed in the following section on training implications of organizational development trends.

Professional/Specialist Training

In this model, the training focus is on awareness and skills for specific clusters of competencies and the development of experts and participants in expert systems. Like training for general competence, some of the training is activities-based, but there is a particularly strong specific results orientation. Those who are trained in this model usually expect to be able to have a repertoire of skills and to be able to accomplish specific sets of tasks. The training may take place in the classroom and may be made more realistic when augmented with worksite instruction as well. Because the focus of the training is narrower, applicability is more limited but more predictable. This type of training, however, may require external validation. Costs are usually higher with this type of training as it involves transfer of special skills.

As there is less pressure to apply the training immediately, professional training shares with general competence training some of the problems of focus, i.e., whether to design for the near-term application or for the longer term. In our experience, those that emphasize the near term may opt for techniques, and those aiming for the longer term may emphasize more theory and process. As the time horizon is also more flexible, prioritization for needs can be a problem and, therefore, also the possibility of inefficient use of resources. In these respects, professional training shares the same problems of general competency training.

Broad-based professional training remains very popular in part because of the economic rewards associated with it for trainees. One recent study (Conrad and Haworth, 1992–93) found that master's degree study, a level at which much professional education takes place, increased by 48% between 1970 and 1990. Because of its success, however, organizational support for it is no longer so broadly based, at least in the United States. For example, states that formerly supported master's degree study in public administration in order to professionalize their civil service ranks, no longer feel the strong need to do so as the goal has largely been accomplished and replenishment can now occur without broad organizational support, e.g., from state agencies. Where support for broad-based professional training does continue, it is usually to entice professional practice in less attractive areas, such as inner cities, reservations, or military services.

A growth area, however, is in professional certification refresher short courses which are either mandated by law or by associations in anticipation of continuing changes in, for example, medical knowledge, tax law, and elementary and secondary education.

Packaged/Handbook Training

This model of training focuses on helping the trainee acquire awareness and skills for generalized or specific techniques, the applications for which are not necessarily unique to particular organizations but may be so. Training can be either activities or results-based or both and can take place in the classroom and/or worksite and may be media-based. Training outcomes may be more predictable but are highly dependent on the fit of the material to the trainee's need and the trainer's interpretation. Handbook training can be validated internally by the organization by whether it works to solve a particular problem.

Although under increasing attack because of its one-size-fits all philosophy or "shrink-wrapped" packaging, this form of training remains very attractive because of its lower cost. Prefabricated training can be cost-effective because sometimes substantial development and production costs can be amortized through low-cost delivery methods, where either less highly trained trainers can be hired to provide the training or, in closed systems, the trainees' supervisors can use this instructional material and deliver the training themselves. As more and more organizations are disinvesting in in-house training units in order to reduce costs, this is one route they are taking to help supervisors do the needed training themselves.

The impact of the information age has led many to see this form of training most amenable to high-technology delivery. Self-instructional video and audio, computer-assisted tutorials, and multimedia approaches using CD-ROM packaging are but some of the innovative training approaches that are based on this mode.

The degree to which the handbook mode can fit a need is the degree to which the training can succeed, although success can be "stretched" by creative use of the material by the trainer. At least one company with which we are acquainted focuses on developing unique handbooks for particular corporate problems. The organization is then free to arrange delivery of training separately. A similar approach is being taken by the United Nations Development Programme (UNDP) in a three-year project to improve its middle management. Here, however, the training delivery will be contracted to regionally-based companies worldwide to lower cost and increase availability of quality programs.

Just-in-Time

This mode focuses on organizationally specific problems, processes, and results. It is customized for specific organizational groups which are often actual teams working on actual problems. It may take place in the classroom and/or on-site and is usually followed with on-site facilitation. This kind of training is more predictable, given strong support from organizational management, but is more narrowly applicable. Because it is designed to meet particular organizational needs, it can be internally validated if the training helps to resolve the problem. The cost of this mode of training tends to be midrange to high depending on the amount of on-site facilitation. Because it is designed to solve particular organizational problems, investment in this kind of training is usually self-amortizing. Indeed, if one takes into account the value of solving the organizational problem simultaneously with the training, the value in the problem solved can yield a very cost-effective approach, perhaps making it even the most cost-effective approach. It has been argued that such problem-solving training projects could be viewed as profit (rather than cost) centers for the organization.

A mode receiving more recent emphasis in training, this approach can permit organizations to deliver training which can be flexibly designed and rapidly applied. It can achieve good results by focusing on limited problems and providing training just to resolve those particular problems. Because it combines classroom training with worksite facilitation of teamwork, the trainer can begin by providing generalized training and then, as teamwork on the problem proceeds, by providing highly targeted training to resolve immediate needs encountered by the teams. As this training is highly particularistic and results-oriented, its success is measured exclusively in terms of organizational satisfaction with the teams' resolution of particular organizational problems.

This kind of training requires a high degree of senior management support to the teams and their members, not only to release them from other commitments while they work on resolution of particular problems but also to provide resources the teams may need to implement their solutions.

Just-in-time training has been successfully used in various quality and continuous improvement initiatives reported in the last decade (see, e.g., Veneziale, 1990). It was applied by MTDI (Management, Training, Development Institute) in an international setting (Nicaragua) in 1995–96 in which several government ministries and related executive agencies worked fairly successfully on small but nagging problems in a politically volatile environment charged with preelection uncertainties and latent animosities left over from a recently ended civil war. The results, in at least one team project, led to a planned revamping of similar activities throughout the country (Argüello, 1996).

The four training models just described are broad conceptual categories and do not exhaust the actual possibilities, which may include combinations of one or more approaches. In our own institute, for example, training provided in our seminars (actually workshops) have utilized all four models to some extent and in varying combinations, as appropriate.

Training Implications of Lessons from Communication and Management Approaches to Achieving Organizational Excellence

The need to deal with an accelerating rate of change and its portent for competition and success of the organization and the individual is a primary source of the onslaught of approaches to excellence in organizational development. When an appropriate response to the need in whole or in part is training, the nature of the approach and philosophy chosen have critical implications for the training to be given and for the likelihood of success of the objectives for which training is given because training is a means, not an end.

The faster changing environment carries the requirement that the training provider be an ever more capable assessor of needs or effective responder to the assessments of others. He, she, or they must also be skilled at informing, involving, and convincing the persons with the power to determine the nature of the intervention. This includes skills at balancing the most effective response to the needs-based challenge at hand and the broader objectives of the stakeholders involved.

Training is often perceived as chasing or anticipating change. It might be argued that training may also simply support maintenance of the present system, but even here, it is a response to anticipated continuing change in the availabilities of skill capacities even at present levels.

Peter Drucker has asserted that, given the speed of change in so many fields and occupations, one of the fastest growing activities in the U.S. will soon be the continuing education of adults. A seeming contradiction of shift by many firms to greater outsourcing and a report in recent surveys of a significant increase in the proportion of firms with stand-alone training departments (Watson Wyatt Communications and Training Survey) is in reality simply reflecting this, and both are correct.

The channels for training are also becoming more diverse. In addition to classroom, workshops, manuals, and internships, more newly introduced and rapidly growing elements such as computer-based and teleconferenced models are being used.

The accelerating pressures *of* and *for* change have generated numerous approaches for achieving organizational development. These management and communication tools have important implications for training. The following are a few examples of these trends that illustrate the diversity of implications for training.

Trend to Reengineering

With restructuring there is a need for training in the nature of the new entity, especially as to changing objectives, culture, expectations, and visions, in addition to the more traditional and technical content usually found in training activities. This is especially true in the pervasive change nature of many reengineering interventions.

An illustration is seen in the desire to shift conceptualization and focus by the worker from seeing his or her job as a specific function which s/he directly provides the organization to viewing it as one part of a process of which his or her activity is an element. This has extensive training implications, ranging from providing greater knowledge about the process and the people and dynamics of it to relationship integration preparation and providing experiences where the conceptualization of being more a part of the whole is enhanced and the contribution of this to performance and productivity is maximized. Thus, we see the greater emphasis on training in team membership, team leadership, and team building.

There are also many instances of reorganization of training structure related to reengineering efforts from such activities as sometimes shifting training responsibilities more to operational levels (hence, increasing the need for training of trainers as well) and to greater outsourcing of training. There is also evidence of greater integration in the latter case in client/training provider activity and sharing of training involvement and responsibilities. This is also seen in more complex training relationships developed by the organization with its suppliers and customers.

Trend to Globalization

The shift from international to multinational to global conceptualization and operations has enormous training demands. Not only the technicalities of informing and facilitating skill acquisition of new systems are involved but also massive shifts in attitudes and conceptualizations of roles and the organizational culture (Marquardt, 1995; Odenwald, 1993).

An illustration of a training approach is that some companies in the course of globalization, in addition to sending persons to practice their roles in several other geographic regions, send teams with members from various regions together to explore and participate in operations at different sites. These activities focus not only on internal functions of their organization in that location but also on exploring the local macroeconomics and political and social characteristics and issues.

Trend to Keeping Inventories Lean and Planning Just Enough Production to Meet Demand

Implications for training are found in the need for many factors such as materials supply, production, distribution, marketing, and administration to be more closely related and synergistic. These factors leverage off each other as an integrated whole, as communicative, and are capable of fast response to changing conditions. The structural and technological changes that are often required each build in changes in training requirements. Further, building systems for such controlled and rapid knowledge operations and change response require more rapid feedback and repeated updating of training input. This includes more complicated systems of formal, informal and on-site training activity than was previously common.

Trend to Creating Learning Organizations

A response to accelerating change, the need for rigorous and more frequent restructuring, the growing importance of flexibility and adjustability in operations and generation and system flow of new ideas, more firms have felt the need to be more receptive to a "learning" orientation in order to stay competitive (Carnevale and Gainer, 1990). An example of the training adaptation is seen in its orientation, organization, and content shift providing a broader spectrum of formal and informal learning activities, much more trainee-determined and executed. Indeed, the expectation seems to be growing that employees will be in charge of identification and managing their own training needs. This includes more self-access training made available through technology and more activity in encouraging the use of it and other training resources.

The character of changes being dealt with may suggest learning be part of continuous improvement or quantum-leap approaches. However, training activity as a whole must clearly represent its role within the organization as being a continuing, never finished, always evolving endeavor.

A recent study of the Learning Organization Network of the American Society for Training and Development (Broad, 1996) identified four factors that most frequently characterized programs in learning organizations:

1. Focus on the whole system
2. Use of multiple and integrated change efforts
3. Goal of team and/or system competence
4. Emphasis given to "double loop" learning (learning how to learn as well as learning new skills and knowledge).

Trend to "Virtualization" of Units or Functions

This increasingly common organizational formulation can provide great flexibility, capabilities that could not be acquired or maintained wholly in-house, and often with greater economy, efficiency, and effectiveness of operation (see, e.g., Day, 1995; Miles and Snow, 1993). Stimulus for the trend includes greater requirements to be adaptable and responsive to changes in the character of the services and products required and time pressures.

An interesting variation is the growing practice among companies to provide services through the personnel of other companies. For example, "consultants on loan" from several companies may attack a problem and instruct one another directly or via telecommunications, creating a temporary virtual workgroup over great distances.

Virtualization transformation not only changes the demands on training for the organization but the training department is often a subject of the virtualization in whole or in part too (McIntosh, 1995). One expression of this is the considerable increase in outsourcing for training services. Sometimes this is with organizations specializing in providing training, but in these cases, it is often less like a purchase of the training commodity as before and often more like having, as one provider put it, a "rent-an-HRD" on an often extended basis. Many firms have done this for economic reasons but are most pleased after involvement with the access it provides them which is wider than they could maintain themselves.

Given the constantly growing demands for more training, some firms are finding their best course to be maintaining and changing the character of their internal training operation and building a system which integrates the use of both internal and outsourced services. This in some cases can create an array of virtual services the firm can offer to its internal or external (customer-related) clients as never before.

One of the great training challenges is to assist organizations adapting the employee community to this new culture and to facilitate cooperation among them and outsourced components of the virtual format. For more about the key issue of communication in this respect, see Darutta (1995).

Trend to More Focus on Transfer of Training Results

This is an area of increased attention in the application of many of the new implementation of communication and management tools in organizational enhancement (Broad and Newstrom, 1992). That is, the fact that needs are identified and training organized and presented is too often the end of planned activity for securing the desired behavioral change at work. The assumption is too often that this will or will not take place depending on the quality and appropriateness of the training. Less formal and systematic attention is given to actual steps to encourage support and enhance transfer, the effectiveness and continuing application of the knowledge and skills gained.

"Full transfer" is indicated when, with practice, the level of skill with which learning is applied has increased beyond that demonstrated at the end of the training period. In part, the movement to more formal attention to transfer is, in today's rapidly changing environment, because there is less latitude for training efforts to take effect.

Recognition of inadequate attention to performance support following training is perhaps best reflected in a recent ASTD HRD Executive Survey (in Broad, 1996). Seventy-three percent of the human resources development executives responding said that current training managers and staff were ill-prepared to provide or develop performance support. Clearly, the challenge is there to integrate training more intimately with organizational problem-solving so that training managers as well as general managers and others in the organization can make such support meaningful and valuable.

Conclusion

Current directions and experimentation in communication and management approaches to achieving excellence in organizations are exciting and promising. Human capital will often play a major role in determining the extent of their success and should receive consideration from the time conceptualization of the interventions is initiated. Training is the primary way to enhance human capital. All members of the organization need to become partners in continuous scanning for nature and levels of training need and opportunities in support of achieving excellence in a changing environment.

References

Argüello, X. (1996). Dirección general de aduanas entra a la calidad total. *El País* (Nicaragua) 38:29–38.

Broad, M. (1996). HRD Innovation for Substance Abuse Prevention. *Training and Development* 50(2):58–66.

Broad M., and Newstrom, J. (1992). *Transfer of Training.* Reading, MA: Addison-Wesley.

Carnevale, A., and Gainer, L. (1990). *The Learning Enterprise.* Alexandria, VA: American Society for Training and Development and U.S. Department of Labor, Washington, D.C.

Conrad, C., and Haworth, J. (1992–93). Master's Programs and Contextual Planning. *Planning for Higher Education* 21(winter):12–18.

Cushman, D., and King, S. (1995). *Communication and High-Speed Management.* Albany: SUNY Press.

Day, K. (1995). Now, The "Virtual Company." *Washington Post,* October 29, pp. H1, 5.

Durutta, N. (1995). Communicating for Real Results in the Virtual Organization. *IABC Communication World,* October, pp. 15–19.

Engler, N. (1995). The (Re)Movable Workforce. *Open Computing,* May, pp. 40–44.

Hoffman, E. (1996). Not for Future CEO's Only. *USAir Magazine* 3/4:18–25.

McIntosh, S. (1995). Envisioning the Virtual Training Organization. *Training and Development,* May, pp. 45–49.

Marquardt, M. (1995). *How to Globalize Your Training.* Alexandria, VA: American Society for Training and Development.

Maslow, A. (1954). *Motivation and Personality.* New York: Harper, pp. 93–98.

Miles, R., and Snow, C. (1993). The New Network Firm: A Spherical Structure Built on a Human Investment Philosophy. *Organizational Dynamics,* 5–17.

Odenwald, S. (1993). *Global Training.* Homewood, IL: Irwin.

Slovacek, C. (1994). Communication Audits: Targeting Winning Education Strategies. *Executive Education in the USA,* 6–8.

Thurow, L. (1996). Preparing Students for the Coming Century. *Washington Post,* April 7, pp. 1–4.

Veneziale, D. (1990). Design-to-Excellence at Beckman Instrument. *Target,* Spring, pp. 30–33.

13

Strategies of Leadership Excellence for Corporate Survival

Richard J. Dieker

Leadership excellence is the key to corporate survival in the twenty-first century. Increasing competitive pressures at both the national and international levels, accelerating technological developments that make the status quo continuously obsolete, shifts by consumers from national patriotism and family brand loyalty to a demand for quality regardless of product source, and a sophisticated workforce that has become frustrated, demoralized, and disillusioned are factors which all corporate leaders, in all marketing arenas, must recognize and respond to.

Given the rapidity of changes taking place in the world marketplace, the focus of corporate leadership must change in dramatic and revolutionary ways. Transcendental leadership changes are needed, requiring a shift from current values and previously successful patterns of leadership behavior, to new ways of envisioning and responding. There are several basic and important differences between current patterns of deficiency need leadership and transcendental leadership (Table 13.1). Those who are capable of making this revolutionary shift in leadership thinking and behavior will more likely survive and prosper. Those who cannot transform themselves into leaders for change inevitably will experience personal and corporate failure.

The ability to transcend the many problems facing organizations will not be easy, and the challenges, frustrations, and failures of organizational leadership in the U.S. are formidable. The U.S. came out of WWII as the richest and most powerful nation on earth; by the mid-1970s, it was rapidly losing its competitive edge. "We lost the edge because, however skillful managers and bureaucrats are at

Table 13.1
Deficiency Need vs. Transcendental Leadership

Deficiency Need Leadership	Transcendental Leadership
• prepares for known and predictable	• prepares for unknown and unpredictable
• determines goals through self-needs and ego gratification	• determine goals through customer and member needs
• builds on prior accomplishments	• expects and plans for obsolescence
• complacency with current profitability and customer satisfaction	• continuous quest for improvement and change
• manages crises as they occur with focus on damage control	• actively scans the environment for problems and prevents crises before they fully develop
• deficiency need–centered; focus on leader's need for status, prestige, and power	• growth-centered; focus on meeting customer and employee needs and realization of self-values
• focus on controlling others and maintaining power	• focus on managing the self and empowering others

holding actions, they have no talent at all for advancing. [The U.S.] no longer leads the world and is itself leaderless" (Bennis, 1989b, p. 35).

The lessons of the recent decline in major market powers in the U.S. help to illustrate the challenges organizations now face. The rise and fall in power of IBM as a world-class leader of the computing world is one example. IBM had established itself for a quarter of a century as the computer giant of the world when the computing industry began to experience dramatic changes. Even IBM's own key research people in personal computers were aware of the potential for rapid growth in this area; IBM steadfastly continued its focus on mainframes and suppressed, rather than encouraged, the development and sales of their own PCs. IBM leadership's inability to comprehend and adapt to this new world resulted in a corporate crisis of immense proportions. While IBM has recently returned to profitability and has gained favor on the stock market, it has achieved renewed profitability only at the cost of drastic downsizing and the loss of nearly half its workforce. GM turned to the use of robots to reduce manufacturing costs in some of their new plants, resulting in a lack of flexibility in adapting production to changing customer needs. Now, state-of-the-art billion-dollar manufacturing plants at GM are idle much of the time. The decline or downfall of organizations in virtually all areas of world commerce due to corporate rigidity, short-sightedness, and lack of progressive leadership could be cited.

While colleges of business in the U.S. were teaching the leaders of the future how to maintain stability and control, utilizing management techniques which were outdated even then, the sleeping giant of world competition and organizational revolution was already awakening. Not only IBM, but many other large and famous U.S. companies, once thought to be invulnerable in the areas of computing, transportation, electronics, and many others, suffered from corporate leadership stagnation. Corporate leaders were preoccupied with preserving the status quo rather than continuously improving products and service and anticipating changes in technology and consumer demands through effective long-term vision and planning.

Many organizational leaders still define their primary function in terms of control, not creativity, and long-term corporate survival is jeopardized in the quest for short-term profitability or stability. The downsizing efforts currently taking place in both public and private organizations, using euphemisms such as "right sizing," "work redesign," "streamlining," and "reengineering," are frequently little more than turn of the *last* century's scientific management approach propounded by Frederick Taylor (1911) to help cut costs and increase profits. Rather than taking a complex, future-oriented look at organizational development, scientific management "describes the way specific organizational tasks should be structured to increase the efficiency of their accomplishment" (Krebs, 1986, p. 75). *Efficiency* of managing people is substituted for leadership *effectiveness*, and members of the organizations are left feeling manipulated, abused, and unappreciated. A new leadership response to organizational development is needed.

This new response must address three major areas of leadership behavior:

1. Leaders of organizations must become increasingly aware of new technology, product, and service developments, must know their competitors, and must exercise leadership in continuous innovation in these areas. They must stay in close touch with customers, not only keeping abreast of but anticipating and responding quickly to changing demands,

meeting and exceeding expectations for product development, performance, and service.

2. Organizations must develop a highly motivated workforce, committed to continuous quality improvement, customer service, and innovative product development.

3. Leaders must become more aware of their own strengths and limitations, particularly as they relate to the accomplishment of the first two objectives. This will require a continuous assessment of their beliefs and behaviors, with the willingness and ability to make needed changes in their approach to organizational leadership.

The importance of product and service development, customer satisfaction, and employee motivation is well-recognized and documented; to fail in any of these areas will inevitably result in organizational crisis and drastic losses in the marketplace, with complete organizational failure a very real potential outcome. However, past approaches to leadership have been too fragmented and insufficient, and efforts to implement changes have often been sporadic, inadequate, and frequently inappropriate. Management training programs have been too centered on increasing managerial control, reducing costs, and improving worker productivity, and have failed to address the need for leadership development with other than manipulative models. An examination of some of the major approaches to leadership will illustrate why they have failed to provide management with the needed analytical and behavioral tools for appropriate leadership behavior, and why they failed to reduce the decline in organizational effectiveness.

A Brief History of the Study of Leadership

The study of leadership has evolved from the rudimentary, unidimensional, linear concept of autocratic, democratic, and laissez-faire leadership styles, investigated extensively by Lewin, Pippitt, and White (1939) and their followers, revisited by Likert (1961) in his leader-centered/worker-centered continuum of management styles, and eventually developed into a focus on participative decision-making (PDM) as a driving principle behind effective leadership. PDM has been extensively critiqued, with numerous characteristics of both leaders and followers found to restrict its effectiveness and generalizability (Conrad, 1994, pp. 245–50). While the participation and commitment of the members of any organization are essential for continued success, *how* to obtain participation has not been sufficiently addressed, and as a result, PDM as a generating force often failed. The focus on management techniques, without fully taking into account the values, beliefs, and motives which undergrade leadership attitudes and behaviors, was unsuccessful.

The unidimensional perspective was gradually replaced by a two-dimensional leadership model, suggested by the studies in the 1950s at Ohio State which focused on "consideration," or the friendliness and supportiveness of the leader, and "initiating structure," or the focus on assignment of tasks and subsequent close supervision to insure that the tasks were accomplished, independently measured by the Leader Behavior Description Questionnaire (Hackman and Johnson, 1991, 32–34.). Although later studies developed several different questionnaires and forms, Yukl (1989) found that "most researchers continued to use only the consideration and initiating structure scales" (p 76).

Blake and Mouton in 1964 used a similar model for their "managerial grid," utilizing "concern for people" and "concern for production" as the two dimensions of the grid. Until later researchers challenged Blake and Mouton's conclusions, the "executive style leader" who manifested both a concern for task and a concern for people was considered the ideal, even though it somewhat resembled the benevolent dictator model of prior decades.

Hersey and Blanchard's (1984) contingency theory took this model into the third dimension by introducing the concept of leader "effectiveness," suggesting that the leadership style of the model which was most effective was determined by the maturity (later renamed to the more politically correct "readiness") level of the followers. According to this model, the combination of concern for task and concern for people that was useful in maximizing production depended on the maturity or readiness level of the subordinates. The high task, high people quadrant of the grid, one of the two-leader-centered combinations, was described as effective only for relatively low maturity members, and would not be as effective as other combinations with either very immature or more mature group members. This cast further doubt on the "executive style" as the ideal propounded by Blake and Mouton.

While the contingency model developed by Hersey and Blanchard suggested that short-term productivity could be affected by different leadership styles for different types of followers, the shift in focus from leader variables to follower variables failed to adequately address many other dimensions central to the explanatory value of the effectiveness dimension of the model. Hersey and Blanchard's conclusions regarding the relationship between leadership style and readiness level of workers, as well as their measuring instrument, have been highly criticized (Graeff, 1983).

The contingency model provided managers with an academic rationale to use heavy-handed techniques with low-readiness workers (low ability and willingness), using a high-task, low-person concern style, without more probing analyses of the motivations and behaviors of both the leader and the followers. Instead of seeking to achieve understanding, ownership, and commitment, the model was willing to accept, if not encourage, short-term behavioral control techniques which required constant and close supervision to achieve productivity. Many problems with product and service quality can be directly traced to workers' rebellion to just such leadership tactics. Rather than providing a long-term solution to organizational development, this model suggested expedient shortcuts which exacerbate rather than alleviate motivational problems for less able and motivated workers.

A different, but related, problem exists with the model on the other end of the "readiness" spectrum, where Hersey and Blanchard suggest a low-task, low-person style for group members with high ability and willingness. At this level, the model confuses *concern for task* with *ability to treat others as equals and share power,* two quite different leader characteristics, and *concern for people* with *ability to treat others with respect and recognition* without being patronizing. No good evidence exists to suggest that any leader, in any situation, will be more effective with a low concern for task and a low concern for people as proposed by the Hershey and Blanchard model. Developing a highly competent and strongly motivated workforce does not mean abandoning concern for task, even when working closely with these individuals, Nor does having a high concern for people, interacting regularly with great respect, caring, and consideration, mean that leaders are interfering with group members in a condescending or solicitous manner. All members of an organization need recognition and social support, even though the nature of this support may vary considerably for different people, and continuous concern with and interaction about group task helps to keep everyone, including the leader, motivated and focused on the organizational mission. This deep and continuous involvement requires that the leader is working *with*, not *over*, the group members, and is not simply trying to control all group outcomes, utilizing patronizing social behaviors. Leaders who are dogmatic and authoritarian may be more effective if they avoid closely supervising their highly competent people; however, considerable evidence suggests that they lack the sensitivity and insight into either themselves or others for long-term leadership effectiveness.

Later leadership theories, frequently referred to as "transformational," have proposed additional leadership qualities, suggesting more specific task or relationship subdimensions, as well as some dimensions, as well as some dimensions which may cut across both task and relationship. The value-driven, principle-centered leadership model of Koestenbaum (1991) focused on the concepts of vision, reality, ethics, and courage, and Covey's (1991) model looked at wisdom, power, guidance, and security. Katzenbach (1995) added commitment, personal initiative, self and other motivation, caring for and enabling others, and a sense of humor. The value of these models is in their broader, more visionary perspective of the role of the leader. Rather than limiting leadership to increasing productivity or improving morale, they suggest the need for setting innovative, future-oriented goals and possessing the personal values and commitment to achieve them. They are not as clear on the specific ways to develop these leadership competencies or how to translate these principles and values into action.

Yukl's (1989) development of an "Integrating Taxonomy of Managerial Behavior," which categorizes leadership effectiveness into four general areas—giving/seeking information, making decisions, influencing people, and building relationships—is a managerial model rather than a leadership model, even though he uses the terms interchangeably in the narrative description of the model (pp 128–46). The focus of Yukl's model is increasing worker productivity, with a concern for control or manipulation of behavior rather than empowerment of workers. Many leaders who perceive themselves to be participatory and delegative continue to insist upon influencing outcomes, either directly or indirectly, by their own persuasive or coercive actions. Even when the demands of change are pressing for innovation, the unique perceptions available to them from all levels of the company remain untapped. Their leader behaviors are seen as manipulative and self-serving, engendering skepticism, distrust, and disloyalty, and seriously eroding motivation and innovation.

Developing countries which have only recently entered the industrial era with factories and manufacturing plants using local labor may profit from some of the earlier industrial leadership models; countries which are making the transition into the postindustrial era will require new approaches. In general, prior leadership models are insufficient to meet the demands of modern, evolving organizations requiring continuous innovation. Further, as long as leaders are operating at deficiency-need levels, they will be unable to achieve leadership greatness (Batten, 1989). Table 13.2 illustrates some typical leader behaviors observed are various deficiency levels of Malsow's hierarchy of needs (Maslow, 1987). The first four levels are all deficiency-motivated leadership behaviors; only the self-actualization level is growth-motivated.

Batten (1989) suggests a level which goes beyond self-actualization for leaders, called "co-actualization," where leaders and members share in meanings, understandings, respect, expectations, and zest for the task with transcendent, stretching goals (p 178).

Table 13.2
Leader Behaviors as Related to Personal Need Level

Need Level	Leader Behavior
Physiological Need Level	Very aggressive or very fearful/defensive leadership style; not a typical need level found in corporate leaders
Security Need Level	Micromanagers, unable to delegate, preoccupied with rules and regulations, fearful of superiors, seeks power based on insecurity and feelings of inadequacy
Belongingness Level	Fearful of offending; lacks courage to take unpopular stands when needed; follows the popular course of action
Esteem Level	Seeks personal recognition for group accomplishments; takes credit for other's work; attempts to maintain image
Self-actualization Level	Strong, healthy values and secure self-concept; trusting, caring, courageous; focus on organization rather than self

The Transcendental Leadership Model: A Proposal

Transformational leadership models have focused on the need to transform the organization; the *transcendental leadership model* focuses on the need for the leader to transform and transcend the self. *To transcend,* in this sense, means the ability to exceed, to excel, to surpass, and to replace the patterns of the past and present, and the ability to develop new and different ways of perceiving and responding to the leadership demands of the future. This model incorporates the lessons learned from those leaders of companies which have been successful in surviving and thriving in an economic environment filled with corporate failure.

Since leadership models have always lagged behind the organizational realities of the present, this proposed model must be considered a work in progress. In many ways, leadership theories may be considered analogous to the modern organization, requiring continuous regeneration, with new paradigms and perspectives regularly replacing old models and beliefs which no longer apply.

Successful *transcendental leaders* have manifested four characteristics, all of which require extraordinary insight and vision related to the key components of long-term leadership effectiveness. These four characteristics are:

1. Perceiving the organization and its mission, with the ability to understand organizational directions needed to achieve greatness, and to accurately perceive and interpret events in the world which might support, hinder, or influence that greatness in any way. The organizational mission and the vision that drives it must have as its central focus providing the highest level of service to its customers, with a relentless commitment to maintain the innovative lead in its field.

2. Perceiving greatness in organizational members, who are considered associates, partners, or colleagues—not subordinates or workers, and acting in ways to release that greatness through all levels of the organization.

3. Perceiving the potential of self in the leadership role, including one's own strengths and limitations, with a passionate concern for ethical obligations, helping others in their development, and continuous self-improvement.

4. Perceiving the realization of organizational greatness. Transcendental leaders must have the ability to translate their values on visions into reality through appropriate leadership behavior.

Perceiving the Organization and Its Mission

Organizational members, including chief executives, in attempting to keep pace with the immediate demands of day-to-day activities, often lose sight of the purpose of the organization's existence. An organization's mission statement may be the organization's most important document, if it is carefully prepared and continuously reviewed, and it should provide focus to everyone in the organization. This is the organization's raison d'être and should reflect the organization's collective vision and direction. Several recent models have focused on the need for leadership vision and the need for continuous innovation to meet customer needs (Covey, 1991; Koestenbaum, 1991; Drucker, 1995; DePree, 1989). Drucker (1995), for example, writes "Every organization—not just business—needs one core competence: *innovation*. And every organization needs a way to record and appraise its *innovative performance*" (p 134)

However, vision and innovation do not occur in a vacuum, nor are they mystical abilities which are bestowed by fate or nature on a selected few. While highly competent and visionary leaders are in short supply, the ability to find, accept, and accurately interpret relevant information are more important than innate intuitive ability. Indeed, reliance on intuition based on experience may be a very costly mistake, as so many CEOs of failed companies have demonstrated. Some authors stress that vision "always refers to a *future* state, a condition that does not presently exist and never existed before" (Bennis and Nanus, 1985, pp 89–90); however, an important component of vision includes accessing and utilizing available data or information from inside and outside the organization, enabling the leader to both see the present and predict the future.

Bennis and Nanus (1985) summarized their interviews with numerous successful leaders: "they *paid attention to what was going on,* they determined what part of the events at hand would be important for the future of the organization, they set a new direction, and they concentrated the attention of everyone in the organization on it" (p 88, italics mine). Donald Beall (1996), CEO of Rockwell Corporation, stated in an interview on CNBC, "I worry about being a leader in every field we're in." In addition to worrying, however, he acts. With the end of the Cold War and military reductions in the

U.S. Rockwell went from 75% dependency on the military in the 1980s to about 25% in 1996; however, visionary planning enabled them to increase production in nonmilitary areas while downsizing the military component of their business, with less negative impact than felt by many other military-dependent companies. They are now positioning themselves as a supplier in the areas of commercial air transport and automotive components, as well as in semiconductor systems. Beall is well-aware of the importance of China as an emerging market and feels that they should be rapidly increasing their presence in that area. The recent focus on the need for high-speed management emphasizes the need for leaders to be able to gather information quickly and act in a timely manner (Cushman and King, 1995). Rockwell appears to be doing just that.

Another component crucial to the success of any vision is the combination of optimism and tenacity associated with that vision. Motorola demonstrated both characteristics in their persistence with successfully entering and competing in the cellular phone market in Japan, gaining access to the Tokyo market by enlisting the intervention of the U.S. government. By the early 1990s they achieved $1 billion a year in sales in Japan, once thought to be an invulnerable market to U.S. electronics manufacturers.

Effective leadership communication involves utilizing information channels to obtain needed data bout all aspects of the organization and its environment, and communicating information to individuals and groups who require data to function knowledgeably and effectively. Those leaders who isolate themselves from information about their customers, their competitors, their employees, or the developing technical knowledge in their field invite disaster. Successful organizations always have as central to the organizational mission satisfying customer needs by meeting and exceeding customer expectations. Leadership models, however, have not primarily defined worker productivity as customer satisfaction, engineers have frequently designed products with neither the production workers nor the customers clearly in mind, and mid and upper-level managers isolated from direct contact with the customers, frequently lose sight of the organization's primary mission in the day-to-day activities of management.

Important lessons can be learned from Sam Walton in his tireless quest for knowledge to bring his Wal-Mart vision to reality. His autobiography is an excellent manual for transcendental leaders to follow. Every opportunity for gaining new information was exploited. Wherever he traveled, Walton would stop in and talk with the executives and managers of retail stores, grilling them for information about successful strategies they used. Even though many of them were his competitors, he found they were almost always willing to spend time and provide valuable insights he could use. (After all, who would perceive the down-to-earth Sam Walton from Bentonville, Arkansas, as any kind of threat?) He would also scout firsthand the new locations for stores, viewing from his airplane the directions that towns were growing to find desirable shopping center locations. He spent time with employees in his stores, gaining more information about what their customers wanted and what the employees needed to do their jobs more effectively (Walton, 1992). He was also wise enough to ignore conventional wisdom, which he heard repeatedly, that discount stores could not succeed in a town of less than 50,000 population.

Perceiving Greatness in Employees

While most leadership theories stressing the need for vision have emphasized organizational change, leadership vision also demands the ability to view employees as having the potential for greatness. Many different concepts have been used to describe the human needs to be taken into account by leaders if they are to be successful "Consideration," "social needs," "higher-level needs," "recognition," and "concern for people" are some attempts to identify or describe these needs.

While all of these social needs are important to people, the visionary concern for employees goes beyond treating people well and recognizing and rewarding task performance. It encompasses several key beliefs, values, and behaviors, including empathy, trust, respect, and faith, which not only make employees "feel good" but also release their potential and develop motivated, innovative, and committed partners in the organization's mission. Beall (1996) acknowledges this importance when he states, "People are our most important asset." This recognition results in a major effort at Rockwell to develop that asset, with continuous learning and training programs for everyone.

This vision is also illustrated by the trust, confidence, and respect which Max DePree of Herman Miller, Inc., shows to his employees, and the return on this respect for employees has been a company with a remarkable record, like Wal-Mart, of continuous growth and profitability. DePree, CEO and son of founder D. J. DePree, knows that people who have a feeling of ownership in a company will be more motivated to work in the company's best interest. However, rather than hearing empty platitudes about company loyalty, 100% of the employees who have been with the company one year own stock in the company. It *is* the employee's company (DePree, 1989).

This value and behavior is also reflected in Sam Walton's respect for his employees, whom he always referred to as his associates or partners. Walton's Rule No. 7 said it most effectively:

> Listen to everyone in your company. And figure out ways to get them talking. The folks on the front lines—the ones who actually talk to the customer—are the only ones who really know what's going on out there. You better find out what they know. This really is what total quality is all about. To push responsibility down in your organization, and to force good ideas to bubble up within it, you *must* listen to what your associates are trying to tell you. (Walton, 1992, p 249)

Perceiving the Self: Integrity, Courage, and Ethics

Effective leaders appear to be those who are capable of knowing their own strengths and weaknesses, and who take the time to reflect on who they are and what they are about. DePree's (1989) book on leadership is an incisive analysis of himself as a leader at Herman Miller, Inc., with a vivid description of the progressive values he holds which permeate the organization. While affirming DePree's ability to practice what he describes in this insightful book, James O'Toole, in his preface to the book, notes "that there is almost always a gap between what a CEO *claims* his philosophy to be and what he, in fact, does on the job" (DePree, 1989, pp xxi–xxii). Despite all the proclamations and slogans, CEOs, unfortunately, frequently do not "walk the talk."

Midlevel managers and CEOs who are concerned with motivation or the problem-solving shortcomings of their employees often lack the self-awareness that their own leadership style is the problem. Self-reflection, openness to information about self from others, and the ability to process positive *and* negative information about the self without defensiveness are extremely important. Self-reflective leaders do not see themselves as finished products but rather as individuals in the continuous process of growth. "Leaders must continually look within to decide what they want, what they value, and what they are willing to be courageous about" (Leider, 1996, p 190). The Marriott Corporation includes an annual pledge to leadership excellence, with a ten-point promise to members of the Marriott "team," beginning with No. 1: "To set the right example for them by my own action in all things" (Batten, 1989, p 18). They promise, in writing, to be leaders who are consistent and fair; have a sincere, personal interest in their team; seek counsel from them; allow them individuality; keep them informed; be appreciative of their efforts and generous in praising their accomplishments; provide training for advancement; and work beside them when needed. This pledge for continuous striving toward leadership excellence is an exemplary model for transcendental leaders to use in developing their own leadership awareness and assessment.

Transcendental personal leadership qualities which emerge from the many leadership studies in recent years, qualities which affect both task and human concerns, include the critical values and behaviors of ethics, integrity, magnanimity, courage, openness, adaptability, creativity, and wisdom (Bennis, 1989b; Koestenbaum, 1991; Covey, 1991; Bennis and Goldsmith, 1994; Drucker, 1995; Nanus, 1992). These qualities are not easily acquired by individuals with hardened views and strong defense systems, nor are they usually measured on the traditional leadership assessment tests used throughout the world. Since levels of self-awareness may vary considerably, self-reporting may be particularly problematic as measures for some or all of them. However, to not self-reflect on these values and behaviors because they are difficult to assess would be to overlook the most critical variables affecting leadership effectiveness.

The concept of ethics includes such traits as honesty, integrity, concern for others rather than just the self, and at times acting against one's own immediate self-advancement or self-interest for a higher, more virtuous reason. Transcendental leaders must exercise this ethical leadership at all levels of the organization and not relegate responsibility or place blame for ethical decisions to someone else in the organizational hierarchy. The middle-level managers who only "carry out orders" and proclaim their own innocence in unethical decisions are themselves unethical and lack courage or integrity. While some CEOs have the motto, "The buck stops here," on their desks, all employees of any organization should wear a badge which declares, "The ethical buck stops here."

Several different methods for gaining insight into the leader's own behavior typify transcendental leaders. Bennis and Goldsmith (1994) suggest four such characteristics:

1. Self-reflection, including the ability and motivation to review critical events during the day for gaining new insights,

keeping journals to log perceptions and learnings and taking the time to reflect;

2. Gaining information through interaction with others, requesting input about how they are perceived as leaders;

3. An openness to learning, with the ability to question and reevaluate prior beliefs and a willingness to change these beliefs when necessary, with a clarity about priorities related to leadership;

4. Internal and external consistency—a continual connection between what leaders believe, what they do, and what they say. Leaders must know who they are and what they want to become, and then practice it with integrity. (pp 70–71).

In summary, transcendental leaders are personally healthy, self-actualizing individuals who are growth rather than deficiency-motivated. They create healthy, growth-oriented organizations, continuously seeking higher levels of understanding and responsiveness. This transcendental characteristic of self-actualizing leadership has been described most effectively by Maslow (1965, 1987).

Integrating Values with Action

Translating vision and values into action requires personal courage, an integral characteristic of great leadership (Koestenbaum, 1991). Integrity reflects moral values which lead to virtuous conclusions; courage reflects the fortitude and tenacity to publicly defend those values and beliefs and to be held accountable for decisions based on those beliefs. This requires withstanding criticism or hostility from superiors or colleagues who may, because of their own deficiencies, pressure the leader to make unethical choices.

Courage also reflects the ability to take actions which may be considered risky or unpredictable in outcome, rather than wait until possible outcomes are absolutely clear. In a fast-changing world, this fear of risk-taking and failure may result in an inability to act in a timely fashion. Courage is also needed to continuously pursue and advocate excellence in the organization, particularly when confronting the norm of mediocrity and complacency found in many companies.

Adaptability refers to the ability to change behaviors and beliefs with changing conditions. This is particularly important in a turbulent environment of new economic, technological, social, and political developments. Adaptability also includes the ability to respond in a positive, productive way to the rapid changes taking place in the diversity of the workforce, challenging traditional stereotypes, biases, and negative beliefs about the nature and potential of any individual or group. Herman Miller, Inc., was one of the leaders in this area, accommodating handicapped workers into its organization before it was either politically correct or legally required (DePree, 1989). Even as corporate leaders are beginning to accept and adapt to the concept of diversity in the organization, more progressive views of equality and community which transcend, yet incorporate, diversity must be developed.

Finally, transcendental leaders, if they are successful in implementing their leadership, will have inspired and helped all members of the organization to achieve self-leadership. This can be accomplished only by sharing information, so members understand their role in the organization and can act intelligently; sharing power, so members can respond to customer needs; sharing recognition, so members feel appreciated; and sharing profits, so members have a viable stake in the outcomes of the organization and are rewarded for their efforts. Transcendental leadership is successful when all members of the organization become leaders, sharing in both the vision for greatness and the responsibility for actions.

Conclusion

Old models of leadership that stressed balancing a concern for task and a concern for people are inadequate for the needs of tomorrow. Leaders must be capable of transcending antiquated habits, beliefs, and world views. Without a vision for continuous change, leaders will find themselves outdated and outpaced in the turbulent and competitive global marketplace. This visionary transcendental leadership must be capable of thinking in totally new directions, yet retain a firm grasp on the realities which must be confronted and the constraints which must be overcome. Sophisticated information systems which bring data in real rather than delayed time from both internal and external sources need to be employed. Crises will be averted only through this continuous monitoring of the environment and taking proactive, visionary steps to read the prodromal signs of potential crises before they develop and circumvent impending organizational disaster (Pauchant and Mitroff, 1992). Information from customers, suppliers, and employees, as well as all of the relevant powers in the external environment—political, scientific, economic, business, and others—must be continuously gathered, processed, and utilized.

Organizational leaders in any field could learn from advances taking place in hospitals and other health care organizations. The health care industry has traditionally not focused on creating *health*, but on curing or treating disease, often intervening only after considerable and sometimes irreparable damage has occurred. The medical world is now beginning to focus more of its energies on creating and maintaining health in people *before* they become sick through more aggressively encouraging and supporting proactive healthy lifestyle choices, rather than on simply treating preventable diseases *after* they occur. In the same way, organizations must focus their leadership energies on creating healthy, committed employees and satisfied consumers, not waiting until morale, motivation, commitment, and work quality decay and customers disappear. Preventing problems by positive organizational leadership will save valuable time and energy on the part of all organizational members; organizational energy can then more productively be spent on meeting the primary mission of the organization—creating the most satisfied customers in the world market.

The characteristics of transcendental leaders are summarized in Table 13.3. Transcendental leaders realize that their organizational mission must have as its central focus meeting and exceeding customer needs. To successfully meet customer needs through continuous innovation and service excellence, they demonstrate to organizational members that they are respected and valued, and teach through example a deep integrity and sense of ethics which places human values above all else. The ultimate leadership goal of the successful organization is to create self-leaders of all employees, with commitment and caring replacing distrust and suspicion throughout the organization. Leaders must also have a clear and healthy knowledge of themselves so their motives and behaviors accurately reflect their deeply held values. Without self-knowledge, their leadership attempts will be immature and manipulative. When leaders have a clear and healthy vision of themselves, their organizations, and their fellow members, and when they nurture and support empowered and committed associates working together for organizational innovation and excellence, transcendental leadership results in fully functioning individuals working together in thriving organizations capable of surviving in a competitive world.

238

Table 13.3
Characteristics of Transcendental Leaders

Main Target: The Leader	Concerning Mission — Customers	Concerning Process — Organizational members	Concerning Leader — Self
Plans	Customer needs met and exceeded through continuous product/service innovation	Member ownership of organization; Members empowered to meet organizational objectives	Continuous self-improvement in knowledge, beliefs, and values about self and others
Envisions	Clear vision of organizational mission; Clear perception of customer wants	Clear vision of member potential as it relates to mission; Clear understanding of human needs	Clear vision of values, priorities, and potential with openness to change; Clear sense of ethics
Primarily Values	Commitment to continuous innovation and outstanding service in all areas	Self-leadership for all members; Helps others to realize their potential	Desire to improve self; Feedback on self-performance; Periodic self-reflection
Primarily Feels	Passion for excellence; Devotion to serving others; Ardent commitment to the organization's mission	Caring and compassion; Deep respect for human dignity; Faith in organizational members	Strong sense of morality; Quiet confidence and humility; Strong courage and integrity; Lack of fear
Communicates	Receives continuous information about customers, members, competitors, and product/service development; Provides honest, complete, and accurate information	Provides needed information, education and training to develop self-leadership in organizational members; Reinforces innovation; Listens and responds to feelings of members	Receives feedback on self from others on a regular basis; Listens to self; takes time for personal reflection; Practices transcendental leadership skills as program of change
Transcends	Transcends focus on short-term success and complacency with current customer satisfaction	Transcends need to control or dominate members and need to place blame for problems on others	Transcends personal ego needs, insecurity, fear, superficiality and pettiness
Achieves	Continuous improvement in meeting organizational mission and improving customer satisfaction in a fully functioning organization	New levels of positive understanding with empowered, fully functioning organizational members who share the organizational mission	Self-actualizing transcendental leadership and new powers of vision, adaptability, courage, ethics and continuous self-improvement

References

Autry, J. A. (1991). *Love and Profit: The Art of Caring Leadership.* New York: Wm. Morrow and Company.

Batten, J. (1989). *Tough-Minded Leadership.* New York: Amacom.

Beall, D. (1996) Interview, CNBC, April 27.

Bennis W. (1989a). *On Becoming a Leader.* Reading, PA: Addison-Wesley.

Bennis, W. (1989b). *Why Leaders Can't Lead.* San Francisco: Jossey-Bass.

Bennis, W., and Goldsmith, J. (1994) *Learning to Lead.* Reading, PA: Addison-Wesley.

Bennis, W., and Nanus, B. (1985). *Leaders.* New York: Harper and Row.

Blake, R., and Mouton, J. (1964). *The managerial grid.* Houston: Gulf., cited in Conrad, C. (1994) *Strategic organization communication.* (3rd ed.). New York: Harcourt Brace.

Conrad, C. (1994). *Strategic Organizational Communication,* 3rd ed. New York: Harcourt Brace.

Covey, S. (1991). *Principle-Centered Leadership.* New York: Simon and Schuster.

Cushman, D., and King, S. (1995). *Communication and High-Speed Management.* Albany: SUNY Press.

DePree, M. (1989). *Leadership Is an Art.* New York: Dell.

Drucker, P. (1995). *Managing in a Time of Great Change.* New York: Penguin.

Drucker, P. (1996). Foreword to Hesselbein, F., et al. (eds.), *The Leaders of the Future.* San Francisco: Jossey-Bass.

Graeff, C. (1983). The Situational Leadership Theory: A Critical View. *Academy of Management Review* 8 (2):285–91.

Hackman, M. and Johnson, C. (1991). *Leadership: A Communication Perspective.* Prospect Heights, IL: Waveland Press.

Hersey, P., and Blanchard, K. (1984). *The Management of Organizational Behavior,* 4th ed. Englewood Cliffs, NJ: Prentice Hall.

Hesselbein, F., Goldsmith, M., and Beckhard R. (eds.) (1996). *The Leaders of the Future: New Visions, Strategies, and Practices for the Next Era.* San Francisco: Jossey-Bass.

Hosmer, L. (1994). *Moral Leadership in Business.* Burr Ridge, IL: Irwin.

Katzenbach, J. (1995). *Real Change Leaders.* New York: Random House.

Koestenbaum, P. (1991). *Leadership: The Inner Side of Greatness.* San Francisco: Jossey-Bass.

Krebs, G. (1986). *Organizational Communication.* White Plains, NY: Longman.

Leider, R. (1996). The Ultimate Leadership Task. In Hesselbein, F., et al. (eds.), *The Leaders of the Future.* San Francisco: Jossey-Bass.

Lewin, K., Lippitt, R. and White R. K. (1939). Patterns of Aggressive Behavior in Experimentally Created "Social Climates." *Journal of Social Psychology* 10:271–99.

Likert, R. (1961). *New Patterns of Management.* New York: McGraw Hill.

Likert, R. (1967). *The Human Organization: Its Management and Value.* New York: McGraw Hill.

Lord, R. G., and Maher, K. J. (1993). *Leadership and Information Processing: Linking Perceptions and Performance.* New York: Routledge

Maslow, A. (1965). *Eupsychian Management: A Journal.* New York: Irwin Dorsey.

Maslow, A. (1987). *Motivation and Personality,* 3rd ed. New York: HarperCollins.

Nanus, B. (1992). *Visionary Leadership.* San Francisco: Jossey-Bass.

Pauchant, T., and Mitroff, I. (1992). *Transforming the Crisis-Prone Organization: Preventing Individual, Organizational, and Environmental Tragedies.* San Francisco: Jossey-Bass.

Taylor, F. (1911). *Scientific Management.* New York: Harper and Row.

Terry, R. (1993) *Authentic Leadership.* San Francisco: Jossey-Bass.

Walton, S. (1992). *Made in America: My Story.* New York: Doubleday.

Yukl, G. (1989). *Leadership in Organizations,* 2nd ed. Englewood Cliffs, NJ: Prentice Hall.

A Checklist for Transcendental Leadership

The following statements reflect some of the major characteristics of transcendental leadership. Indicate the extent to which you agree or disagree with each item as it applies to yourself in your organization.

SA = Strongly Agree   A = Agree   N = Neutral
D = Disagree   SD = Strongly Disagree

I. Organizational vision
   IA. Clarity of vision

Positive:	SA	A	N	D	SD
I can see clear, achievable goals for my organization which will assure its continued growth and health.					
I enjoy thinking about the unlimited, although challenging, possibilities that exist for my organization.					
I continuously search for better ways to accomplish organizational objectives.					
I enjoy utilizing my creativity and intuition in visualizing a better future for my organization.					
I am capable of breaking a problem into its many subsidiary issues.					
I actively look for and reward innovation in my organization					

Negative:	SA	A	N	D	SD
Others in the organization are responsible for the overall direction of the organization.					
I tend to be pessimistic about my organization's future.					
I do not enjoy "blue sky" thinking.					
Many of the factors affecting my organization's future are out of our control.					

A Checklist for Transcendental Leadership *(continued)*

IB. Bringing vision into reality

Positive:	SA	A	N	D	SD
I pay meticulous attention to detail.					
I know and strictly adhere to professional standards.					
I never stop learning more about my organization.					
I know all aspects of my organization or job well.					
I work out the details of plans or see that they are done by capable people.					
I am persistent in following through on my ideas.					

Negative:	SA	A	N	D	SD
I prefer to think of the big picture but leave the details to others.					
I do not make the effort to learn more than I need to know to do my job.					

IC. Communicating and receiving information about task vision

Positive:	SA	A	N	D	SD
I use many systems for gaining information about customer needs and satisfaction.					
I stay in close touch with my suppliers and keep them informed about forthcoming needs.					
I am continuously looking for more information sources about developments in my organization's field.					
I look for ways to build bridges with my competitors where it might be mutually beneficial.					

A Checklist for Transcendental Leadership *(continued)*

	SA	A	N	D	SD
I seek continuous input from my workers about their perceptions and feelings through established channels of communication, including personal contact.					
I continuously scan the information environment for information which might be valuable to my organization.					
I keep my employees informed about all relevant information.					
When a task must be done in a certain way, I always explain why a certain procedure must be followed.					
I always seek input from those doing the job about ways to improve their job.					
I provide continuous training to help workers improve their job skills.					
I provide a full report of all factors affecting our organization to my subordinates.					
I make training available to further my workers' career advancement.					

Negative:	SA	A	N	D	SD
My subordinates do not need to know all the reasons behind my decisions.					
I will not provide information and assistance to those who do not show initiative.					
I do not always have time to provide reasons for work-related decisions.					

A Checklist for Transcendental Leadership *(continued)*

IIA. Vision of other's potential: Trust

Positive:	SA	A	N	D	SD
My subordinates can be trusted to carry out their tasks without my supervision.					
I am comfortable leaving my subordinates unsupervised for extended periods of time.					
I am capable of bringing out the best in all of the members of my organization with whom I come in contact.					
I have a deep and abiding faith in the motivation of the workers in my organization.					

Negative:					
People require close supervision to do well.					
My subordinates, when left on their own, will not perform well.					

IIB.   Vision of other's potential: Recognition/reward

Positive:	SA	A	N	D	SD
I often praise my subordinates for their performance.					
I frequently write personal notes of appreciation to my subordinates.					
I actively look for opportunities to recognize good performance.					
I am generous with my praise of others.					

A Checklist for Transcendental Leadership *(continued)*

Negative:	SA	A	N	D	SD
I don't have time to write notes of support to my subordinates.					
I praise only the few who show outstanding performance.					
My subordinates do not need praise from me.					
I criticize as much as I praise others in the organization.					

IIC. Vision of others: Empathy

Positive:	SA	A	N	D	SD
I offer sympathetic help with the personal problems of my subordinates.					
I show workers special consideration when they are having problems in their personal lives.					
I make great effort to understand the negative emotions of my workers.					

Negative:	SA	A	N	D	SD
I do not feel it is my job to get involved with subordinates' personal safety problems.					
I keep a safe, impersonal distance from my subordinates.					
My subordinate should not tell me their personal problems.					
My job as a manager/leader does not include being a personal counselor to my workers.					
I get defensive when others disagree with me.					

A Checklist for Transcendental Leadership *(continued)*

IIIA. Vision of self as leader

Positive:	SA	A	N	D	SD
I know my limitations as well as my strengths as a leader.					
I actively seek information from my subordinates about my impact as a leader.					
I often reflect on my conflicts with others and seek to understand my leadership behavior.					
I welcome criticism as a way to growth and understanding.					
I spend time away from my job reflecting on what I might be doing better as a leader.					
My statements and behaviors always reflect what I believe.					

Negative:	SA	A	N	D	SD
I do not know, or really care, how others perceive me.					
I do not have time for self-reflection as a leader.					
I am puzzled by others' reactions to me.					
I tend to get defensive when I am criticized as a leader.					
I sometimes must play a role as leader which is not the real me.					

IIIB. Vision and personal ethics

Positive:	SA	A	N	D	SD
I place my concerns for the welfare of my subordinates above the demands of the organization.					
I keep my subordinates fully informed about any factors that may adversely affect them, even if ordered by my superiors to do otherwise.					

A Checklist for Transcendental Leadership *(continued)*

	SA	A	N	D	SD
I find personal, fulfilling meaning in my work.					
I have the highest integrity, morality, and principles in my dealings with my job and others.					
I approach my job with a sense of love and service.					
I find it easy to forgive people who offend me.					
I do not hold grudges or seek revenge.					

Negative:	SA	A	N	D	SD
The duties of my job force me to do things I personally feel are not in the best interests of my subordinates at times.					
I must, at times, compromise my personal values to be a team player for my superiors.					
I will not convey personally relevant information to my subordinates if I am ordered not to by my superiors.					
I will distort the truth to my workers in order to prevent or deflect possible hostile reactions.					
I do not believe that a sense of service is necessary in my job.					

IIIC. Vision and courage

Positive:	SA	A	N	D	SD
I am not concerned about the personal fallout from controversial positions I sometimes need to take on my job.					
I am able to accept considerable personal rejection in taking stands on controversial issues.					

A Checklist for Transcendental Leadership *(continued)*

	SA	A	N	D	SD
I am comfortable taking significant actions I feel are right, though risky.					
I have the ability to persistently pursue and advocate excellence.					
I am able to tolerate maximum amounts of anxiety without fear.					
I manage my anxiety productively.					

Negative:	SA	A	N	D	SD
I am interested in pleasing my superiors and my subordinates so they will like me.					
My fear of antagonizing others may keep me from being as effective as I would like to be.					
I like to be very certain of the correctness of my decisions before I act.					
I don't handle anxiety very well.					
I find that trying to change my organization goes unrewarded.					

IIIB. Vision and personal adaptability

Positive:	SA	A	N	D	SD
I enjoy the challenge of significant change in my job or life.					
I am not bothered by the rapid changes taking place in the world.					
I respond proactively to change by welcoming and dealing with it.					
I can successfully adapt to a broad range of changes in my organization.					
I see changes in the organization as opportunities for personal growth.					
I welcome increased diversity in the workforce in my organization.					

A Checklist for Transcendental Leadership *(continued)*

Negative:	SA	A	N	D	SD
I much prefer stability and predictability in my life and job.					
I dislike the changes taking place in my organization.					
I often think with nostalgia about the "good old days" when things were more stable.					
I fear becoming obsolete because of changes taking place in the work world.					
I feel threatened by the increasing diversity of the work force.					

For self-improvement:

1. Analyze those positive items which you rated yourself as less than Strongly Agree, and those negative items which you rated yourself as Strongly Disagree, to identify attitudes, beliefs, values, or behaviors which may interfere with transcendental leadership.

2. Identify the positive attitudes, beliefs, values, or behaviors you might wish to consider to improve yourself as a transcendental leader.

3. Visualize the potential impact of these attitudes, beliefs, values, or behaviors on yourself and on those you interact with in the organization.

4. Practice instilling these attitudes, beliefs, values, or behaviors in your own life, and act in ways which would inspire similar attitudes, beliefs, values, or behaviors in others.

14

A Summary and Conclusion to Excellence in Communicating Organizational Strategy

Donald P. Cushman and Sarah Sanderson King

We began this book with a brief summary of each chapter designed to whet the reader's appetite for the gourmet main courses provided by each chapter in this book. We now conclude by providing the dessert in the form of the rich, subtle, and satisfying lessons provided by each chapter. These lessons are lines of analysis in an ongoing inquiry into excellence in communicating organizational strategy.

Lesson No. 1: Excellence in the communication of an organization's strategy rests upon two general propositions. First, reducing the cycle time an organization takes in getting the products and/or services to customers, clients, voters, or aid recipients yields significant organizational outcomes. Second, improving a firm's organizational communication in High-Speed Management processes are the central ingredients necessary for reducing organizational cycle time.

Lesson No. 2: Attempts to effectively reduce organizational cycle time involve (1) environmental scanning, (2) value chain analysis, and (3) continuous improvement—the three stages of High-Speed Management.

Lesson No. 3: Excellence in the communication of organizational leadership strategy involves the clear and complete articulation of a firm's visions, targets, and implementing structures. The latter involves putting in place a proactive corporate culture, rapid-response communication system, and an effective continuous improvement system.

Lesson No. 4:   Excellence in communicating an organization's marketing strategy can develop effective implementing structures which (1) link the structure of a product and service development team to the customer; (2) build a consensus on standards which favor your firm; (3) employ a marketing strategy which involves low-cost pricing and high-quality products, exclusive contracting, and product bundling which competitors cannot imitate; and (4) leverage the use of standards to limit competitor sales, so that firm can dominate a market by preventing competitor entry.

Lesson No. 5:   When excellence in communication can be employed to build a corporate culture with values like (1) emphasizing a Christian culture, (2) involving a youth movement, (3) emphasizing male/female equality, and (4) developing a learning culture, then the company can attract, energize, and adapt its managers in such a manner as to develop a sustainable competitive advantage.

Lesson No. 6:   Excellence in communicating organizational crises strategies involves understanding (1) the underlying sources of friction which generated the crisis, (2) the organizational manifestations of that friction and stress, (3) the mass media's immediate response, and (4) the effects of the crisis on organizational stakeholders.

Lesson No. 7:   Excellence in handling organizational crises involves establishing trust and building credibility with a firm's stakeholders and the press. Open and rapid communication must be established before, during, and after a potential crisis by (1) having a crisis management plan, (2) responding quickly, (3) being honest, (4) listening carefully, (5) admitting when you don't know the answer or what is happening, and (6) distributing printed responses to hold interpretations constant.

Lesson No. 8:   Excellence in communicating governmental strategy should not mistake speed of technology information exchange for the communication of understanding based on respect for cultural differences and mutual support.

Lesson No. 9:   Excellence in communicating national strategies for establishing global competitiveness can be influenced by (1) labor management rules tied to local productivity; (2) flexibility in communication, motivation, and entrepreneurship; (3) revamping public education and private training to be a skills based program based on national competency standards; and (4) organization rewards for skills attainment.

Lesson No. 10: The organizational strategies which define an industry require a great deal of energy which frequently has harmful effects on its leaders and which begins a process of evolution which has a life of its own.

Lesson No. 11: Strategies and implementing programs which integrate a board of directors, the CEO, and professional staff in fundraising allow such efforts to achieve stretch goals.

Lesson No. 12: Intuition plays an important constructive role in successful management communication when subjected to positive and negative feedback and the development of ethical standards. This implementing process, in turn, yields the integrity, courage, and moral choice necessary for developing dynamic visions, values, and organizational actions.

Lesson No. 13: Emotions can affect a manager's decision-making in a productive manner so as to enhance flexible planning, creative thinking, and motivation under certain circumstances.

Lesson No. 14: An organization's training strategies are tied to its organizational needs and time frame in meeting those needs. Four different types of strategies and implementing structures can be considered based on a two-level analysis of both organizational needs and time frames: (1) a general competency, (2) a packaged/handbook, (3) a professional/specialist, or (4) a just-in-time model.

Lesson No. 15: A transcendental strategy of leadership is required to deal with rapid change in unpredictable directions if a firm is to be successful in its rapidly changing environment.

This then is the richness of our inquiry, the lessons we learned, and the knowledge we create.

Contributors

Donald P. Cushman, Ph.D., is Professor Emeritus of Communication at the State University of New York at Albany and CEO of the Cushman Group, a communication consulting firm. He has authored, coauthored, or edited sixteen books and over 150 articles in journals and/or chapters in books. He has been named a Senior Research Scholar by the Ford Foundation, the National Endowment for the Humanities, and the U.S. Fulbright Commission. He has received the Charles Woolbert Award from the National Communication Association "for research of exceptional originality and influence which has stood the test of time." He has received the Gerald M. Philips Award from the National Communication Association for Distinguished Applied Research which is "impressive for the breadth and originality of work in rhetorical, interpersonal, and organizational communication theory."

Richard J. Dieker, Ph.D., is Professor of Communication at Western Michigan University, Kalamazoo, where he served as department chairperson for seventeen years. He has published numerous journal articles and has presented over thirty papers at state, regional, national, and international professional conferences. He has also been a review editor for state and national journals in the discipline and is a certified curriculum consultant for the Speech Communication Association. He has served as a communication consultant to many private and public organizations, both in the U.S. and abroad, and has been a visiting professor at several major universities. As a consultant to the country of Belize, he worked with the Chamber of Commerce and several national agencies in the area of improving the tourist industry. Most recently, he has been conducting leadership development seminars for mid- and upper-level managers in Europe.

B. Thomas Florence is the president and CEO of ARPC, a research and consulting firm located in Washington, DC. His Ph.D. is in communication from Michigan State University. Dr. Florence has over twenty years of experience in management consulting and policy research. He has served as a consultant and advisor to multinational corporations, trust funds, courts, and government agencies. His work in the area of crisis management has included the Love Canal superfund site, Three Mile Island nuclear incident, Times Beach dioxin spill, as well as numerous product liability problems involving asbestos, IUDs, breast implants, and automotive safety. He is currently an advisor to the trust funds established to distribute over $6 billion to individuals injured by exposure to asbestos products.

Robyn Johnston, B.A. Dip Ed (Syd), M.A. (MacQ), is a lecturer at the University of Technology, Sydney, Australia. She is currently involved in teaching students undertaking degrees in Human Resource Development. Prof. Johnston has had considerable experience as a consultant to industry and as a researcher. She is currently a senior researcher with the Research Centre for Vocational Education and Training based at the university. Her current research interests include organizational communication and human resource development practice.

Yanan Ju is Professor of Communication at Central Connecticut State University. He earned his Ph.D. in political science from the University of Belgrade. Ju has taught in China's Fudan University in Shanghai, University of Connecticut, and University of North Carolina at Chapel Hill. He has authored or coauthored a dozen books and numerous articles. His most recent publications include *Understanding China: Center Stage of the Fourth Power* and *Organizational Teamwork in High-Speed Management* (coauthored with Donald P. Cushman), both published by SUNY Press. Ju also consults for organizations in the area of intercultural communication and cross-cultural organizational management.

Yong-Chan Kim is a Ph.D. student at the Annenberg School for Communication at the University of Southern California. His research focuses on media sociology, new media technology, media organizations, and globalization and includes such topics as interorganizational relations among stakeholders in the media industry, communication media ecology in urban environments, global news value chain, and ethnic media in the United States. He earned a M.A. in organizational communication from State University of New York at Albany in 1996 and a B.A. in mass communication from Yonsei University (Seoul, Korea) in 1990.

Sarah Sanderson King, Ph.D., is Professor Emeritus of Communication at Central Connecticut State University and CFO of the

Cushman Group, a communication consulting firm. She has authored, coauthored, or edited ten books and over forty-five articles in journals and/or chapters in books. She has been the recipient of $400,000 in grants from NEH, NIHM, State of Connecticut, East-West Center, Harvard University, University of Hawaii, and Central Connecticut State University to investigate such areas as the role of communication in alleviating stress, training programs for managers of minority programs, alternatives on development, and multicultural curricula. In addition, her awards include Fellowships or Research positions at the University of Chicago, Ohio State University, University of Hawaii, and Harvard University. She has served as Head of the Division of Communication Arts at Marist College, Chair of the Department of Communication at the University of Hawaii, and Chair of the Department of Communication at Central Connecticut State University.

Branislav Kovačić is an Associate Professor of Communication in the School of Communication at the University of Hartford. He received his Ph.D. in communication and sociology from SUNY-Albany. He was a former journalist and magazine editor in Yugoslavia. He has edited and coedited three books published by SUNY Press. He has written journal articles and book chapters on organizational communication, mental health and communication, and rhetoric of social sciences. He is currently working on communication in Internet-based organizations.

Ernest F. Martin Jr., is Associate Professor of the College of Communication and Media Science at Zayed University, Abu Dhabi, United Arab Emirates. He received his Ph.D. in 1971 from the University of Missouri. He previously held positions at Hong Kong Baptist University, Syracuse University, University of Kansas, and Iowa State University. Industry positions have included vice-president/general manager of KDNL-TV (Preview), director of research with Cox Broadcasting, senior research project director with Frank Magid Associates, and director of research and marketing for KPLR-TV. Publications include two books, ten book chapters, and various articles in international journals, including *Asian Journal of Communication, Australian Journalism Review, Gazette, World Communication, Journal of Broadcasting,* and *Journal of Communication and Media Arts.*

Rod Miller advises educational and other nonprofit enterprises on institutional advancement. His assignments include leading capital campaigns, as well as advancement operations and staff development in the United States, Australia, Canada, and New Zealand. He has been a core faculty member of the Fund Raising School at Indiana

University's Center on Philanthropy and was the founding editor of *Australian Journal of Communication.*

Susanne R. Morris, Ph.D., is Deputy Director of the Management Training and Development Institute, Washington, DC, an organization providing short-term, intensive seminar/workshops for participants from throughout the world. Prior to joining the institute, she administered the master's degree program in Public Policy and Administration at Michigan State University, where she also taught for a number of years. She has over twenty years' experience in designing, implementing, and evaluating training programs for public and private-sector participants.

Robert C. Morris, Ph.D., is Executive Director of the Management Training and Development Institute. He has worked in project management and evaluation in various parts of the world for the past thirty years. This included, among other activities, several positions with the U.S. Peace Corps, work as consultant in various capacities to the U.S. Agency for International Development, and the Swedish International Development Agency as a Social Science Research Fellow at the International Center for Tropical Agriculture, Colombia. He has taught cross-cultural communication at Michigan State University and is the author of various published works. With Susanne Morris, he edits the SUNY series on Management and Communication in the Workplace. He is particularly interested in the role of communication in project management and technology transfer.

John Penhallurick received his Ph.D. from Columbia University and is currently Associate Professor of Communications at the University of Canberra. As Head of School, he built the largest and most successful communication program in Australia, introduced the first Honours degree in Communication, and the first master's degree in Marketing Communication. He teaches and publishes in the fields of Mass Communication, Audience Analysis (including Geodemographics and Cognitive Mapping), Marketing Communication, and Organizational Communication. He is married with two children and is ranked among the world's top hundred birdwatchers.

Joseph T. Pillittere II is the Manager of the Nuclear Communication Services department for Northeast Nuclear Energy Company's Millstone Nuclear Power Station. In this position, Mr. Pillittere provides leadership and guidance to an eleven-member communication staff, and strategic direction for programs, projects, and business plans. He also coordinates the department's Emergency Planning and media relations efforts, oversees the financial budget and implements both internal and external communications to inform, update, and maintain a positive corporate image. Previously, Mr. Pillittere served as the communication liaison for the Millstone Unit 2 Recovery Officer during the company's recovery effort. Prior to that, he worked at their Connecticut Yankee nuclear power plant as a senior nuclear information representative (the plant is being decommissioned). Before joining NU, Mr. Pillittere worked for ten years with the New York Power Authority in various positions that involved outreach to the community, government, and news media. Pillittere received a B.S. degree from State University College at Buffalo and his master's degree in Communication and Organizational Management from Central Connecticut State University.

Index